Transnational Islam in
Interwar Europe

THE MODERN MUSLIM WORLD

Series Editor: Dietrich Jung of the Center for Contemporary Middle East Studies, University of Southern Denmark

The modern Muslim world is an integral part of global society. In transcending the confines of area studies, this series encompasses scholarly work on political, economic, and cultural issues in modern Muslim history, taking a global perspective. Focusing on the period from the early nineteenth century to the present, it combines studies of Muslim majority regions, such as the Middle East and parts of Africa and Asia, with the analysis of Muslim minority communities in Europe and the Americas. Emphasizing the global connectedness of Muslims, the series seeks to promote and encourage the understanding of contemporary Muslim life in a comparative perspective and as an inseparable part of modern globality.

Migration, Security, and Citizenship in the Middle East: New Perspectives
 Edited by Peter Seeberg and Zaid Eyadat

Politics of Modern Muslim Subjectivities: Islam, Youth, and Social Activism in the Middle East
 Dietrich Jung, Marie Juul Petersen and Sara Cathrine Lei Sparre

Transnational Islam in Interwar Europe: Muslim Activists and Thinkers
 Edited by Götz Nordbruch and Umar Ryad

TRANSNATIONAL ISLAM IN INTERWAR EUROPE

Muslim Activists and Thinkers

Edited by

Götz Nordbruch and Umar Ryad

palgrave
macmillan

TRANSNATIONAL ISLAM IN INTERWAR EUROPE
Copyright © Götz Nordbruch and Umar Ryad, 2014.

First published in 2014 by
PALGRAVE MACMILLAN®
in the United States—a division of St. Martin's Press LLC,
175 Fifth Avenue, New York, NY 10010.

Where this book is distributed in the UK, Europe and the rest of the world,
this is by Palgrave Macmillan, a division of Macmillan Publishers Limited,
registered in England, company number 785998, of Houndmills,
Basingstoke, Hampshire RG21 6XS.

Palgrave Macmillan is the global academic imprint of the above companies
and has companies and representatives throughout the world.

Palgrave® and Macmillan® are registered trademarks in the United States,
the United Kingdom, Europe and other countries.

ISBN: 978–1–137–38703–5

Library of Congress Cataloging-in-Publication Data

Transnational Islam in interwar Europe : Muslim activists and thinkers /
edited by Götz Nordbruch & Umar Ryad.
    pages cm
    ISBN 978–1–137–38703–5 (hardback : alk. paper)
    1. Muslims—Europe. 2. Islam—Europe—History. 3. Europe—
History—1918–1945. I. Nordbruch, Götz. II. Ryad, Umar.
BP65.A1T73 2014
305.6′9709409041—dc23   2013048521

A catalogue record of the book is available from the British Library.

Design by Newgen Knowledge Works (P) Ltd., Chennai, India.

First edition: June 2014

10 9 8 7 6 5 4 3 2 1

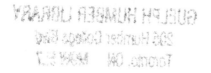

Contents

Acknowledgments

We would like to deeply thank Leiden University Center for the Study of Islam and Society (LUCIS), the Centre for Contemporary Middle East Studies of the University of Southern Denmark, the Danish Council for Independent Research—Humanities, The Leids Universiteits Fonds (LUF) and the Netherlands-Flemish Institute in Cairo for their generosity and financial support to organize the conference "Transnational Islam in Interwar Europe" at the University of Leiden in December 2011.

Introduction: Toward a Transnational History of Islam and Muslims in Interwar Europe

Götz Nordbruch and Umar Ryad

The study of Muslim encounters with and experiences in interwar Europe is still in its initial phase. Many aspects about the history of Muslim interaction with Europe before the influx of Muslim immigrant workers are still entirely unknown. With the exception of the edited volume *Islam in Interwar Europe* and a number of references in the secondary literature,[1] no conclusive research has been conducted as yet about the meaning of the intellectual and political out/input of Muslims to the history of Europe itself. The present volume contains eight case studies that were presented and discussed during the international conference "Transnational Islam in Interwar Europe." The conference was organized by the two editors at Leiden University in a collaboration between Leiden University Center for the Study of Islam and Society (LUCIS) and the Centre for Contemporary Middle East Studies of the University of Southern Denmark (12–14 December, 2011).[2]

A group of scholars and historians from different disciplines was invited to investigate the evolution of Muslim networks and activities in interwar Europe. The various contributions focused on the transnational dimension of such activities in Europe in the interwar period by analyzing the significant sociopolitical ideals and religious affiliations of the actors within these networks. World War I was chosen as a point of departure, as it was the catalyst in encouraging the migration of Muslims to Europe as a result of the demands of the war. We took 1946 as the end of our period of interest, since most political and cultural activities of individual Muslims and Muslim organizations declined by the end of World War II, and reemerged only with the coming of guest workers in the late 1950s and early 1960s. Particular focus was placed on research on personal archives and contemporary writings that so far have widely been ignored in the study of European history. The conference intended to place Muslim activities in interwar Europe within world history by combining the historical data and the patterns of social, political, religious, as well as cultural mobility of Muslims as new social actors in Europe of that era.

Indeed, both world wars were huge transnational cataclysms in human modern history. Despite the extensive literature on the history of interwar Europe, however, much more remains to be said. After the end of World War I, the Paris Conference of 1919 represented the beginning of a new connectivity in modern international relations that should cherish the principle of national sovereignty. This year witnessed a shift in our understanding of the concept of "internationalism" by imposing new analytical frameworks of what is now known as "transnational history."[3] As for the Muslim presence in Europe during the interwar period and World War II, it is observed that their stories have been mostly dealt with as part of Middle-Eastern and Asian history, colonial studies or—briefly—as related to European migration history.[4] Previous research focused either on the accounts of Arab/Muslim travelers and residents in Europe in the nineteenth century or on the later Muslim labor migration in the post–World War II period. Such approaches doubtlessly have their justification, as Muslim actors in interwar Europe often considered themselves as part of the political and cultural movements in the geographical Muslim world. Yet these studies tend to overlook the impact of Muslims as transnational actors in Europe itself.

Muslims were no key players in Europe of that time; however, the contribution of individual Muslims and Muslim movements to European interwar history represents a remarkable laboratory for our understanding of the religious needs and sociopolitical demands of a minority group in Europe in the colonial era. The present book therefore stresses the importance of this history for the colonized as well as for the colonizers. Precisely because the politics of the interwar years had momentous impact on European and world history, the volume tries to unearth original insights into the history of Muslim interactions and encounters *with* and *in* European societies. It also highlights how such interactions coincided with emerging geopolitical and intellectual East-West networks that transcended national, cultural, and linguistic borders.

Owing to its multifaceted nature, the subject of Muslims in interwar Europe is well-suited for a collection of chapters. In the present volume, Muslims in interwar Europe are perceived as subjects formed by their participation in different religious and political ideologies in their historical setting. The articles aim at formulating new approaches to Muslim-European history. Muslim presence in interwar Europe was tied to emerging discourses of transnational and at times global reach and impact. As it will become clear, in their pursuit of global religious and political transformation in the interwar period, Muslims made various attempts to reinforce the manifestation of their self-consciousness in the land of the European colonial powers. The main link between Muslims in interwar Europe was their mobilization in various entities, such as religious institutions and political structures of power, that provided meeting points for activities and exchanges across borders. Although they aggregated specific religious entities and political properties and relations, they were in many cases cribbed by the societies of which they were members.

This volume intends to fill in a lacuna by mapping out this history of Muslims by using interwar Europe as a point of departure, and by analyzing how they laid the groundwork for new political and religious ideas on European soil. By focusing on links and encounters, it considers Muslim actors in interwar Europe as part of European and global intellectual and political history.

As we shall see, the interwar period was an intriguing moment in time when Muslims in Europe were confronted with immense challenges within the course of world history. The chapters discuss individuals, communities, institutions, and formal or informal networks. These studies are based on previously unexplored sources, adding a new historical inquiry about the evolution of Islam in the increasingly transnational context of the early twentieth century. They collectively create new directions for the questioning of established categories that have been applied in descriptions and analytical reconstructions of Muslim communities in interwar Europe. Taking the history of Muslims in interwar Europe into consideration adds an intriguing case study that will enriches the ongoing conceptual debates regarding the meaning of transnational and national boundaries, human agency between local conditions and global contexts of history, the *histoire croisée*, *Transfergeschichte*, and so on.

EUROPE AS "THE OTHER"?

In the nineteenth and early twentieth century, Europe was a crucial point of reference in contemporary debates among Muslim scholars and activists. Arab and Muslim engagement with Europe was often characterized by ambiguity that implied both fascination and rejection.[5] For Muslims actors in the interwar period, Europe was a colonial space and a "cradle" for modern civilization and culture at the same time. Their experiences illustrate the complexity of interwar societies in the context of global transformation. While colonialism and an increasing secularization of society were perceived as representing the repressive and antireligious tendencies of European intellectual traditions, the advance of modern sciences and the institutionalization of political liberties were regarded as achievements providing potential signposts for reform in Muslim societies. Europe, however, was no entity with clearly marked delimitations. Rather, it often stood as a shifting metaphor that was interpreted as a mirror image for elaborating one's own identity and defining one's own ambitions.

Internationally, Muslims regularly drew an image of a "declining West" while searching for alternative civilizational discourses that would take up Islamic history and traditions. However, Pan-Islamic appeals were challenged by the decline and unmaking of empires and the appearance of two alternate political claims that promised to reshape the imperial world order—namely, the Bolshevik Revolution and the principles of President Wilson that inspired anti-imperialist, socialist, or nationalist European movements.[6] These principles also resounded among Muslims in interwar Europe.

It is obvious that the interwar era was a significant watershed for the development of various intellectual, cultural, and political networks that developed across national borders and in the context of the new international relations. It was the very moment when intriguing questions were posed concerning individual and collective identities and their relevance within the emerging local and transnational intellectual discourses and political networks.

Following the collapse of the Ottoman Empire, Muslim sociopolitical and intellectual transnational networks discovered Europe as a suitable ground where they could set up and seek to defend their respective interests and promote their thoughts and ideologies. Their activities in Europe were also linked to a wider Arab nationalist movement that had gained ground in the interwar period, and included Christian and Muslim nationalists belonging to upper-status or elite families.[7] The study of Muslim activities in Europe in this era provides intriguing examples of the interplay between their understanding of nationalism, populism, and religion in interwar Europe, and how their experiences shaped their conceptualization of ideology and Islamic traditions. In order to realize their goals, Muslim activists attempted to exploit their scholarly, professional, social, and political positions in lobbying, campaigning, and making alliances with Western politicians, diplomats, Orientalists, publishers, but also with the wider public.

As Muslim activists in interwar Europe engaged culture and politics, European cities increasingly turned into a new locus for Pan-Islamist aspirations. These ideas were thus not fully detached from their proponents' vision of Europe. Muslims as an *international minority* of that age pursued this idea in Europe itself again due to their new experiences and imaginations in the West. Pan-Islamism was seen by many Muslim political actors, intellectuals, and propagandists in Europe as the only practical way to continue their activities.[8] Maybe the most significant figure among them was the Lebanese Druze prince Shakib Arslan (1869–1946), who made his place of exile Geneva "the umbilical cord of the Islamic world."[9] In collaboration with other Muslim nationalists inside and outside Europe (such as Rashid Rida [1865–1935], Amin al-Husayni [1897–1974], and many others), Arslan laid the foundation for reformist religiopolitical ideas that gained wide circulation among many elite groups in the Muslim world.

These Muslim networks were mobilized by the abolition of the caliphate (1924) and colonial politics in the Muslim world. They created an informal community of intellectual/activists beyond national boundaries that helped foster an ethos of transnational Pan-Islamism. Yet, Muslims in interwar Europe were no homogeneous group. They belonged to various ethnicities and classes, but many of them understood their shared religious ideas and political aspirations in the European context. However, by studying their activities and thoughts, the role of other nationalists, Pan-Arabists or secularist liberals belonging to the boundaries of the Muslim world should be taken into consideration. In early twentieth century Muslim thought, the "umma" is often considered as a single entity with established traits of religious belonging and solidarity. Yet, Muslim intellectuals and activists who interacted with European societies also inevitably experienced a sense of Muslim diversity through their contacts with fellow Muslims of different origins. At the same time, they became aware of many similarities with non-Muslims that went against notions of religious distinctiveness and cultural authenticity.

This volume thus studies the redefinitions of religious community as articulated in the thoughts and activities of Muslim activists in Europe; it aims at investigating the question whether religion was a well-embedded framework of reference to the self-identification of Muslims in Europe. Did the activists and thinkers in question perceive Islam in the singular, and as something distinct? Or did they consider their Muslim identity as merely one aspect of their complex experience as individuals living in Europe? How did Muslims define Islam (for instance, with regard to the diversity of Islamic schools, ethnic origins, etc.) and the Muslim community (for instance, with regard to class differences, educational background, urban/rural background, migrants/ indigenous Muslims)? How did such actors relate to non-Muslim communities, movements, or intellectual trends? What kind of loyalties did they develop (with regard to cities, nations, religion, etc.)?

Agency between Local Conditions and Global Contexts

Muslims in interwar Europe were no passive strangers to local politics and public debate. Like their non-Muslim European peers of that period, many intellectuals and activists among them had a variety of ways to articulate, such as letters, memoirs, and newspapers. Besides, they actively engaged with European and international institutions, social actors, and political movements—all while their politics and networking were subject to local influences and restrictions.

The idea of international conventions was the single most striking phenomenon that connected Pan-Islamists in the interwar era. The congresses of Mecca (1924) and (1926), Cairo (1926), and Jerusalem (1931) had their affiliates in Europe.[10] Likewise, Muslim religious and political associations were established in interwar Europe as well. Examples of these were: Society for the Progress of Islam; Islamische Zentralinstitut, Islamische Gemeinde, and Verein für islamische Gottesverehrung (Berlin); Alliance Musulmane Internationale, La Fraternité Musulmane, Association des oulémas musulmans en Algérie (Paris); Orientbund and Islamische Kulturbund (Vienna); and the European Muslim Congress (Geneva).

In a similar way, during the interwar years the local controversies and prevailing social and political concerns impacted on the intellectual outlook and political visions formulated by Muslim thinkers. The ideas and visions formulated by Muslims in interwar Europe were closely related to prevailing discourses in Muslim societies. Most Muslim political mediators chose Switzerland, Germany, Britain, and France as points of departure for their political mobility. Germany in particular offered many of them an exceptional opportunity for fraternal ties after World War I. North African political actors in Europe were also able to build long-standing ties with many French and Spanish socialists and anti-imperialist activists. In the meantime, through the establishment of journals and newspapers in Europe[11] and enormous contributions to the Arab and Muslim press, Muslims participated in the popularization of the European political, sociore- ligious and intellectual thought in the wider Muslim world.

This volume puts forward a series of arguments to highlight the multiple layers of identification and political action that reflect this complex intersection of local and global conditions. Many of the Muslim groups and individuals explored in this volume indicate how the new transnational and global setting collided with local struggles for identity. Muslims and their networks in interwar Europe cannot be reduced to a single Muslim identity; instead, their transnational activ- ism often implied a revision and redefinition of boundaries that were paralleled by merging intellectual concepts and political visions.

The Contributions

Against this background, the chapters reconstruct the intellectual and political contributions of Muslim individuals and organizations in interwar Europe and place them in the wider context of global transformations.

In chapter 1, David Motadel starts the discussions by analyz- ing how Muslim life flourished and was institutionalized for the first time during the interwar period. In most western European metropolises, Muslims organized themselves for the first time in that period. Focusing on Great Britain, France, and Germany, the chapter outlines processes of formal organization and institutionalization of Muslim life. It looks at the building of mosques and prayer houses, the creation of organizations and associations, and the foundation of Islamic newspapers and journals. More generally, the chapter enquires into the ways in which Muslim life was shaped by both the majority society and the wider Muslim world and explores entangle- ments and connections between different local Muslim communities in Europe. Drawing on various local and regional studies, Motadel attempts to provide the framework of a comparative history of Islam in modern western Europe. He concentrates on the institutionaliza- tion and formal organization of these communities, particularly the creation of (1) physical spaces (mosques); (2) legal spaces (associations and organizations); and (3) communicative and intellectual spaces (journals). The creation of these communities involved a transfer and translation of codes, meanings, and organizing principles from one place (Muslim countries) to another (western Europe). The purpose is therefore to examine influences from home countries, as well as from international Muslim organizations and networks. This contribution builds on original sources and enhances our understanding of diaspora communities, cross-cultural migration and religious minorities in the global age.

While David Motadel discusses the institutional global aspects of Islam in western Europe, Nathalie Clayer studies the impact of the transnational connections in building an "indigenous" Albanian and European Islam in interwar Albania. In that building process of a "national," "European" and "modern" Islam in interwar Albania, transnational networking activities played an important role. They offered possibilities for the elaboration of a new corpus of religious texts and, more widely, texts about Islam. Moreover, they provided opportunities for the emergence of new religious leaders and thinkers. These transnational connections mainly linked Muslims in Albania with their coreligionists in Turkey, India, Egypt, and in Europe itself, but also in the United States. Such networking activities were very often based on personal exchanges, but also involved institutional dimensions. These networks were not static; they have to be seen in their interplay between their local, national, and transnational dimensions. In the Albanian case, the multiplicity of networks activated by local actors is striking.

In chapter 3, Richard van Leeuwen looks afresh at the question of how the intensification of the interaction between Europe and the Middle East during the nineteenth century contributed to the formation of migrant communities on both sides of the Mediterranean and various kinds of transnational networks in the early twentieth century. Religious scholars in the Muslim world were among the groups to be most affected by such cross-border interactions. They were not only involved in migration, but also became familiar with European societies through travel and studies. The growing interaction coincided with and influenced efforts at reform that, especially in the second half of the nineteenth century and the early twentieth century, dominated debates among the *ulama* throughout the Islamic world. These tendencies of increasing mobility and intensifying reform efforts were deeply affected by French and British interventions in north African and Middle Eastern affairs since the second half of the nineteenth century. Van Leeuwen recounts the experiences of two *ulama* traveling from French North Africa to France in the early twentieth century to analyze these interactions. Focusing on the scholars Muhammad al-Wartatani and Muhammad Ibn 'Abd al-Salam al-Sa'ih from Tunisia and Morocco respectively, his study exposes the complexities of the transnational networks that existed in the first half of the twentieth century in relation to European expansion in the Maghreb.

In chapter 4, Götz Nordbruch draws on the intellectual contributions of Arab/Muslim scholars at the Institut de Droit Comparé in Lyon, 1920–1939, to exemplify these intellectuals' reasoning across various legal traditions. As a case study of a particular group of thinkers, his paper sheds light on an important facet of Arab-Islamic intellectual networks and exchanges across the Mediterranean that challenges established notions of distinct intellectual traditions. In contrast to the claims to "cultural authenticity" and "distinct origins" that had marked most contemporary political movements of this period, many of these scholars drew on universalist understandings of law and justice.

Umar Ryad discusses how Taqi al-Din al-Hilali (1894–1987), a *Salafi* Muslim student, was able to build a successful career both in German Orientalist milieus as well as in the Nazi German propaganda institution Radio Berlin. This chapter places Hilali's role in Nazi Germany within a broader political and cultural context. In the Nazi period, Germany hosted a significant number of foreign students, among them many Arabs. This case study of Hilali's German period introduces a unique figure who was caught between two different worlds, since he was subjected to National Socialism while also strongly engaged in propagating anticolonial ideas and *Salafi* populism in the Muslim world. As we shall see, Hilali's experience stands for a telling example of what Peter Wien has called the "culpability of exile"—"A moral dilemma that affects foreigners who take up residence in a villainous country such as Nazi Germany."[12]

While most papers discuss activities and aspirations of students and intellectuals of Sunni origin, Mohammed Alsulami, in contrast, deals with Iranian self-exiled intellectuals who were active in a number of European countries, and Germany in particular. It shows how twentieth-century Iranian nationalist groups in exile, particularly in Europe, played an important role in the later modernization, secularization, and reforms in Iran. Focusing on the journals *Kaveh* and *Iranshahr* that were published in Berlin, this paper traces the changing intellectual visions of these exiled circles and relates them to contemporary intellectual discourses in Iran. As it becomes clear, these two journals played a vital role in constructing and reconstructing Iranian identity in modern times.

The differing political conditions in interwar Europe, in turn, profoundly shaped Muslim politics in that era. In chapter 7, Humayun Ansari analyzes a transnational case study at the intersection of Pan-Islamism, colonialism, and radical politics in England. He argues that in the late nineteenth century, Muslims in India as elsewhere became acutely aware of how the expansion of European power was increasingly subjecting their coreligionists to Christian rule. Barkatullah (1859–1927) was one of the Muslims who had adopted radical Pan-Islamism to fight against Western control and the conquest of the Islamic world. This chapter investigates this activist's experience in England as a seminal moment in the shaping of his ideological and political development. Barkatullah's political journey is located in the context of late nineteenth and early twentieth centuries' global politics; it provides valuable insights into Muslim sensibilities in the context of European-Muslim encounters and places the struggle against colonial rule in a wider transnational intellectual and political context.

In contrast to the other contributions, Ali Al Tuma does not focus on social or political elites; instead, he investigates the history of Moroccan soldiers in the Spanish Civil War (1936–1939). His study specifically examines the integration of these soldiers into the Spanish army and the contacts that these troops developed with the Spanish civilian population, as well as the policy practiced by the Spanish military institutions in an effort to regulate the interaction of these culturally different colonial troops with their environment in Spain.

The studies of this volume reflect a growing scholarly interest in the history of Muslims in interwar Europe and their role in transnational politics in that crucial period of world history. This collection does not provide a comprehensive account that would cover Muslims' experiences and trajectories in this period. As case studies that place a particular emphasis on the transnational dimensions of these actors' thoughts and actions, these studies provide important stimuli for a rereading of the existing literature on European-Muslim encounters, and for a reframing of its premises and underlying perspectives.

NOTES

1. See, for example, Nathalie Clayer and Eric Germain, eds., *Islam in Inter-war Europe* (London: Hurst, 2008); Humayun Ansari, ed., *The Making of the East London Mosque, 1910–1951: Minutes of the London Mosque Fund and East London Mosque Trust Ltd* (Cambridge: Cambridge University Press, 2011); Humayun Ansari, "Between Collaboration and Resistance: Muslim Soldiers' Identities and Loyalties in the Two World Wars," *Arches Quarterly* 4 (2011): 18–29; Umar Ryad, "Among the Believers in the Land of the Colonizer: Mohammed Ali Van Beetem's Role among the Indonesian Community in the Netherlands in the Interwar Period," *Journal of Religion in Europe* 5.2 (2012), 273–310; Umar Ryad, *Documents on the German Arms Trade in the Arabian Peninsula: Readings in the*

Archive of Zeki Kiram (Arabic) (Cairo: National Archives of Egypt, Documentary Studies Series, no. 2, 2011); Umar Ryad, "From an Officer in the Ottoman Army to a Muslim Publicist and Armament Agent in Berlin: Zekî Hishmat Kirâm (1886–1946)," *Bibliotheca Orientalis* 63.3–4 (2006), 235–268.

2. http://www.hum.leidenuniv.nl/lucis/eerder-bij-lucis/conference -islam-interwar-europe.html (last accessed October 20, 2013)

3. See, for example, Tyler Stovall, *Paris and the Spirit of 1919: Consumer Struggles, Transnationalism, and Revolution* (Cambridge: Cambridge University Press, 2012); Erez Manela, *The Wilsonian Moment: Self-Determination and the International Origins of Anticolonial Nationalism* (Oxford: Oxford University Press, 2007).

4. Clayer and Germain, *Islam in Inter-war Europe*, 1–2.

5. See, for example, Ian Coller, *Arab France: Islam and the Making of Modern Europe, 1798–1831* (Berkeley: University of California Press, 2010); Sandra Naddaf, "Mirrored Images: Rifa'ah al-Tahtawi and the West," *Alif: Journal of Comparative Poetics* 6 (Spring, 1986), 73–83; Anwar Louca, *Voyageurs et ecrivains egyptiens en France aux XIXe siecle* (Paris: Didier,1970); Albert Hourani, *Arabic Thought in the Liberal Age 1798–1939* (Oxford: Oxford University Press, 1970).

6. Cemil Aydin, *The Politics of Anti-Westernism in Asia* (New York: Colombia University Press, 2007).

7. Ernest C. Dawn, "The Formation of Pan-Arab Ideology in the Interwar Period," *International Journal of Middle East Studies* 20.1 (1988), 67–90.

8. Jacob M. Landau, *The Politics of Pan Islamism: Ideology and Organization* (Oxford: Clarendon Press, 1990), 228–230.

9. William L. Cleveland, *Islam against the West: Shakib Arslán and the Campaign for Islamic Nationalism the West* (Austin: University of Texas Press, 1985), 67.

10. Landau, *The Politics of Pan Islamism*, 234–235.

11. Gerhard Höpp, *Arabische und islamische Periodika in Berlin und Brandenburg 1915 bis 1945: geschichtlicher Abriss und Bibliographie* (Berlin: Das Arabische Buch, 1994).

12. Peter Wien, "The Culpability of Exile: Arabs in Nazi Germany," *Geschichte und Gesellschaft* 37 (2011), 332–358.

References

Ansari, Humayun. "Between Collaboration and Resistance: Muslim Soldiers' Identities and Loyalties in the Two World Wars." *Arches Quarterly* 4 (2011): 18–29.

———, ed. *The Making of the East London Mosque, 1910–1951: Minutes of the London Mosque Fund and East London Mosque Trust Ltd*. Cambridge: Cambridge University Press, 2011.

Aydin, Cemil. *The Politics of Anti-Westernism in Asia.* New York: Colombia University Press, 2007.

Clayer, Nathalie and Eric Germain, eds. *Islam in Inter-war Europe.* London: Hurst, 2008.

Cleveland, W. L. *Islam against the West: Shakib Arslan and the Campaign for Islamic Nationalism.* Austin: University of Texas Press, 1985.

Coller, Ian. *Arab France: Islam and the Making of Modern Europe, 1798–1831.* Berkeley: University of California Press, 2010.

Dawn, E. C. "The Formation of Pan-Arab Ideology in the Interwar Period." *International Journal of Middle East Studies* 20.1 (1988): 67–90.

Höpp, Gerhard. *Arabische und islamische Periodika in Berlin und Brandenburg 1915 bis 1945: geschichtlicher Abriss und Bibliographie.* Berlin: Das Arabische Buch, 1994.

Hourani, Albert. *Arabic Thought in the Liberal Age 1798–1939.* Oxford: Oxford University Press, 1970.

Landau, Jacob M. *The Politics of Pan Islamism: Ideology and Organization.* Oxford: Clarendon Press, 1990.

Louca, Anwar. *Voyageurs et ecrivains egyptiens en France aux XIXe siecle.* Paris: Didier, 1970.

Manela, Erez. *The Wilsonian Moment: Self-Determination and the International Origins of Anticolonial Nationalism.* Oxford: Oxford University Press, 2007.

Naddaf, Sandra. "Mirrored Images: Rifa'ah al-Tahtawi and the West." *Alif: Journal of Comparative Poetics* 6 (Spring, 1986): 73–83.

Ryad, Umar. "Among the Believers in the Land of the Colonizer: Mohammed Ali Van Beetem's Role Among the Indonesian Community in the Netherlands in the Interwar Period." *Journal of Religion in Europe* 5.2 (2012): 273–310.

———. *Documents on the German Arms Trade in the Arabian Peninsula: Readings in the Archive of Zeki Kiram* (Arabic). Cairo: National Archives of Egypt, Documentary Studies Series, no. 2, 2011.

———. "From an Officer in the Ottoman Army to a Muslim Publicist and Armament Agent in Berlin: Zeki Hishmat Kiram (1886–1946)." *Bibliotheca Orientalis* 63.3–4 (2006): 235–268.

Stovall, Tyler. *Paris and the Spirit of 1919: Consumer Struggles, Transnationalism, and Revolution.* Cambridge: Cambridge University Press, 2012.

Wien, Peter. "The Culpability of Exile: Arabs in Nazi Germany." *Geschichte und Gesellschaft* 37 (2011): 332–358.

CHAPTER 1

The Making of Muslim Communities in Western Europe, 1914–1939

David Motadel

I. Introduction

Muslim presence in western Europe is not a recent phenomenon resulting from the postcolonial and worker migrations of the 1950s and 1960s. In most western European metropolises, Muslim life flourished and was institutionalized for the first time during the interwar period. In France, the *Grande Mosquée de Paris* was inaugurated in July 1926, immediately fuelling debates in London about launching a similar project in the British capital. In 1928, the first mosque opened in Berlin-Wilmersdorf. Muslims across western Europe began to organize themselves, setting up institutions varying from mosques and schools to cemeteries and publications.

Although there is a vast and rapidly growing body of literature on Muslims in contemporary Europe, this research usually lacks a historical perspective, generally containing little information about the history of Islam in western European societies.[1] This is surprising given the profound research in the field over the last decade.[2] The major historiographical problem is, however, that most of the research done so far is scattered, limited to local and regional studies, and has so far not been connected. Addressing this problem, this article is an attempt to provide the first comprehensive, though concise, account of the history of Muslim life in western Europe before World War II.

Most scholars perceive Muslim presence in western Europe as a result of the labor and postcolonial mass migrations of the postwar period. It is certainly true that Islam became more visible in the public sphere in western Europe as a result of Muslim mass immigration to major European industrial countries in the second half of the twentieth century. Another reason why only few studies have addressed the issue is because their research has focused on national or ethnic rather than religious categories, examining the histories of Turks, Persians, Indians, or Arabs in countries like Germany, France, and Great Britain.[3] The Muslim identities and Islamic practices of these communities have been considered to be of secondary importance, outpaced by language, color, or nationality, which were seen as the key signifiers of individual and collective difference. Looking through the lens of religion, the following pages focus on the founding of local Muslim communities in Germany, Great Britain, and France during and after World War I.

The making of these early Muslim communities was part of the much wider historical phenomenon of migration and the emergence of new minorities in the global age. Since the late nineteenth and early twentieth centuries, small minority groups started to appear worldwide—Chinatowns in Hamburg or Chicago, Japanese communities in Hawaii or Sao Paolo, Russian groups in Shanghai or Helsinki or, say, Lebanese communities in Senegal. Some of these groups organized themselves not only on ethnic or national, but also on religious grounds—Sikh communities in Manchester, Buddhist groups in Berlin or Muslim minorities in South Shields or Paris, for instance. While much research has been done on ethnic diaspora communities in the global age, we know less about the birth of these faith communities. These groups formed new kinds of religious minorities, characterized by mobility and embedded in global religious networks.

Indeed, the history of Muslim minorities in interwar western Europe is, after all, a history of global interconnection and mobility. Most of the religious minorities that have been studied, such as Jews in Europe, Christians in the Middle East, or Muslims in Russia, India, or East Asia, have a long history within their majority societies. Accordingly, religious minority history has been written primarily as local (or national) history, addressing the relationship between minority and majority society. The presence of organized Muslim communities in western European countries is a relatively new phenomenon, however, forming part of the worldwide integration processes that began in the late nineteenth century. A history of Muslim communities in western Europe during the late nineteenth and early twentieth centuries is, first of all, a history of migration and settlement, the creation of Muslim space and the implementation of Muslim presence in a non-Muslim environment. The making of these communities involved a transfer of cultural practices, lifestyles, codes, meanings, and organizing principles from one place (Muslim countries) to another (western European cities). In the new setting, a unique and hybrid Muslim space was created that was shaped both by the new, non-Muslim environment and the wider Muslim world. Even in the period following the actual settlement, these minorities maintained international links.[4] In fact, Muslim minorities in interwar Europe were characterized by a continuous flow of people and information. Consequently, they cannot be studied as a local phenomenon, shaped by their relationship with the majority society alone. Rather, their study needs also to take into account influences from the wider Islamic world. Furthermore, the few Muslim communities that did take root in interwar Europe were also entangled with one another.

The following pages address the actual processes of formal organization and institutionalization of Muslim life in western Europe, as it was shaped by both the majority society and the wider Islamic world. The institutionalization of Muslim life, as reflected in the formal organization of Muslim communities, is a classic characteristic of Islamic diaspora communities. In Islamic societies, the creation of distinctive Muslim spaces was essentially unnecessary. In the diaspora, however, the physical and legal place of minorities within the majority society and state as well as the organization of religious life became crucial issues. An institutional framework provided a safe space for religious practices and rituals like feasts, marriages, and funerals.

The "making of Muslim space" will be discussed in three parts.[5] First, the emergence of mosques as *physical religious spaces*; second, the development of associations and organizations as *legal spaces*; and finally, the construction of *communicative and intellectual spaces*, expressed in Islamic newspapers and journals.

The scope of this chapter has limitations. First, it concerns only those individuals who identified themselves as "Muslims." Thus, it draws on a cultural rather than a theological definition of "Muslim." Second, it concentrates primarily on Muslims who organized themselves in Islamic organizations and formed groups identifiably organized by religion within the majority society. "Muslim community" is defined as a network of these individuals (often of diverse ethnic and linguistic backgrounds) based on their common faith.[6] The following pages will not concentrate on the many Muslims who had not organized themselves in religious groups, or who were not affiliated with any official organization. To be sure, many Muslims were neither organized in a formal religious community nor were they affiliated with any official organization. Finally, the expression "Muslim diaspora" will be used with reservation since the traditional and perhaps defining characteristic of "diaspora" is a common *geographic* origin. Instead of a common home country, Muslims of interwar western Europe shared a more or less similar *religious* background, at best forming what could be called a "religious diaspora."

II. Origins

Although in the *long durée* Islamic globalization began as early as in the late Middle Ages, in Europe Muslim presence occurred only on the fringes of the continent.[7] In the early eighth century, Muslim soldiers and settlers landed on the Iberian Peninsula and, soon after, along the Mediterranean shores of other parts of Southern Europe. In the early modern period, parts of the Ottoman-ruled Balkans became Muslim. Tatar settlers brought Islam to the Baltic region. In the heartlands of western Europe, though, there was no permanent Muslim presence until the late nineteenth and early twentieth centuries.[8] The settlement of Muslim migrants at this time was the result both of structural changes and events. Structurally, Muslim immigration resulted from increasing globalization, especially of the labor market, mobility, and European imperialism. Eventually, major events—most notably World War I and, to a lesser extent, the Russian Revolution and the collapse of the Ottoman Empire—caused increasing migration and led to a period of formal organization of Muslim life in western Europe.

In the late nineteenth century, Muslim migration to western Europe was in large part connected with the empires. Colonial migration brought Muslims to French and British seaports and capitals, whereas Germany experienced relatively insignificant levels of Muslim immigration. Still, the Muslim presence in all three countries was highly atomized. First clusters and networks of individuals emerged only after 1918. In fact, the institutionalization of Islam was an immediate result of the war, which brought thousands of Muslims to Europe. By the early 1920s, more than 10,000 Muslims were living in Britain, especially in Manchester, Liverpool, South Shields, Cardiff, and London.[9] Most of them had South Asian backgrounds, but many also came from the Arab world and Africa. They included industrial workers and seafarers, like the legendary Yemeni and Somali sailors of Cardiff and South Shields, as well as students and merchants. At the same time, more than 100,000 Muslims, mostly from North Africa, now lived in France, particularly in Marseilles and Paris, and their numbers were growing rapidly.[10] In Germany, a Muslim community emerged prisoner of war camps at Wünsdorf and Zossen, towns close to Berlin, where more than 4,000 Muslim soldiers, who had fought in the Entente armies, were detained.[11] Some of them, especially Tatars from Eastern Europe, stayed after the war. In the interwar period, the numbers of Muslims in Berlin, the centre of Muslim life in Germany, were highly fluid, varying between 1,800 and 3,000.[12] Most were students, merchants, diplomats, refugees, and political activists, coming from all parts of the Muslim world. Even Islamic missionaries—mainly members of the *Ahmadiyya* movement, an Indian Muslim sect—arrived in the German capital, and also in other metropolises of western Europe, during that time. In all three countries, the interwar years became a formative period in regard to the formal organization and institutionalization of Islamic life.

III. Physical Spaces: Building Mosques

The making of physical Muslim places, brick-and-mortar buildings, which were clearly visible to the majority society, began during World War I. In Britain, France, and Germany, the government authorities mostly supported the creation of these Muslim spaces in order to show their gratitude for Muslim support during the war.

In France, the first functional mosque was built by the military government in Nogent-sur-Marne, a small town near Paris, during World War I.[13] Inaugurated by a military imam in April 1916, it was to serve Muslim colonial soldiers who fought in the French army. Around the same time, another centre of Muslim soldiers from northern Africa emerged in the Mediterranean town of Fréjus in Southeast France.[14] The so-called *Camp de Caïs* was not closed after the war, and thousands of Muslims remained there, and in 1928, on the initiative of the Muslim officer Abd al-Qadir Madenba, they built the *Mosquée "Missiri" de Fréjus*. The centre of Muslim life in interwar France, however, became Paris. On July 15, 1926, the French president Gaston Doumergue opened the *Grande Mosquée de Paris*, situated on the Left Bank in the fifth *arrondisement* facing the *Jardin des Plantes*.[15] Again, the mosque was built as a sign of gratitude to Muslims soldiers for their loyalty in the war. It included a library, a *hamam*, study and conference rooms, and a restaurant. The prayer hall of the mosque was only to be used by Muslims, creating an exclusive Islamic space in the French capital. Headed by the charismatic French-Algerian religious leader and civil servant Si Kaddour Benghabrit, the mosque quickly became a religious and cultural centre of Muslims in Paris. The massive support the project received from the secular French republic, particularly the *Quai d'Orsay*, provoked jokes that Muslims were treated better by the authorities than Christians. Unsurprisingly, the mosque evoked bitter protest from Catholic and right-wing nationalists of the *Action Française*.[16] In the 1930s, finally, a fourth mosque was planned for Marseilles, a town hosting the second largest Muslim population in France at that time.[17] Due to various political struggles, however, the project was not realized before the outbreak of World War II. Only in 1942, for strategic and political reasons, Vichy authorities started a new initiative to build the mosque, but before these plans could become more concrete, Anglo-American troops invaded southern France.

In Germany, the first mosque was opened in the prisoner of war camp in Wünsdorf in July 1915.[18] The imperial government was at pains to provide good conditions and to ensure that the prisoners could follow their religious customs, as German officials hoped to recruit them into their own armies. As in Fréjus, some prisoners, especially Tatars, sometimes joined by their families, remained in the "Muslim village" of the camp after the war. The Wünsdorf mosque served the growing Muslim community in Berlin as a prayer room until it became dilapidated and was closed down in 1924. Afterwards, Muslims used a number of provisional places for worship, as described by the German convert Chalid Albert Seiler-Chan:

> After the closure of the Wünsdorf Mosque, celebratory services were held at various locations in greater Berlin, including Schloß Wannsee, the Humboldthaus, the Orientalische Club, the Hindustanhaus, the Tiergartenhof, as well as on the rooftop of the observatory in Treptow. Spread out before the pious Muslims at this naturally beautiful place lay the world city of Berlin, framed by Treptow Park and by the green squares of fields, bordered by meadows and forests. Nature's book of revelation was opened before the eyes of the praying men and women, and shimmered green in the holy colour of Islam, a carpet of Allah.[19]

Finally, in April 1925, the prayer hall of a new mosque on the *Fehrbelliner Platz* in Berlin's Wilmersdorf district was inaugurated.[20] The mosque was opened in March 1928. Proposed and financed by the Lahori branch of the *Ahmadiyya*, it soon became the centre for all Muslims living in Berlin during the interwar period. In fact, the founders of the mosque tried hard to make sure that the building provided an ecumenical centre for all Muslims in Berlin. Sticking out in the neighborhood of Wilmersdorf, the German press showed immense interest in the building and its worshippers.[21]

The initial purpose of the Berlin mosque was to support the missionary work of the *Ahmadiyya* in Germany. In the eyes of many who wished to promote Islam in western Europe, Germany seemed to provide the most fertile soil. In May 1922, the *Mohammadan*, a major English-language newspaper in British India, underlined this view in an article entitled "The Need for the Propagation of Islam in Germany":

> Among all the countries of Europe, there does not appear to be as much scope for the propagation of Islam as there is in Germany. She suffered defeat in the War, and now she is seriously thinking of re-building her future course in order to usher in a new era of peace and prosperity. Everyone here is convinced that rebirth is not possible without following true religion. Christianity has met with complete failure. Germany is in a much better position to reach to the core of the veritable reality underlying false and baseless propaganda...Germany is the centre of Europe and to achieve success here will have very healthy influence on the neighbouring countries...I am writing my observations after studying current events in Germany. And thus I feel that I would be disloyal to Islam if I did not inform the Indian Muslims of this great opportunity for propagating Islam in this country.[22]

The author of the article was the Indian political activist and Islamic scholar Abdus Sattar Kheiri who, together with his older brother, Abdul Jabbar Kheiri, played a leading role in the organization of Muslims in the German capital in the early 1920s. Not members of the *Ahmadiyya*, however, they soon fiercely opposed the foundation of the Wilmersdorf mosque—though without success. Next to the mosque were built a community hall and a residential building for the imam. The first imam became the Indian Maulana Sadr ud-Din, who, prior to his stay in Germany, had worked at the mosque in Woking, near London.[23] In fact, the Woking mosque had served as an example for the Berlin mission.

In Britain, the organization of community life around mosques also began after World War I. The only serious attempt to establish an organized Muslim congregation before the war had been made in Liverpool, where the eccentric British convert, Henry William (Abdullah) Quilliam, had founded a mosque as early as 1891.[24] Dependent on its founder's funding, the Liverpool congregation fell into decline when Quilliam left Britain in 1908. Following World War I, attempts to build mosque communities were more successful.

The most important mosque in interwar Britain became the Shah Jahan Mosque in Woking.[25] The picturesque building on 149 Oriental Road had been constructed in the late nineteenth century by the famous Orientalist and convert Gottlieb Wilhelm Leitner, who had run it like a private club. Then, in 1913, the Lahori branch of the *Ahmadiyya* movement, represented by the Indian barrister Khwaja Kamal ud-Din, bought the building and, after the war, built an additional prayer house, and successfully turned the mosque into a centre of religious practice in Britain. In October 1926, the Qadiani branch of the *Ahmadiyya* opened a small prayer house in London— the so-called *Fazl Mosque*. As in Berlin, the congregation of Woking too was at pains to strengthen the nonsectarian character of their mosque. Their vision was to build an organized Muslim community in Britain. Yet, London itself still lacked a major mosque comparable to the Paris mosque. In the British capital, Muslims had to meet for prayer in provisional prayer rooms, like the so-called London Muslim Prayer House on Campden Hill Road. The opening of the *Grande Mosquée de Paris* in 1926, though, encouraged Muslim dignitaries in Britain to promote a similar project in London.[26] Initially, the petitioners were successful. In the same year, as a temporary measure, three houses in the Stepney district were converted into a mosque, fundraising was intensified and, in 1928, even a site in Kensington was purchased. In the end, however, the plans to set up a Kensington mosque never materialized. During World War II, finally, with the support of the Churchill war cabinet, the East London Mosque was inaugurated.[27] Moreover, in 1944, the British government granted land and money for the building of the London Central Mosque in Regent's Park.[28] Both projects were heavily instrumentalized by British war propaganda in the Muslim world. In contrast to Germany and France, no mosques were built in the provinces, although in the port cities of Cardiff and South Shields prayer rooms were established in Arab boarding houses.[29] Here, the Yemeni and Somali sailors were organized under the auspices of the Yemeni religious scholar Shaykh 'Abd Allah Ali al-Hakimi of the *Alawiyya* Sufi order, who had gained experience in organizing Muslim exile communities in Marseilles and Rotterdam before arriving in Britain in 1936. Al-Hakimi set up *zawiya*s with prayer rooms and bathrooms for ablutions, providing the first properly institutionalized spaces of worship in these port cities.

In western Europe, the newly built mosques and prayer houses became the lynchpins of the new Muslim communities. Their cultural function went far beyond functioning as mere places of worship. They became cultural centers, connecting Muslim individuals within the European metropolises and port cities. Scholars of Islam in contemporary western European societies have described this diaspora phenomenon as "mosque culture."[30] Whereas the communities in France were religiously (and ethnically) fairly homogenous, the mosques of London and Berlin united Muslims from various religious backgrounds in a kind of ecumenical union.

The building of mosques in western Europe involved a transfer of architectural style, cultural meaning, and iconography.[31] In their urban environment, the buildings clearly stuck out. The Wünsdorf mosque, for instance, was modeled after the famous *Dome of the Rock* in Jerusalem, an Islamic shrine built in the Umayyad style in the centre of the *Al-Aqsa Mosque*, whereas the mosque of Berlin-Wilmersdorf, with its two 32-metre minarets, was clearly influenced by its Indian creators.[32] Designed by a German architect, it was constructed in the style of *Mughal* burial buildings. According to the German convert Albert Seiler-Chan, its architecture was influenced by the *Taj Mahal* of Agra. To ordinary Berlin citizens it soon became known as the "Jewel Box" ("Schmuckkästchen"). The same label would certainly be appropriate to describe the Woking mosque, which was built by the Victorian architect William Isaac Chambers in the style of Indian *koubbas*.[33] The French mosques differed entirely from those in Berlin and London, reflecting the different backgrounds of Muslims in France. The mosque of Fréjus was more or less a replica of the *Great Mosque of Djenné* in Mali, which had been built after the turn of the twentieth century and remains the world's largest mud brick building.[34] Like its African model, the Fréjus mosque had an open interior and was made entirely of red mud brick and mud mortar. Similarly, the Paris mosque was heavily influenced by north African architecture. Again, the mosque was planned and constructed by European architects.[35] It was patterned after the *madrasa*s of Fez, particularly the famous *Bou Inania Madrasa*, built in the fourteenth century. Finally, also the architecture of the planned mosque in Marseilles was intended to reflect the culture of north African Islam.[36]

The mosques became the clearest markers of physical Muslim space in western Europe. Often, their territory was also marked by other Islamic symbols such as flags or banners. In 1934, for instance, on the occasion of the death of the German president Paul von Hindenburg, the local Berlin papers reported that "the green banner of the prophet" with "mourning bands" was flown "at half-mast" on the mosque at the *Fehrbelliner Platz*.[37] In fact, this episode also hints at another dimension of the mosques—their political significance.

The newly founded mosques were frequently transformed into diplomatic places. From the European perspective, they were a symbol of the worldwide Muslim community, representing Islam in Germany, Britain, and France. As imaginative cultural bridges to the Muslim world, European governments were eager to make political use of the buildings. Diplomats, heads of state, and religious dignitaries from across the Muslim world all made a point of attending the mosques during their visits to the West. During the interwar period, the visitors to the Berlin mosque included the princes of Hyderabad, the Amir of Afghanistan, the Lebanese Druze prince Shakib Arslan, and the Aga Khan who visited Berlin in his role as the president of the League of Nations in 1937.[38] A year earlier, in 1936, the Nazi regime had made extensive use of the Wilmersdorf mosque during the Olympic Games, when the building was used to welcome Muslim athletes. And when the Grande Mosquée opened in Paris, the French president received Sultan Yusef of Morocco.[39] Delegations from the sultan of Morocco, the maharaja of Kapurthala, Istanbul, and Angora were among the guests present during the festivities that surrounded the laying of the foundation stone in 1922.[40] In 1930, the Albanian ambassador Ilyas Vrioni used the Paris Mosque as a stage to proclaim the secularist Zogist state as "a fortress of the Islamic traditions in Europe."[41] In Woking, the Aga Khan, Amir Faisal of Saudi Arabia, King Faruq of Egypt, and chiefs from northern Nigeria attended services at the mosque.[42] The mosques became part of the international diplomatic stage. They became political buildings, buildings that were ultimately used in propaganda efforts during World War II by both Axis and Allies.[43]

Although they were the most important physical markers of Islam, mosques were not the only Muslim buildings constructed in interwar western Europe. In March 1935, sponsored by the state, a Muslim hospital, *L'Hôpital Franco-Musulman* (since 1978, *Hôpital Avicenne*) opened in Bobigny, near Paris.[44] It included a prayer room and, from 1937, an adjoining Islamic cemetery. Burial places, in fact, became another major physical sign of Muslim presence in interwar western Europe. Like mosques, Islamic graveyards were highly symbolic places.[45] Characterized by distinctively shaped and decorated gravestones, which were directed towards Mecca, they provided not only a territory for burial, but also for funerary rites and rituals of remembrance. Prior to World War I, Muslims who died in France, Germany, or Britain were usually buried in Christian graveyards. Between 1914 and 1918, Islamic cemeteries for Muslim soldiers were laid out in all three countries. In France, a number of Muslim graveyards were founded in the Parisian area, in Bagneux, Pantin, Ivry, and one close to the newly constructed mosque in Nogent-sur-Marne.[46] On the burial place site in Nogent-sur-Marne a *koubba*, inscribed with two verses from the Qur'an (sura 3, verse 169 and 170), was built in 1919.[47] The founding of the Islamic site in Nogent-sur-Marne was a direct response to the construction of the German mosque in the Wünsdorf prisoner camp. The camps in Wünsdorf and Zossen, in fact, also included a Muslim cemetery.[48] Germany's first Muslim graveyard, though, had already opened in 1866 in Berlin's Neukölln district, as a gesture from the German emperor to Constantinople, allowing the Ottoman sultan to bury his diplomats in Prussia.[49] Yet, it was not until the interwar period that the graveyard became more widely used by Muslims, and, between 1921 and 1922, a German architect, assigned by the Turkish embassy in Berlin, even constructed a small prayerhouse on the site. As in France and Germany, British authorities also established an Islamic cemetery during World War I.[50] Intended for the burial of colonial soldiers, it was laid out in close proximity to the Woking mosque. In 1937, finally, a year after his arrival in Britain, al-Hakimi managed to convince the local authorities to create a Muslim section in Harton cemetery in South Shields.[51]

IV. LEGAL SPACES: ESTABLISHING ASSOCIATIONS AND ORGANIZATIONS

Muslim life in interwar Europe was not only characterized by mosque-building projects, but also by the emergence of associations, clubs, and unions that organized Muslims according to membership, statutes, rules, and hierarchies. This was a new phenomenon, one that had not existed before 1914. The creation of these legal spaces within the majority society had at least two functions. First, formal organizations were used to represent Muslims and to defend their causes in the non-Muslim state. Moreover, the organizational frame-work held the community together, generating a cultural island, a space for Muslim religious practice, debate, and sociability. Generally, Muslims in non-Muslim societies tended to be more organized than in Muslim countries. We can therefore hardly describe the making of Islamic legal spaces in simple terms of cultural transfer. Islamic organizations were hybrid constructs, combining Islamic purposes with European forms of organization. This phenomenon was most prevalent in Germany, where German *Vereinskultur* fused with Islam. Most Muslim groups there were registered as "eingetragener Verein," a standard designation in the German legal framework. Even a Berlin Sufi group became registered as *Sufi Order e.V.*

In the German capital, the "Islamic Community of Berlin" (*Islamische Gemeinde zu Berlin e.V.*), founded by Abdul Jabbar Kheiri in April 1922, became an early centre of organized Muslim life.[52] In 1927, the community opened the "Islam Institute of Berlin" (*Islam Institut zu Berlin*).[53] Attempts by diplomats of the embassies from several Muslim countries to organize Berlin's Muslims within a "Society for Islamic Worship" (*Verein für Islamische Gottesverehrung*), led by the former Ottoman officer Zeki Kiram, were unsuccessful.[54] In the mid-1920s, the *Ahmadiyya* mission established the "Muslim Community" (*Moslemische Gemeinschaft*), later renamed "German-Muslim Society" (*Deutsch-Moslemische Gesellschaft*), which was the official organization of the Wilmersdorf mosque.[55] Although it was met with suspicion by some of Berlin's Muslims, especially the group around the Kheiri brothers, the "German-Muslim Society" largely succeeded in uniting Muslims from various backgrounds in an ecumenical union. Nevertheless, tensions between the "Islamic Community of Berlin" and the "German-Muslim Society" remained unresolved. Throughout the 1920s and 1930s, various smaller Muslim groups also founded organizations and associations, which, however, often did not comprise more than a dozen members, such as the Berlin Sufi group (*Sufi Orden e.V.*), the "Society for the Support of Muslim Students from Russia" (*Verein zur Unterstützung der muslimischen Studenten aus Rußland*) and the Islamic student union *Islamia Studentenvereinigung* of the Frederick William University (today Humboldt University).[56] Given that the Muslim community in Germany was smaller by far than that in France or Britain, the extent of the formal organization of Islam in Germany is remarkable. The year 1933 had no significant effect on the Islamic associations. Although they were now closely monitored by the Nazi regime, the organizations were not restricted.[57] In France, by comparison, Muslims organized themselves into fewer associations, most notably the "Islamic Institute" (*Institut Musulman*), which was opened by Benghabrit in a Paris apartment close to the Place de la Concorde during World War I, and a number of smaller societies that had emerged since the beginning of the century, such as the Paris-based *Fraternité Musulmane*.[58] In the 1930s, French authorities anxiously observed the members of the Islamic reformist *Association des Oulémas Musulmans Algériens*, who had founded educational and discussion groups.[59] In Britain, too, there was no all-encompassing association like the "German-Muslim Society."[60] Shortly after the outbreak of World War I, the "British Muslim Society" was set up under the patronage of Lord Headley, an influential British convert. Headley cooperated closely with the Woking mission, conferring a great deal of prestige on the *Ahmadiyya* institution. After World War I, other influential associations emerged: the "Islamic Society," led by the Cambridge-educated barrister Maulvi Abdul Majid, and the "Western Islamic Association," headed by the British convert Khalid Sheldrake. Both had links to the Woking mosque, but also branched out to the British seaports. Moreover, smaller groups, such as the "Muslim Literary Society" were established. In the 1930s, Shaykh 'Abd Allah Ali al-Hakimi institutionalized his *Alawiyya* Sufi *zawiya*s as "Zaouia Islamia Allawouia Religious Society of the United Kingdom."

It is remarkable that for so many exile groups, religion remained a key notion of identification. Some, of course, joined or grouped themselves into nonreligious organizations, which were often nationalist or organized along ethnic lines and at times even openly dismissed religion. In Britain, for instance, national associations such as the Somali Club, the Arab Club, the Indian Workers Association or the All-India Union of Seamen included Muslim members, who were not necessarily organized in religious organizations. On the occasion of the inauguration of the Wilmersdorf mosque in Berlin, a group of Egyptian nationalists distributed pamphlets denouncing the mosque as a "nest of spies" before they were arrested by the Berlin police.[61] Kemalist groups in the German capital clashed with Muslims of the "Islamic Community of Berlin" following the abolishment of the caliphate in March 1924.[62] In Paris, the nationalist Algerian *L'Étoile Nord-Africaine* vehemently criticized the foundation of the Grand Mosquée as an act of French colonial propaganda, and denounced the lavish inauguration as "mosquée-réclame."[63] Still, compared with national organizations, the number of religious associations that were founded in interwar western Europe is striking.

Eventually, several of these local Muslim organizations became translocally connected. Moreover, French, British, and German Muslim associations were often well-embedded within transnational Islamic organizations that had been emerging since the late nineteenth century. The *Ahmadiyya* branches in India, for example, influenced the activities of the missions in both Woking and Berlin-Wilmersdorf. In 1932, a Berlin section of the Islamic World Congress was opened.[64] Around the same time, a vehement controversy erupted among German and Italian Muslim students over the question whether the centre of the European Muslim Student League should be located in Berlin or in Rome. The most important transnational event for European Muslims during that period was certainly the *European Muslim Congress*, held in Geneva in August 1935, where Muslim activists from various western European countries promoted a cosmopolitan sense of Muslim solidarity.[65] Organized by the Geneva-based Muslim émigré circle around Shakib Arslan, the congress was the first attempt to gather under one roof these local activists from across the continent.

Overall, German, French, and British authorities dealt quite benevolently with Muslim attempts to organize themselves in associations. In the eyes of many European officials, dealing with the Muslim minority could have direct influence on their country's relationship with the wider Muslim world. European governments regularly took foreign policy implications into consideration when dealing with their Muslim minorities. Consequently, policies toward the Muslim minorities were made not only at the municipal, but often even at a national level, at the foreign ministries and colonial offices. It was the *Quai d'Orsay*, the *Auswärtiges Amt*, the Colonial Office and the India Office, rather than the offices of the interiors, which were involved in issues regarding the Muslim organizations. The files on the "Islamic world" of the German Foreign Office, for instance, contain significant numbers of documents on the Muslim community in Berlin.[66] Overall, the state played a major role in shaping Muslim communities in interwar western Europe, granting permission for buildings and associations, and at times even supporting them financially.

V. Communicative and Intellectual Spaces: Creating Journals and a Muslim Public

Finally, the interwar period witnessed the spread of Islamic newspapers and journals throughout western Europe. Through them, Muslims attempted to create an Islamic public within their majority societies and connect Muslim individuals within imagined and now fomenting Muslim exile communities. In fact, journals were perceived to be crucial instruments of community building by their publishers.

In Britain, two Muslim journals had already been in circulation in the 1890s—the weekly *The Crescent* (*1893) and the monthly *The Islamic World* (*1893), both founded by William Quilliam's Liverpool congregation.[67] During the interwar period, a number of new papers appeared, among them the widely read *Islamic Review* (*1913), published by the Woking mission, and smaller publications like the so-called *Sufi Magazine* (*1915).[68] The Islamic press also flourished in the French capital, exemplified, for instance, by the journals *France-Islam: Revue Mensuelle Illustrée des Pays de l'Orient et de l'Islam* (*1923), *Al-Islam: Journal d'Information et d'Éducation*

(*1930) and *Chroniques Brèves: Informations Mensuelles de la Revue en Terre d'Islam* (*1938). During World War I, the French government had authorized a French Muslim paper, as had the Germans, who distributed the journals *Al-Jihad* (Holy War) (*1915) and *Jaridat al-Asara Mata Halbmondlager* (Camp Paper of the Halbmondlager) (*1916) among its Muslim prisoners of war.[69] Most Muslim papers in the 1920s and 1930s were published in Berlin, an intellectual hub of European Islam.[70] In fact, more than a dozen periodicals explicitly labeled "Islamic" were created during that time, although most of them were relatively short-lived. They included not only *Islam: Ein Wegweiser zur Rettung und zum Wiederaufbau* (*1922) of Kheiri's "Islamic Community of Berlin" and the famous *Die Moslemische Revue* (*1924) of the *Ahmadiyya* mission, but also titles like *Liwa al-Islam* (Banner of Islam) (*1921), *Azadi Sharq* (Freedom of the East) (*1921), *Die Islamische Gegenwart: Monatszeitschrift für die Zeitgeschichte des Islam* (*1927), *Islam-Echo* (*1927), and the Muslim student journal *Der Islamische Student* (*1927). For a short period of time, Muslims in Berlin even published the English-language papers *The Crescent: The Only Muslim Organ in Europe* (*1923) and *The Muslim Standard* (*1924), which distinctly targeted a European Muslim audience.

According to the pretensions and conceptions of their makers, the journals were intended to reach a readership beyond the orbit of local communities, connecting Muslims from all over western Europe and linking them to the heartlands of the Islamic world. In many respects, the journals reflected an emerging Islamic internationalism, which was particularly promoted by Muslims in Europe. Indeed, among diaspora groups, the imagined global *umma* seemed to be more important as a reference point than it was in the Islamic world itself. This is reflected in the journals' languages, their subjects, their contributors, and their distribution. Most of them were published in European—some in non-European—languages. A number of papers contained articles in different languages. They frequently discussed global Muslim issues, such as the caliphate question, pan-Islamic anti-imperialism, or the Palestine conflict. Writers from all parts of the world contributed. For instance, authors of *Die Moslemische Revue* included international religious figures like Muhammad Ali of Lahore; similarly, the imam of the Berlin mosque, Maulana Sadr-ud-Din, also wrote in London's *Islamic Review*. Both publications advertised in each other. Finally, many of these journals were available in various European metropolises and beyond. The German publications *Liwa al-Islam* and *Azadi Sharq* were distributed in India, Iran, Egypt, Dubai, Qatar, Oman, and the Najd.[71]

Already, at the turn of the century, the first British-Islamic paper *The Crescent* had subscribers in India, Turkey, China, the United States, Egypt, Switzerland, Morocco, West Africa, Germany, New Zealand, Afghanistan, Iran, Australia, Syria, and Canada.[72] Clearly, the history of these new local religious minorities was also a global history.

CONCLUSION

The emergence of Muslim minority communities in western Europe in the interwar years continues to be a fruitful field of historical inquiry. Although the previous pages have focused on the minorities of France, German, and Britain, future research may examine the history of Muslim communities in other parts of interwar western Europe. Although in countries like Italy, Belgium, or the Netherlands the first mosques were only built after World War II, they were still home to considerable Muslim minorities before the war.[73] In the successor states of the Danube Monarchy, Islam had already been institutionalized long before World War I. Ultimately, the further study of the history of these Muslim minorities will contribute more generally to our understanding of diaspora communities, cross-cultural migration, and religious minorities in the global age.

NOTES

1. The body of literature on Muslim minorities in contemporary Europe is vast. A comprehensive overview is given by Yvonne Yazbeck Haddad, "The Globalisation of Islam: The Return of Muslims to the West," in *The Oxford History of Islam,* ed. John L. Esposito (Oxford: Oxford University Press, 1999), 601–641. One of the first comparative introductions is Jørgen S. Nielsen, *Muslims in Western Europe* (Edinburgh: Edinburgh University Press, 1992); see also Jørgen S. Nielsen, *Towards a European Islam* (London: Palgrave Macmillan, 1999); Bernard Lewis and Dominique Schnapper, *Muslims in Europe* (London and New York: Pinter, 1994); Jan Rath, et al., *Western Europe and its Islam* (Leiden, Netherlands: Brill, 2001); Iftikhar H. Malik, *Islam and Modernity: Muslims in Europe and the United States* (London: Pluto, 2004); and Joel S. Fetzer and J. Christopher Soper, *Muslims and the State in Britain, France and Germany* (Cambridge: Cambridge University Press, 2005). Notable studies on Britain are Mohammad S. Reza, *Islam in Britain: Past, Present and the Future* (Leicester: Volcano, 1991); Philip Lewis, *Islamic Britain: Religion, Politics and Identity among British Muslims* (London: IB Tauris, 1994); Daniele Joly, *Britannia's Crescent: Making a Place*

for Muslims in British Society (Aldershot, UK: Avebury, 1995); Peter E. Hopkins, *Muslims in Britain: Race, Place and Identities* (Edinburgh: Edinburgh University Press, 2009); and Sophie Gilliat-Ray, *Muslims in Britain: An Introduction* (Cambridge: Cambridge University Press, 2010); on France, see Annie Krieger-Krynicki, *Les Musulmans en France: Religion et Culture* (Paris: Maisonneuve et Larose, 1985); Gilles Kepel, *Le Banlieues de l'Islam* (Paris: Seuil, 1987); Jocelyne Cesari, *Être Musulman en France: Associations, Militants et Mosquées* (Paris: Karthala, 1994); on Germany, see Ursula Spuler-Stegemann, *Muslime in Deutschland: Nebeneinander oder Miteinander?* (Freiburg: Herder, 1998); Alacacioglu Hasan, *Deutsche Heimat Islam* (Munich: Waxmann, 2000); and Faruk Şen and Hayrettin Aydin, *Islam in Deutschland* (Munich: C. H. Beck, 2002). For the early literature in the field, see also Felice Dassetto and Yves Conrad, *Muslims in Western Europe: An Annotated Bibliography* (Paris: Harmattan, 1996).

2. The literature on the history of Muslim minorities in western Europe includes, on Britain: Humayun Ansari, *The Infidel Within: Muslims in Britain since 1800* (London: Hurst, 2004); Humayun Ansari, ed., *The Making of the East London Mosque, 1910–1951* (Cambridge: Cambridge University Press, 2011); Humayun Ansari, "The Woking Mosque: A Case Study of Muslim Engagement with British Society since 1889," *Immigrants and Minorities* 21.3 (2002), 1–24; Humayun Ansari, "Processes of Institutionalization of Islam in England and Wales, 1830s–1930s," in *Muslims in Europe: From Margin to the Centre*, ed. Jamal Malik (Münster: Lit, 2004), 35–48; Humayun Ansari, "'Burying the Dead': Making Muslim Space in Britain," *Historical Research* 80 (2007), 545–566; Richard Lawless, "Religion and Politics among Arab Seafarers in Britain in the Early Twentieth Century," *Islam and Christian-Muslim Relations* 5.1 (1994), 35–56; A. L. Tibawi, "History of the London Central Mosque and of the Islamic Cultural Centre 1910–1980," *Die Welt des Islams* 21.1–4 (1981), 192–208; Ron Geaves, *Islam in Victorian Britain: The Life and Times of Abdullah Quilliam* (Leicester: Kube, 2010); Muhammad Mumtaz Ali, *The Muslim Community in Britain: An Historical Account* (Kelana Jaya, Malaysia: Pelanduk, 1996); and M. M. Ally, *History of Muslims in Britain 1850–1980* (MA dissertation, Birmingham, 1981). On Germany, see Bernd Bauknecht, *Muslime in Deutschland von 1920 bis 1945* (Cologne, Germany: Teiresias, 2001); M. Salim Abdullah, *Die Geschichte des Islams in Deutschland* (Graz: Styria, 1981); M. Salim Abdullah, *Und gab ihnen sein Königswort: Berlin-Preußen-Bundesrepublik: Ein Abriß der Geschichte der islamischen Minderheit in Deutschland* (Altenberge, Germany: Cis, 1987); Gerhard Höpp, *Muslime in der Mark: Als Kriegsgefangene und Internierte in Wünsdorf und Zossen, 1914–1924* (Berlin: Das Arabische Buch, 1997); Gerhard Höpp, "Muslime in Märkischer Heide: Die Wünsdorfer Moschee,

1915 bis 1924," *Moslemische Revue* 1 (1989), 21–28; Gerhard Höpp, "Die Wünsdorfer Moschee: Eine Episode Islamischen Lebens in Deutschland, 1915–1930," *Die Welt des Islams* 36.2 (1996), 204–218; Gerhard Höpp, "Zwischen Moschee und Demonstration: Muslime in Berlin, 1920–1930," *Moslemische Revue* 3 (1990), 135–146; 4 (1990), 230–238; and 1 (1991), 13–19; Gerhard Höpp, "Muslime unterm Hakenkreuz: Zur Entstehung des Islamischen Zentralinstituts zu Berlin e.V.," *Moslemische Revue* 1 (1994), 16–27; and Britta Richter, "Islam in Deutschland der Zwischenkriegsjahre," *Zeitschrift für Türkeistudien* 2 (1996), 257–266. On France: Alain Boyer, *L'Institut Musulman de la Mosquée de Paris* (Paris: Cheam, 1992); Michel Renard, "Aperçu sur l'Histoire de l'Islam à Marseille, 1813–1962: Pratiques Religieuses et Encadrement des Nord-Africains," *Outre-Mers* 90.340–341 (2003): 269–296; Michel Renard, "Gratitude, Contrôle, Accompagnement: Le Traitement du Religieux Islamique en Métropole (1914–1950)," *Bulletin de l'Institut d'Histoire du Temps Présent* 83 (2004): 54–69; Michel Renard, "Les Débuts de la Présence Musulmane en France et son Encadrement," in *Histoire de l'Islam et des Musulmans en France du Moyen Age à Nos Jours*, ed. Mohammed Arkoun (Paris: Albin Michel, 2006), 712–740; Pascal le Pautremat, *La Politique Musulmane de la France au XXe Siècle: De l'Hexagone aux Terres d'Islam* (Paris: Maisonneuve et Larose, 2003), 277–308 and 327–342; Sadek Sellam, *La France et Ses Musulmans: Un Siècle de Politique Musulmane (1895–2005)* (Paris: Fayard, 2006), esp. 177–184; and Naomi Davidson, *Only Muslim: Embodying Islam in Twentieth-Century France* (Ithaca, NY: Cornell University Press, 2012), 36–85. A landmark volume is Nathalie Clayer and Eric Germain, eds., *Islam in Inter-War Europe* (London: Hurst, 2008), especially the introduction and the articles on Muslim minorities in western Europe by Eric Germain, Sebastian Cwiklinski, Humayun Ansari, and Richard Lawless.
3. Among the most notable historical studies of ethnic and national minorities are Neil MacMaster, *Colonial Migrants and Racism: Algerians in France, 1900–62* (London: Palgrave Macmillan, 1997); Paul A. Silverstein, *Algeria in France: Transpolitics, Race, and Nation* (Bloomington: Indiana University Press, 2004); Fred Halliday, *Arabs in Exile: Yemeni Migrants in Urban Britain* (London: IB Tauris, 1992) (republished in 2010 as *Britain's First Muslims: Portrait of an Arab Community*); Idem, "The *Millet* of Manchester: Arab Merchants and Cotton Trade," *British Journal of Middle Eastern Studies* 19.2 (1992), 159–176; Richard I. Lawless, *From Ta'izz to Tyneside: An Arab Community in the North-East of England during the Early Twentieth Century* (Exeter: University of Exeter Press, 1995); David Byrne, "Class, Race and Nation: The Politics of the 'Arab Issue' in South Shields 1919–39," in *Ethnic Labour and British Imperial Trade: A History of Ethnic Seafarers*

in the UK, ed. Diane Frost (London: Routledge, 1995), 89–103;
Kathleen Hunter, *History of Pakistanis in Britain* (Norwich: Page
Bros, 1963); Rozina Visram, *Ayahs, Lascars and Princes: Indians in
Britain, 1700–1947* (London: Pluto, 1986); Rozina Visram, *Asians
in Britain: 400 Years of History* (London: Pluto, 2002); Shompa
Lahiri, *Indians in Britain: Anglo-Indian Encounters, Race and
Identity, 1880–1930* (London: Routledge, 2000); Denis Wright,
The Persians amongst the English: Episodes in Anglo-Persian History
(London: IB Tauris, 1985); Kris Manjapra, *The Mirrored World:
Cosmopolitan Encounter between Indian Anti-Colonial Intellectuals
and German Radicals, 1905–1939* (PhD dissertation, Harvard
University, 2007); Gerhard Höpp, "Arabs in Berlin: The Political
and Journalistic Activities of Arab Anti-Colonialists in the Capital
of the Reich, 1918–1928," *Asia, Africa, Latin America*, Special
Issue 18 (1986), 94–110; Iskander Gilyazov, "Die Wolgatataren
und Deutschland im ersten Drittel des 20. Jahrhunderts," in *Muslim
Culture in Russia and Central Asia from the 18th to the Early 20th
Centuries*, eds. Michael Kemper et al. (Berlin: Klaus Schwarz, 1996–
1998), vol. 2, 335–353; and Ingeborg Böer, Ruth Haerkötter, and
Petra Kappert, eds., *Türken in Berlin, 1871–1945: Eine Metropole
in den Erinnerungen osmanischer und türkischer Zeitzeugen* (Berlin
and New York: Walter de Gruyter, 2002).
4. On Islamic networks in contemporary Europe, see articles in Stefano
Allievi and Jørgen S. Nielsen, eds., *Muslim Networks and Transnational
Communities in and across Europe* (Leiden, Netherlands: Brill, 2003);
on transnational and global interrelations of religious communities
in general, see articles in Susanne Hoeber Rudolph and James P.
Piscatori, eds., *Transnational Religion and Fading States* (Boulder,
CO: Westview, 1997).
5. Barbara Daly Metcalf, ed., *Making Muslim Space in North America
and Europe* (Berkeley: University of California Press, 1996).
6. Although a problematic concept, the following pages will refer to
"community." Amitai Etzioni, "Creating Good Communities and
Good Societies," *Contemporary Sociology* 29.1 (2000), 188–195; and
Steven Brint, "Gemeinschaft Revisited: A Critique and Reconstruction
of the Community Concept," *Sociological Theory* 19.1 (2001), 1–23
provide critical examinations of the concept. E. P. Thompson, *The
Making of the English Working Class* (London: Victor Gollancz,
1963) remains the seminal historical study of the cultural construction of community.
7. Amira K. Bennison, "Muslim Universalism and Western globalisation," in *Globalization in World History*, ed. A. G. Hopkins (London:
W. W. Norton, 2002), 74–97; and Marshall G. S. Hodgson,
*Rethinking World History: Essays on Europe, Islam, and World
History* (Cambridge: Cambridge University Press, 1993), 97–243;
see also Everett Jenkins Jr., *The Muslim Diaspora: A Comprehensive*

Reference to the Spread of Islam in Asia, Africa, Europe and the Americas 1500–1799 (New York: Mcfarland, 2000).

8. On the early presence of individuals and small groups, see Ian Coller, *Arab France: Islam and the Making of Modern Europe, 1798–1831* (Berkeley: University of California Press, 2009); Nabil Matar, *Islam in Britain, 1558–1685* (Cambridge: Cambridge University Press, 1998); Nabil Matar and Gerald MacLean, *Britain and the Islamic World, 1558–1713* (Oxford: Oxford University Press, 2011); and, more generally on Europe's early encounters with Islam, Bernard Lewis, *Islam and the West* (New York and Oxford: Oxford University Press, 1993); Franco Cardini, *Europe and Islam* (Cambridge: Blackwell, 2001); and Jack Goody, *Islam in Europe* (Cambridge: Blackwell, 2004).

9. Ansari, *Infidel Within*, 24–51; on Muslims in Liverpool, Manchester, Cardiff, and South Shields, see also Geaves, *Islam in Victorian Britain*; Halliday, *Britain's First Muslims*; Halliday, "The *Millet* of Manchester"; Lawless, *From Ta'izz to Tyneside*; Lawless, "Religion and Politics"; Lawless, "Islam in the Service of Social Control: The Case of Arab Seamen in Britain during the Inter-War Years," in *Islam*, eds. Clayer and Germain, 229–252; and Byrne, "Class, Race and Nation."

10. It is estimated that more than 100,000 Algerians were living in France by 1930, in addition to the many thousands of Tunisians, Moroccans, and Muslims from other parts of the French Empire, see Gérard Noiriel, *Immigration, Antisémitisme et Racisme en France (XIXe-XXe Siècle): Discours Publics, Humiliations Privées* (Paris: Fayard, 2009), 313.

11. Höpp, *Muslime in der Mark*, on the numbers, see 44–45; see also articles in Gerhard Höpp, ed., *Fremde Erfahrungen: Asiaten und Afrikaner in Deutschland, Österreich und in der Schweiz bis 1945* (Berlin: Klaus Schwarz, 1996); and Gerhard Höpp and Brigitte Reinwald, eds., *Fremdeinsätze: Afrikaner und Asiaten in Europäischen Kriegen 1914–1945* (Berlin: Das Arabische Buch, 2000); for a summary, see Höpp, "*Muslime* in *Märkischer Heide*"; Höpp, "Die Wünsdorfer Moschee"; and Abdullah, *Geschichte des Islams*, 23–27.

12. For the 1920s, see Höpp, "Zwischen Moschee und Demonstration" I, 136; for the 1930s, see M. Salim Abdullah, "Zwischen Anbiederung und Friedenspredigt," *Moslemische Revue* 3 (1999): 129–138, 137.

13. Renard, "Présence Musulmane," 716–717; see also Belkacem Recham, *Les Musulmans Algériens dans l'Armée Française (1919–1945)* (Paris: Harmattan, 1996); and Belkacem Recham, "Les Musulmans dans l'Armée Française, 1900–1945," in *Histoire de l'Islam*, ed. Arkoun, 742–761.

14. Renard, "Présence Musulmane," 730–731.

15. Renard, "Présence Musulmane," 718–730; Michel Renard, "Gratitude, Contrôle, Accompagnement"; Boyer, *L'Institut Musulman de la Mosquée de Paris*, 19–33; Pautremat, *La Politique Musulmane de la France au XXe Siècle*, 333–342; Sellam, *La France et Ses Musulmans*,

178–184; and Davidson, *Only Muslim*, 36–61; for a contemporary account, see René Weiss, *Réception à l'Hôtel de Ville de Sa
Majesté Moulay Youssef, Sultan du Maroc: Inauguration de l'Institut
Musulman et de la Mosquée* (Paris: Imprimerie Nationale, 1927).
Hamza Ben Driss Ottmani, *Kaddour Benghabrit: Un Maghrébin hors
du Commun* (Rabat: Marsam, 2010) provides a sympathetic account
of the mosque's rector.

16. Renard, "Présence Musulmane," 727–728.
17. Renard, "Présence Musulmane," 732–734; and Renard, "Aperçu sur
l'Histoire de l'Islam à Marseille," 281–286.
18. Höpp, *Muslime in der Mark*, esp. 113–129; and the literature in
note 11.
19. Chalid-Albert Seiler-Chan, "Der Islam in Berlin und Anderwärts im
Deutschen Reiche," *Moslemische Revue* 2–3 (1934): 47–56; and 4
(1934), 112–119, quote from part II, 114–115.
20. Bauknecht, *Muslime in Deutschland*, 59–65; Höpp, "Zwischen
Moschee und Demonstration," I, 141–146; II, 230–232; and
Abdullah, *Geschichte des Islams*, 28–34; on the wider context of the
Ahmadiyya Lahore in Europe, see Eric Germain, "The First Muslim
Missions on a European Scale: Ahmadi-Lahori Networks in the
Inter-War Period," in *Islam*, eds. Clayer and Germain, 89–118.
21. An overview of German press articles on Islam can be gained in the
collections of the *Reichslandbund Pressearchiv*, stored in the German
Federal National Archives in Berlin-Lichterfelde (BA), R8034 II/2787
(Kirchen und Sekten, 1915–1919); R8034 II/2788 (Kirchen und
Sekten, 1919–1931); R8034 II/2789 (Kirchen und Sekten, 1931–
1935); and R8034 II/2790 (Kirchen und Sekten, 1935–1944).
22. Quoted in Manfred Backhausen, *Die Lahore-Ahmadiyya-Bewegung
in Europa: Geschichte, Gegenwart und Zukunft der als 'Lahore-
Ahmadiyya-Bewegung zur Verbreitung islamischen Wissens' bekannten
internationalen islamischen Gemeinschaft* (Lahore and Wembley, UK:
Ahmadiyya Anjuman Lahore Publication, 2008), 51–52; see also
Nasir Ahmad, *A Brief History of the Berlin Muslim Mission (Germany)
(1922–1988)* (n.p., 2004); on the Kheiri brothers, see Heike Liebau,
"The Kheiri Brothers and the Question of World Order after World
War I," *Orient Bulletin: History and Cultures in Asia, the Middle East
and Africa* (December 13, 2007): 3–4; and Majid Hayat Siddiqi,
"Bluff, Doubt and Fear: The Kheiri Brothers and the Colonial State,
1904–1945," *Indian Economic and Social History Review* 24.3
(1987): 233–263.
23. Bauknecht, *Muslime in Deutschland*, 64.
24. Ansari, *Infidel Within*, 82–84, 121–126; and Geaves, *Islam in
Victorian Britain*, esp. 59–130.
25. Ansari, *Infidel Within*, 126–134; and Ansari, "The Woking Mosque,"
6–13; H. Ansari, "Making Transnational Connections: Muslim
Networks in Early Twentieth-Century Britain," in *Islam*, eds. Clayer

and Germain, 31–63; and, on the wider context, Germain, "The First Muslim Missions."

26. Ansari, *Infidel Within*, 134; Ansari, "Introduction," in Ansari, *East London Mosque*, 1–80; and Tibawi, "London Central Mosque."
27. Ansari, ed., *East London Mosque*.
28. Tibawi, "London Central Mosque."
29. Ansari, *Infidel Within*, 135–143; Lawless, *From Ta'izz to Tyneside*, esp. 207–244; Lawless, "Religion and Politics"; Lawless, "Islam in the Service of Social Control"; and Halliday, *Britain's First Muslims*, 27–39, 137–139.
30. Haddad, "The Globalisation of Islam," 615–620.
31. Christian Welzbacher, *Euroislam-Architektur: Neue Moscheen des Abendlandes* (Amsterdam: Sun Architecture, 2008).
32. On the Wünsdorf mosque, see Martin Gussone, "Die Moschee im Wünsdorfer Halbmondlager: Die symbolische Inbesitznahme einer Architektonischen Ikone" (Paper, 3rd Colloquium of the Ernst-Herzfeld-Gesellschaft, Vienna, 2007); on the Wilmersdorf mosque, see Seiler-Chan, "Der Islam in Berlin," II, 115–116.
33. Mark Crinson, "The Mosque and the Metropolis," in *Orientalism's Interlocutors: Painting, Architecture, Photography*, eds. Jill Beaulieu and Mary Roberts (Durham, NC: Duke University Press, 2002), 79–102, 81–82; and S. Brown, "The Shah Jahan Mosque, Woking: An Unexpected Gem," *Conservation Bulletin* 46 (2004), 32–34.
34. Renard, "Présence Musulmane," 731.
35. Renard, "Présence Musulmane," 723.
36. Renard, "Présence Musulmane," 734.
37. Quoted in Bauknecht, *Muslime in Deutschland*, 87.
38. Bauknecht, *Muslime in Deutschland*, 69.
39. Renard, "Présence Musulmane," 724.
40. Renard, "Présence Musulmane," 723–724.
41. Quoted in Nathalie Clayer, "Behind the Veil: The Reform of Islam in Inter-War Albania or the Search for a 'Modern' and 'European' Islam," in *Islam*, eds. Clayer and Germain, 128–155, 151.
42. Ansari, *Infidel Within*, 133.
43. David Motadel, "Germany's Policy towards Islam, 1941–1945" (PhD dissertation, University of Cambridge, 2010).
44. Jalila Sbai, "L'Hôpital Franco-Musulman," in *Histoire de l'Islam*, ed. Arkoun, 741; see also Katia Kukawka and Sophie Daynes, eds., *L'Hôpital Avicenne, 1935–2005: Une Histoire sans Frontières* (Paris: Musée de l'Assistance Publique-Hôpitaux de Paris, 2005); Josiane Chevillard-Vabre, "Histoire de l'Hôpital Franco-Musulman" (MA dissertation, Paris VI, 1982); and Marie-Ange d'Adler, *Le Cimetière Musulman de Bobigny: Lieu de Mémoire d'un Siècle d'Immigration* (Paris: Autrement, 2005).
45. G. Jonker, "The Knife's Edge: Muslim Burial in the Diaspora," *Mortality* 1.1 (1996), 27–43.

46. Renard, "Présence Musulmane," 715–716.
47. Renard, "Présence Musulmane," 716–717.
48. Höpp, *Muslime in der Mark*, 131–137.
49. Gerhard Höpp and Gerdien Jonker, eds., *In fremder Erde: Zur Geschichte und Gegenwart der Islamischen Bestattung in Deutschland* (Berlin: Klaus Schwarz, 1996); and Karl-Robert Schütze, *Von den Befreiungskriegen bis zum Ende der Wehrmacht: Die Geschichte des Garnisonfriedhofs am Rande der Hasenheide in Berlin-Neukölln* (Berlin: Bezirksamt Neukölln, 1986).
50. Ansari, *Infidel Within*, 128; and Ansari, "Burying the Dead", 559–561.
51. Ansari, *Infidel Within*, 141; Ansari, "'Burying the Dead", 557–558; and Lawless, *From Ta'izz to Tyneside*, 209–212.
52. On the Muslim Community in Berlin, see Municipal Archive (Landesarchiv) Berlin (LArchB), B Rep. 042 (Amtsgericht Charlottenburg), No. 26590 (Islamische Gemeinde zu Berlin, 1922–1955); and A Pr. Br. Rep 030–04 (Polizeipräsidium Berlin, Vereine), No. 513 (Islamische Gemeinde zu Berlin, 1936); see also Bauknecht, *Muslime in Deutschland*, 58–59, 107–117.
53. On the Islam Institute, see LArchB, A Pr. Br. Rep 030–04 (Polizeipräsidium Berlin, Vereine), No. 2314 (Islam-Institut, 1939–1940); and LArchB, A Pr. Br. Rep. 030–04 (Polizeipräsidium Berlin, Vereine), No. 2840 (Islamisches Zentral-Institut zu Berlin).
54. Höpp, "Zwischen Moschee und Demonstration," I.140; on Zeki Kiram, see also Umar Ryad, "From an Officer in the Ottoman Army to a Muslim Publicist and Armament Agent in Berlin: Zekî Hishmat Kirâm (1886–1946)," *Bibliotheca Orientalis* 63.3–4 (2006), 235–268.
55. On the German-Muslim Society, see LArchB, A Pr. Br. Rep. 030–04 (Polizeipräsidium Berlin, Vereine), No. 1350 (Deutsch-Muslimische Gesellschaft zur Förderung des Islam durch Aufklärungsarbeiten, 1936–1939); see also the file of the Ahmadiyya Anjuman Ishat-i-Islam, in the German Federal National Archives in Berlin-Lichterfelde (BA), R87/2080.
56. On the Sufi Society of Berlin, see LArchB, B Rep. 042 (Amtsgericht Charlottenburg), No. 9021 (Sufi-Bewegung Berlin, 1925–1935); see also Bauknecht, *Muslime in Deutschland*, 94–95; on the Islamic student union, see Höpp, "Zwischen Moschee und Demonstration," II, 234–235.
57. The monitoring reports of the SS are stored in BA, R58/5955 (SS Reichssicherheitshauptamt, Beobachtung der islamischen Gemeinde in Berlin, 1933–1937) and BA, R58/5633 (SS Reichssicherheitshauptamt, Beobachtungen der Tätigkeit nichtchristlicher Religionsgemeinschaften, 1939–1944).
58. Renard, "Présence Musulmane," 718–721.
59. Renard, "Présence Musulmane," 737–740.

60. Ansari, *Infidel Within*, 130–143; Ansari, "Making Transnational Connections", 49–50, 58–59; Lawless, *From Ta'izz to Tyneside*, 219; Lawless, "Religion and Politics"; Lawless, "Islam in the Service of Social Control," 237–250; and Halliday, *Britain's First Muslims*, 28.
61. Höpp, "Zwischen Moschee und Demonstration," I, 142–146.
62. Höpp, 139–140.
63. Renard, "Présence Musulmane," 727.
64. On the Berlin Section of the Muslim World Congress, see LArch, A Pr. Br. Rep 030–04 (Polizeipräsidium Berlin, Vereine), No. 1523 (Islamischer Weltkongress zu Berlin, 1933–1941).
65. Martin Kramer, *Islam Assembled: The Advent of the Muslim Congresses* (New York: Columbia University Press, 1986), 142–153; Jacob M. Landau, *The Politics of Pan-Islam: Ideology and Organization* (Oxford: Clarendon, 1990), 242–245; Reinhard Schulze, *Islamischer Internationalismus im 20. Jahrhundert: Untersuchungen zur Geschichte der Islamischen Weltliga* (Leiden, Netherlands: Brill, 1990), 102–103; Raja Adal, "Shakib Arslan's Imagining of Europe: The Coloniser, the Inquisitor, the Islamic, the Virtuous, and the Friend," in *Islam*, eds. Clayer and Germain, 156–182, 171–174; and, for contemporary accounts, Anonymous, "Der Muslimische Kongreß von Europa: Genf, September 1935", *Die Welt des Islams* 17.3–4 (1936), 99–104; and "Au Congrès Musulman d'Europe," *La Tribune d'Orient*, reprinted in *Die Welt des Islams* 17.3–4 (1936), 104–111.
66. On the case of the German Foreign Office involvement and monitoring of the Muslim community in Berlin and its international connections and networks, see Political Archives of the German Foreign Office (PA), R78240 (*Religions- und Kirchenwesen: Islam*, 1924–28); PA, R78241 (*Religions- und Kirchenwesen: Islam*, 1928–31); PA, R78242 (*Religions- und Kirchenwesen: Islam*, 1932–36); and PA, R104801 (*Religions- und Kirchenwesen: Islam*, 1936–39).
67. Ansari, *Infidel Within*, 83, 122.
68. Ansari, *Infidel Within*, 88, 129–130; and Ansari, "The Woking Mosque," 8–9; Ansari, "Making Transnational Connections," 48, 53.
69. Höpp, *Muslime in der Mark*, 101–112.
70. Gerhard Höpp, *Arabische und Islamische Periodika in Berlin und Brandenburg 1915–1945: Geschichtlicher Abriß und Bibliographie* (Berlin: Das Arabische Buch, 1994); see also Höpp, *Texte aus der Fremde: Arabische politische Publizistik in Deutschland, 1896–1945: Eine Bibliographie* (Berlin: Klaus Schwarz, 2000); Höpp, "Arabische und Islamische Periodika in Deutschland: Initiatoren und Ziele (1915–1929)," *Moslemische Revue* 3 (1991), 150–155; 4 (1991), 224–232; and 1 (1992) 49–58; and Johannes Benzing, "Berliner politische Veröffentlichungen der Türken aus der Sowjetunion," *Die Welt des Islams* 18 (1936), 122–131.
71. Höpp, *Arabische und Islamische Periodika*, 29.

72. Ansari, *Infidel Within*, 123.
73. Ismail Hakki Bey Tevfik, "Der Islam in Belgien und Luxemburg," *Der Islam* 18.3–4 (1929), 319–320 provides insights into the small Muslim minorities, mostly miners and workers, in interwar Belgium and Luxemburg.

REFERENCES

Abdullah, M. Salim. *Die Geschichte des Islams in Deutschland*. Graz: Styria, 1981.

———. *Und gab ihnen sein Königswort: Berlin-Preußen-Bundesrepublik: Ein Abriß der Geschichte der islamischen Minderheit in Deutschland*. Altenberge, Germany: Cis, 1987.

———. "Zwischen Anbiederung und Friedenspredigt." *Moslemische Revue* 3 (1999): 129–138.

Ahmad, Nasir. *A Brief History of the Berlin Muslim Mission (Germany) (1922–1988)*. n.p., 2004.

Ali, Muhammad Mumtaz. *The Muslim Community in Britain: An Historical Account*. Kelana Jaya, Malaysia: Pelanduk, 1996.

Allievi, Stefano and Jørgen S. Nielsen, eds. *Muslim Networks and Transnational Communities in and across Europe*. Leiden, Netherlands: Brill, 2003.

Ally, M. M. *History of Muslims in Britain 1850–1980*. MA dissertation, University of Birmingham, 1981.

Anonymous. "Au Congrès Musulman d'Europe." *La Tribune d'Orient*, reprinted in *Die Welt des Islams* 17.3–4 (1936): 104–111.

———. "Der Muslimische Kongreß von Europa: Genf, September 1935." *Die Welt des Islams* 17.3–4 (1936): 99–104.

Ansari, Humayun. "'Burying the Dead': Making Muslim Space in Britain." *Historical Research* 80 (2007): 545–566.

———. *The Infidel Within: Muslims in Britain since 1800*. London: Hurst, 2004.

———, ed. *The Making of the East London Mosque, 1910–1951*. Cambridge: Cambridge University Press, 2011.

———. "Processes of Institutionalisation of Islam in England and Wales, 1830s-1930s." In *Muslims in Europe: From Margin to the Centre*, edited by Jamal Malik, 35–48. Münster, Germany: Lit, 2004.

———. "The Woking Mosque: A Case Study of Muslim Engagement with British Society since 1889." *Immigrants and Minorities* 21.3 (2002): 1–24.

Arkoun, Mohammed, ed. *Histoire de l'Islam et des Musulmans en France du Moyen Age à Nos Jours*. Paris: Albin Michel, 2006.

Backhausen, Manfred. *Die Lahore-Ahmadiyya-Bewegung in Europa: Geschichte, Gegenwart und Zukunft der als 'Lahore-Ahmadiyya-Bewegung zur Verbreitung islamischen Wissens' bekannten internationalen islamischen Gemeinschaft*. Lahore and Wembley, UK: Ahmadiyya Anjuman Lahore Publication, 2008.

Bauknecht, Bernd. *Muslime in Deutschland von 1920 bis 1945*. Cologne, Germany: Teiresias, 2001.

Bennison, Amira K. "Muslim Universalism and Western Globalisation." In *Globalization in World History*, 74–97. London: W. W. Norton, 2002.

Benzing, Johannes. "Berliner politische Veröffentlichungen der Türken aus der Sowjetunion." *Die Welt des Islams* 18 (1936): 122–31.

Böer, Ingeborg, Ruth Haerkötter, and Petra Kappert, eds. *Türken in Berlin, 1871–1945: Eine Metropole in den Erinnerungen osmanischer und türkischer Zeitzeugen*. Berlin and New York: Walter de Gruyter, 2002.

Boyer, Alain. *L'Institut Musulman de la Mosquée de Paris*. Paris: Cheam, 1992.

Brint, Steven. "Gemeinschaft Revisited: A Critique and Reconstruction of the Community Concept." *Sociological Theory* 19.1 (2001): 1–23.

Brown, S. "The Shah Jahan Mosque, Woking: An Unexpected Gem." *Conservation Bulletin* 46 (2004): 32–34.

Byrne, David. "Class, Race and Nation: The Politics of the 'Arab Issue' in South Shields 1919–39." In *Ethnic Labour and British Imperial Trade: A History of Ethnic Seafarers in the UK*, edited by Diane Frost, 89–103. London: Routledge, 1995.

Cardini, Franco. *Europe and Islam*. Oxford: Blackwell, 2001.

Cesari, Jocelyne. *Être Musulman en France: Associations, Militants et Mosquées*. Paris: Karthala, 1994.

Chevillard-Vabre, Josiane. *Histoire de l'Hôpital Franco-Musulman*. MA dissertation, University Paris VI, 1982.

Clayer, Nathalie and Eric Germain, eds. *Islam in Inter-War Europe*. London: Hurst, 2008.

Coller, Ian. *Arab France: Islam and the Making of Modern Europe, 1798–1831*. Berkeley: University of California Press, 2009.

Crinson, Mark. "The Mosque and the Metropolis." In *Orientalism's Interlocutors: Painting, Architecture, Photography*, edited by Jill Beaulieu and Mary Roberts, 79–102. Durham, NC: Duke University Press, 2002.

d'Adler, Marie-Ange. *Le Cimetière Musulman de Bobigny: Lieu de Mémoire d'un Siècle d'Immigration*. Paris: Autrement, 2005.

Dassetto, Felice and Yves Conrad. *Muslims in Western Europe: An Annotated Bibliography*. Paris: Harmattan, 1996.

Davidson, Naomi. *Only Muslim: Embodying Islam in Twentieth-Century France*. Ithaca, NY: Cornell University Press, 2012.

Etzioni, Amitai. "Creating Good Communities and Good Societies." *Contemporary Sociology* 29.1 (2000): 188–195.

Fetzer Joel S. and J. Christopher Soper. *Muslims and the State in Britain, France and Germany*. Cambridge: Cambridge University Press, 2005.

Geaves, Ron. *Islam in Victorian Britain: The Life and Times of Abdullah Quilliam*. Leicester: Kube, 2010.

German Federal National Archives Berlin-Lichterfelde (BA), R87/2080 (Ahmadiyya Anjuman Ishat-i-Islam).

German Federal National Archives Berlin-Lichterfelde (BA), R8034 II/2787 (*Reichslandbund Pressearchiv*: Kirchen und Sekten, 1915–1919).

German Federal National Archives Berlin-Lichterfelde (BA), R8034 II/2788 (*Reichslandbund Pressearchiv*: Kirchen und Sekten, 1919–1931).

German Federal National Archives Berlin-Lichterfelde (BA), R8034 II/2789 (*Reichslandbund Pressearchiv*: Kirchen und Sekten, 1931–1935).

German Federal National Archives Berlin-Lichterfelde (BA), R8034 II/2790 (*Reichslandbund Pressearchiv*: Kirchen und Sekten, 1935–1944).

German Federal National Archives Berlin-Lichterfelde (BA), R58/599 (Reichssicherheitshauptamt, Beobachtung der islamischen Gemeinde Berlin, 1933–1947).

Gilliat-Ray, Sophie. *Muslims in Britain: An Introduction*. Cambridge: Cambridge University Press, 2010.

Gilyazov, Iskander. "Die Wolgatataren und Deutschland im ersten Drittel des 20. Jahrhunderts." In *Muslim Culture in Russia and Central Asia from the 18th to the Early 20th Centuries*, edited by Michael Kemper et al., 2 vols, vol. 2, 335–353. Berlin: Klaus Schwarz, 1996–1998.

Goody, Jack. *Islam in Europe*. Oxford: Blackwell, 2004.

Gussone, Martin. "Die Moschee im Wünsdorfer Halbmondlager: Die symbolische Inbesitznahme einer Architektonischen Ikone." Paper, 3rd Colloquium of the Ernst-Herzfeld-Gesellschaft, Vienna, 2007.

Haddad, Yvonne Yazbeck. "The Globalisation of Islam: The Return of Muslims to the West." In *The Oxford History of Islam*, edited by John L. Esposito, 601–641. Oxford: Oxford University Press, 1999.

Halliday, Fred. *Arabs in Exile: Yemeni Migrants in Urban Britain*. London: IB Tauris, 1992 (republished in 2010 as *Britain's First Muslims: Portrait of an Arab Community*).

———. "The *Millet* of Manchester: Arab Merchants and Cotton Trade." *British Journal of Middle Eastern Studies* 19.2 (1992): 159–176.

Hasan, Alacacioglu. *Deutsche Heimat Islam*. Munich: Waxmann, 2000.

Hodgson, Marshall G. S. *Rethinking World History: Essays on Europe, Islam, and World History*. Cambridge: Cambridge University Press, 1993.

Hopkins, Peter E. *Muslims in Britain: Race, Place and Identities*. Edinburgh: Edinburgh University Press, 2009.

Höpp, Gerhard. "Arabs in Berlin: The Political and Journalistic Activities of Arab Anti-Colonialists in the Capital of the Reich, 1918–1928." *Asia, Africa, Latin America*, Special Issue 18 (1986): 94–110.

———. *Arabische und Islamische Periodika in Berlin und Brandenburg 1915–1945: Geschichtlicher Abriß und Bibliographie*. Berlin: Das Arabische Buch, 1994.

———. "Arabische und Islamische Periodika in Deutschland: Initiatoren und Ziele (1915–1929)." *Moslemische Revue* 3 (1991): 150–155; 4 (1991): 224–232; and 1 (1992): 49–58.

———. "Die Wünsdorfer Moschee: Eine Episode Islamischen Lebens in Deutschland, 1915–1930." *Die Welt des Islams* 36.2 (1996): 204–218.

————, ed. *Fremde Erfahrungen: Asiaten und Afrikaner in Deutschland, Österreich und in der Schweiz bis 1945*. Berlin: Klaus Schwarz, 1996.

————. *Muslime in der Mark: Als Kriegsgefangene und Internierte in Wünsdorf und Zossen, 1914–1924*. Berlin: Das Arabische Buch, 1997.

————. "Muslime in Märkischer *Heide*: Die Wünsdorfer Moschee, 1915 bis 1924." *Moslemische Revue* 1 (1989): 21–28.

————. "Muslime unterm Hakenkreuz: Zur Entstehung des Islamischen Zentralinstituts zu Berlin e.V." *Moslemische Revue* 1 (1994): 16–27.

————. *Texte aus der Fremde: Arabische politische Publizistik in Deutschland, 1896–1945: Eine Bibliographie*. Berlin: Klaus Schwarz, 2000.

————. "Zwischen Moschee und Demonstration: Muslime in Berlin, 1920–1930." *Moslemische Revue* 3 (1990): 135–146; 4 (1990): 230–238; and 1 (1991): 13–19.

Höpp, Gerhard and Brigitte Reinwald, eds. *Fremdeinsätze: Afrikaner und Asiaten in Europäischen Kriegen 1914–1945*. Berlin: Das Arabische Buch, 2000.

Höpp, Gerhard and Gerdien Jonker, eds. *In fremder Erde: Zur Geschichte und Gegenwart der Islamischen Bestattung in Deutschland*. Berlin: Klaus Schwarz, 1996.

Hunter, Kathleen. *History of Pakistanis in Britain*. Norwich: Page Bros, 1963.

Jenkins, Everett Jr. *The Muslim Diaspora: A Comprehensive Reference to the Spread of Islam in Asia, Africa, Europe and the Americas 1500–1799*. New York: Mcfarland, 2000.

Joly, Daniele. *Britannia's Crescent: Making a Place for Muslims in British Society*. Aldershot, UK: Avebury, 1995.

Jonker, G. "The Knife's Edge: Muslim Burial in the Diaspora." *Mortality* 1.1 (1996): 27–43.

Kepel, Gilles. *Le Banlieues de l'Islam*. Paris: Seuil, 1987.

Kramer, Martin. *Islam Assembled: The Advent of the Muslim Congresses*. New York: Columbia University Press, 1986.

Krieger-Krynicki, Annie. *Les Musulmans en France: Religion et Culture*. Paris: Maisonneuve et Larose, 1985.

Kukawka Katia and Sophie Daynes, eds. *L'Hôpital Avicenne, 1935–2005: Une Histoire sans Frontières*. Paris: Musée de l'Assistance Publique-Hôpitaux de Paris, 2005.

Lahiri, Shompa. *Indians in Britain: Anglo-Indian Encounters, Race and Identity, 1880–1930*. London: Routledge, 2000.

Landau, Jacob M. *The Politics of Pan-Islam: Ideology and Organization*. Oxford: Clarendon, 1990.

Lawless, Richard. *From Ta'izz to Tyneside: An Arab Community in the North-East of England during the Early Twentieth Century*. Exeter: University of Exeter Press, 1995.

————. "Religion and Politics among Arab Seafarers in Britain in the Early Twentieth Century." *Islam and Christian-Muslim Relations* 5.1 (1994): 35–56.

Lewis, Bernard. *Islam and the West.* New York and Oxford: Oxford University Press, 1993.

Lewis Bernard and Dominique Schnapper. *Muslims in Europe.* London and New York: Pinter, 1994.

Lewis, Philip. *Islamic Britain: Religion, Politics and Identity among British Muslims.* London: IB Tauris, 1994.

Liebau, Heike. "The Kheiri Brothers and the Question of World Order after World War I." *Orient Bulletin: History and Cultures in Asia, the Middle East and Africa* (December 13, 2007): 3–4.

MacMaster, Neil. *Colonial Migrants and Racism: Algerians in France, 1900–62.* London: Palgrave Macmillan, 1997.

Malik, Iftikhar H. *Islam and Modernity: Muslims in Europe and the United States.* London: Pluto, 2004.

Manjapra, Kris. *The Mirrored World: Cosmopolitan Encounter between Indian Anti-Colonial Intellectuals and German Radicals, 1905–1939.* PhD dissertation, Harvard University, 2007.

Matar, Nabil. *Islam in Britain, 1558–1685.* Cambridge: Cambridge University Press, 1998.

Matar and Gerald MacLean. *Britain and the Islamic World, 1558–1713.* Oxford: Oxford University Press, 2011.

Metcalf, Barbara Daly, ed. *Making Muslim Space in North America and Europe.* Berkeley: University of California Press, 1996.

Motadel, David. "Germany's Policy towards Islam, 1941–1945." PhD dissertation, University of Cambridge, 2010.

Municipal Archive (Landesarchiv) Berlin (LArchB), B Rep. 042 (Amtsgericht Charlottenburg), No. 26590 (Islamische Gemeinde zu Berlin, 1922–1955).

Municipal Archive (Landesarchiv) Berlin (LArchB), A Pr. Br. Rep 030–04 (Polizeipräsidium Berlin, Vereine), No. 513 (Islamische Gemeinde zu Berlin, 1936).

Municipal Archive (Landesarchiv) Berlin (LArchB), A Pr. Br. Rep 030–04 (Polizeipräsidium Berlin, Vereine), No. 2314 (Islam-Institut, 1939–1940).

Municipal Archive (Landesarchiv) Berlin (LArchB), A Pr. Br. Rep. 030–04 (Polizeipräsidium Berlin, Vereine), No. 2840 (Islamisches Zentral-Institut zu Berlin).

Municipal Archive (Landesarchiv) Berlin (LArchB), A Pr. Br. Rep. 030–04 (Polizeipräsidium Berlin, Vereine), No. 1350 (Deutsch-Muslimische Gesellschaft zur Förderung des Islam durch Aufklärungsarbeiten, 1936–1939).

Municipal Archive (Landesarchiv) Berlin (LArchB), B Rep. 042 (Amtsgericht Charlottenburg), No. 9021 (Sufi-Bewegung Berlin, 1925–1935).

Municipal Archive (Landesarchiv) Berlin (LArchB), A Pr. Br. Rep 030–04 (Polizeipräsidium Berlin, Vereine), No. 1523 (Islamischer Weltkongress zu Berlin, 1933–1941).

Nielsen, Jørgen S. *Muslims in Western Europe.* Edinburgh: Edinburgh University Press, 1992.

———. *Towards a European Islam*. London: Palgrave Macmillan, 1999.

Noiriel, Gérard. *Immigration, Antisémitisme et Racisme en France (XIXe–XXe Siècle): Discours Publics, Humiliations Privées*. Paris: Fayard, 2009.

Ottmani, Hamza Ben Driss. *Kaddour Benghabrit: Un Maghrébin hors du Commun*. Rabat. Morocco: Marsam, 2010.

Pautremat, Pascal le. *La Politique Musulmane de la France au XXe Siècle: De l'Hexagone aux Terres d'Islam*. Paris: Maisonneuve et Larose, 2003.

Political Archives of the German Foreign Office (PA), R78240 (*Religions- und Kirchenwesen: Islam*, 1924–28).

Political Archives of the German Foreign Office (PA), R78241 (*Religions- und Kirchenwesen: Islam*, 1928–31).

Political Archives of the German Foreign Office (PA), R78242 (*Religions- und Kirchenwesen: Islam*, 1932–36).

Political Archives of the German Foreign Office (PA), R104801 (*Religions- und Kirchenwesen: Islam*, 1936–39).

Rath, Jan Rinus Penninx, Kees Groenendijk, and Astrid Meyer. *Western Europe and Its Islam*. Leiden, Netherlands: Brill, 2001.

Recham, Belkacem. *Les Musulmans Algériens dans l'Armée Française (1919–1945)*. Paris: Harmattan, 1996.

Reichslandbund Pressearchiv, (BA), R58/5955 (SS Reichssicherheitshauptamt, Beobachtung der islamischen Gemeinde in Berlin, 1933–1937).

Renard, Michel. "Aperçu sur l'Histoire de l'Islam à Marseille, 1813–1962: Pratiques Religieuses et Encadrement des Nord-Africains." *Outre-Mers* 90.340–341 (2003): 269–296.

———. "Gratitude, Contrôle, Accompagnement: Le Traitement du Religieux Islamique en Métropole (1914–1950)." *Bulletin de l'Institut d'Histoire du Temps Présent* 83 (2004): 54–69.

———. "Les Débuts de la Présence Musulmane en France et son Encadrement." In *Histoire de l'Islam et des Musulmans en France du Moyen Age à Nos Jours*, edited by Arkoun, Mohammed, 712–740. Paris: Albin Michel, 2006.

Reza, Mohammad S. *Islam in Britain: Past, Present and the Future*. Leicester: Volcano, 1991.

Richter, Britta. "Islam im Deutschland der Zwischenkriegsjahre." *Zeitschrift für Türkeistudien* 2 (1996): 257–266.

Rudolph, Susanne Hoeber and James P. Piscatori, eds. *Transnational Religion and Fading States*. Boulder, CO: Westview, 1997.

Ryad, Umar. "From an Officer in the Ottoman Army to a Muslim Publicist and Armament Agent in Berlin: Zeki Hishmat Kiram (1886–1946)." *Bibliotheca Orientalis*, 63.3–4 (2006): 235–268.

Schulze, Reinhard. *Islamischer Internationalismus im 20. Jahrhundert: Untersuchungen zur Geschichte der Islamischen Weltliga*. Leiden, Netherlands: Brill, 1990.

Schütze, Karl-Robert. *Von den Befreiungskriegen bis zum Ende der Wehrmacht: Die Geschichte des Garnisonfriedhofs am Rande der Hasenheide in Berlin-Neukölln*. Berlin: Bezirksamt Neukölln, 1986.

Seiler-Chan, Chalid-Albert. "Der Islam in Berlin und Anderwärts im Deutschen Reiche." *Moslemische Revue* 2–3 (1934): 47–56; and 4 (1934): 112–119.

Sellam, Sadek. *La France et Ses Musulmans: Un Siècle de Politique Musulmane (1895–2005)*. Paris: Fayard, 2006.

Şen Faruk and Hayrettin Aydin. *Islam in Deutschland*. Munich: C. H. Beck, 2002.

Siddiqi, Majid Hayat. "Bluff, Doubt and Fear: The Kheiri Brothers and the Colonial State, 1904–1945." *Indian Economic and Social History Review* 24.3 (1987): 233–263.

Silverstein, Paul A. *Algeria in France: Transpolitics, Race, and Nation*. Bloomington: Indiana University Press, 2004.

Spuler-Stegemann, Ursula. *Muslime in Deutschland: Nebeneinander oder Miteinander?* Freiburg: Herder, 1998.

Tevfik, Ismail Hakki Bey. "Der Islam in Belgien und Luxemburg." *Der Islam* 18.3–4 (1929): 319–320.

Thompson, E. P. *The Making of the English Working Class*. London: Victor Gollancz, 1963.

Tibawi, A. L. "History of the London Central Mosque and of the Islamic Cultural Centre 1910–1980." *Die Welt des Islams* 21.1–4 (1981): 192–208.

Visram, Rozina. *Asians in Britain: 400 Years of History*. London: Pluto, 2002.

———. *Ayahs, Lascars and Princes: Indians in Britain, 1700–1947*. London: Pluto, 1986.

Weiss, René. *Réception à l'Hôtel de Ville de Sa Majesté Moulay Youssef, Sultan du Maroc: Inauguration de l'Institut Musulman et de la Mosquée*. Paris: Imprimerie Nationale, 1927.

Welzbacher, Christian. *Euroislam-Architektur: Neue Moscheen des Abendlandes*. Amsterdam: Sun Architecture, 2008.

Wright, Denis. *The Persians amongst the English: Episodes in Anglo-Persian History*. London: IB Tauris, 1985.

CHAPTER 2

Transnational Connections and the Building of an Albanian and European Islam in Interwar Albania

Nathalie Clayer

When speaking about Muslims in Europe, one generally focuses on Muslims in western Europe, ignoring the case of their coreligionists living in northern, eastern, and southeastern Europe. In this part of the continent, Muslims represent a large group of people formed during the Ottoman period as the result of migrations and conversions. The end of the Ottoman rule—which occurred at different periods of time in the different regions—caused the death (during conflicts) and departure of many Muslims, flying to the remaining parts of the Ottoman Empire, for religious and sociopolitical reasons. However, despite these significant waves of migration, large communities of Muslims remained in Serbia, Montenegro, and in the Austro-Hungarian province of Bosnia-Herzegovina (after World War I these territories being included into the Yugoslav kingdom, together with the present territory of Macedonia and Kosova). Large groups of Muslims also remained in Bulgaria, and to a lesser extent in Greece and Romania, while the Albanian state was the only state formed (1912–1913) in the region having a Muslim majority, with approximately 70 percent of the total population.

With the creation of these new states during the nineteenth century and at the beginning of the twentieth century, the new political authorities generally tried to control and nationalize the Islamic hierarchies, and western Europe (sometimes also Russia) became a pole of attraction for some segments of the local population. However, until WWI, this did not prevent the Balkan Muslims from remaining strongly attached to Istanbul and the sultan-caliph. After the abolition of the sultanate and the caliphate, and the creation of the Turkish Republic in 1923, the horizon of the Balkan Muslims was considerably transformed. Connections with the new Turkish republic were not totally cut: waves of migration continued to mark the fate of many Muslims from southeastern Europe, and Kemalism had a noticeable impact on both Muslims and Balkan state authorities. Transformations in Turkey as well as the policies of nationalization that were implemented by authoritarian or quasi-authoritarian regimes in the region during this period generally coincided with attempts to institutionalize Islam and to nationalize the administration of Islam. Yet, Muslims also had to cope with the quasi-abolition of higher Islamic education in Turkey and to adapt themselves to new national and international networks involved in the diffusion of Islamic (and non-Islamic) knowledge; such adaptation was framed by the possibilities and the constraints they encountered in daily life, at different levels (micro and macro), in societies where Christians were the majority and where nation-building processes were marked by a wish to de-Ottomanize and de-Islamize the public sphere in order to Europeanize it.

In the Albanian case, in spite of a Muslim majority in the population, the nation-building process was characterized by similar attempts to institutionalize and nationalize the Islamic institutions. Moreover, the fact that the majority of the population was Muslim led some political and religious actors not only to try to Albanianize, but also to "Europeanize" and "modernize" Islam in the country.[1] For this, they used transnational connections to Muslims in Turkey and western Europe, and even in India and Egypt.

To understand this phenomenon, I analyze in this chapter the reconfiguration of transnational connections of Muslim actors in Albania that aimed at shaping Islam in the country in the 1920s and 1930s. Beginning with a study of publications and education policies of the leaders of the Albanian Islamic institutions during that period, this chapter decenters the approach and exemplarily investigates the activities of prominent independent Albanian Muslim scholar Hafiz Abdullah Zëmblaku, an active propagator of Islam through booklets and training courses for young Muslims.[2]

Tracing back the transnational connections in question faces some major obstacles, most prominently the lack of sources (diaries, correspondence, etc.). Contrary to studies on Islamic networks in earlier periods,[3] this study also accounts for impersonal connections created by the diffusion of printed matter (periodicals and books), which fostered the circulation of ideas, facts, and images within the Islamic world during the interwar period.[4]

I. From Ottoman Islamic Networks to the Building of Albanian Islamic Institutions

In post-Ottoman Albania (i.e. after 1912–1913), Islam became more deeply institutionalized. The first step toward reorganization was made during the Austro-Hungarian occupation of two-thirds of the new Albanian territory between 1916 and 1918, on the model of the administration in Bosnia-Herzegovina. The position of great mufti was created and a Sharia High Council was formed with the great mufti and two other *ulamas*, on the model of the *ulama-medžlis* of Sarajevo, in order to administer the Islamic cult in the whole occupied zone with the help of three regional qadi-muftis in Shkodër, Elbasan, and Berat. With the re-creation of the Albanian state after the Peace Conference in 1920, new national institutions were set up, with their centre in Tirana. Continuities to the previous institutional settings were important. The three members of the high council remained at the top of the religious hierarchy until 1924, the great mufti until 1929. From 1923 onward, some lay Muslims entered these institutions (they already were involved in the administration of the *waqfs*). After 1929 and a third congress, new statuses were elaborated and the position of head of the Islamic institutions was given to a layman, a lawyer.[5]

During this period, as a result of internal and external dynamics, a heterogeneous group of Muslims (clerics and laymen) formed the nucleus of the Albanian Islamic institutions, supposed to administer and control the diffusion and the practice of Islam in the country; yet, for various reasons, these representatives of official Islam had difficulty imposing themselves on the whole Islamic sphere. Cooperation between these representatives, and with the political authorities, was tense and often subject to conflicts over objectives and definition of the religious policies. While Muslim leaders agreed with state attempts to nationalize Islam, and to use it for both modernization and social control purposes, they opposed political authorities when they attempted to reduce the prerogatives of Islamic institutions and the place of Islam in the society.[6] Their main efforts were directed toward the training of new clerics and the diffusion of an Islamic education and Islamic values among the Muslim of the countries (in 1928–1929, with the introduction of the civil code, they lost their prerogative in the field of family law).

In this regard, their positions and strategies—which were not univocal—toward the state, Islam and its institutions shifted according to time and context.[7] In many instances, their discourses and approaches were influenced by transnational contacts with the wider Muslim world and resources this gave to them.

As a result of their training and careers, most of the first official Muslim actors in the 1920s and at the beginning of the 1930s had been part of Ottoman networks. They had generally been trained first in their native villages and towns and later on in Istanbul, the Ottoman capital. They had then begun their careers as *ulamas* (*müderris*, qadi, or mufti) in their home country or in different places of the empire. Some of them had a mixed—religious and secular—training, again linking many of them to Istanbul. These careers are illustrated by the following personalities: Vehbi Dibra, the great mufti, born in 1867, had studied in Dibër, his hometown, and then in Istanbul. He became a mufti in Dibër, like his father. Later, he was appointed head of the Albanian Islamic hierarchy with its centre successively in Vlorë (1913–1914), in Shkodër (1916–1919) and then in Tirana (1919–1929).[8] Hafiz Ali Korça was born in Korçë in 1873. After his studies in the local gymnasium, he went to Istanbul to study at the university where he learned Arabic, Persian, French, and Islamic sciences, before returning to the Albanian province and working in different educational and religious institutions.[9] Born in 1860 in Libohova—now in southern Albania—not far from Gjirokastër, Vejsel Naili had studied in the *madrasas* of Libohova, Gjirokastër, and Janina, before frequenting the new school of qadis (the *Mekteb-i nüvvab*) in Istanbul. He was then appointed qadi in the Arab provinces, in the Balkans, in Anatolia, and then again in the Balkans.[10] Salih Vuçitërni, the director of the Waqfs, born in 1880 in present Kosovo, had studied at a lyceum and later followed theological studies in Istanbul. Even Behxhet Shapati, who was born in Vlorë and succeeded to Vehbi Dibra at the head of the Islamic Community, studied law in Istanbul.[11]

In the light of such careers, the intellectual horizon of most official Islamic leaders—as different as they could be from one person to another—had been shaped by the Ottoman educational network (religious and secular), by the religious and secular life in late Ottoman Istanbul, and by ideas conveyed by Ottoman newspapers and books that were circulating in the Ottoman realm. Turning again to the example of Hafiz Ali Korça: in Istanbul and the Balkans, in the first years of the twentieth century he had written in different Ottoman and Albanianist newspapers. In 1909, he published an article on the much-needed reforms of *madrasas* in the Istanbul-based reformist journal, *Sırat-ı müstakim*.[12] Even after the end of Ottoman rule, he continued reading Turkish Islamist newspapers. A booklet he wrote in 1925 to denounce Bolshevism as the destruction of humanity shows that his arguments were largely inspired by information and ideas transmitted by the Istanbul based journal *Sebilürreşad*.[13] The Turkish journal was also one of the resources for the elaboration of the official journal of the Albanian Islamic institutions, *Zani i naltë* (*The supreme voice*), to which he was one of the main contributors.[14]

The geopolitical changes engendered by the Balkan wars, World War I, and the end of the Ottoman Empire contributed to the transformation of the horizons of these people. The evolutions, as we shall see, present important discontinuities, but also continuities.

There were discontinuities, mainly because of the changes in Turkey itself. The abolition of the caliphate, but above all the closing down of the *madrasas* in 1924, pushed the Albanian Muslims toward a reorientation. At least for higher Islamic education, leaders of the new Albanian institutions and parents had to send their students to other Islamic centers. On the Albanian side, official spiritual connections with centers abroad were hindered by state authorities. Already in 1923, before the abolition of the Ottoman caliphate, the Albanian Muslims had proclaimed their independence and had built up sovereign religious institutions. Official contacts with foreign institutions were forbidden: in 1926, when the shaykh of al-Azhar invited the Albanian Islamic institutions to send a delegation for the caliphate Congress to be held in Cairo, the Ministry of Justice did not give the authorization, arguing that the election for a caliph was not a Sharia prescription and that the Albanian institutions were autocephalous. In 1931, Albanian muftis were asked to decline the invitation to the Jerusalem Congress. Similarly, in 1935, no delegate represented the Muslims of Albania at the Geneva Congress.[15]

Yet, these restrictions did not mean that the Albanian Islamic leaders were unconnected to the external Muslim world. To provide higher Islamic education or to quickly build up an Islamic corpus in the Albanian language (a relatively new written language in which only a few Islamic catechisms, Mevluds, and booklets for the time of the Ramadan existed), they extensively drew on outside resources. Due to the changes in Turkey, their networks were increasingly reoriented toward the Ahmadi network in India and Europe, as well as toward Cairo.

II. Toward New Horizons:
Europe-India and Cairo

The *Ahmadiyya Anjuman Isha'at al-Islam* (Ahmadiyya society for the propagation of Islam) from Lahore was a branch of the Ahmadi movement, born in Punjab at the end of the nineteenth century. Soon after the death of its founder, Mirza Ghulam Ahmad, in 1908, the movement split. On one side, the majority of the Ahmadis formed the Qadiyani branch, considering Mirza Ghulam Ahmad as a prophet. The other group, numerically less important, saw in Mirza Ghulam Ahmad only a renewer (*mujaddid*). This last group, known as the Lahori society and a very active missionary organization, took the initiative to write to the editor of *Zani i naltë*, the journal of the Albanian Islamic institutions, in the summer of 1927. As such, this contact illustrates the importance of these impersonal networks created by the diffusion of printed matter. The Lahori-Ahmadi missionaries sent their printed production in English and German and asked their Albanian coreligionists to translate the Qur'an in an edition published and commented on by their spiritual master Mawlana Muhammad Ali. For the Ahmadis, already operating in Great Britain and Germany,[16] Albania was to serve as a relay for the spread of their works and ideas in neighboring countries, among Muslims as well as among Christians.[17]

As a result of these epistolary contacts and the diffusion of Ahmadi printed matter, the leaders of Albanian Islamic institutions, and mainly the director of the Waqfs, Salih Vuçitërni, who was at that time the promoter of reforms, took an increasing interest in translating these publications with the financial support of believers (a method used and promoted by the Ahmadi missionaries). From 1927 onward, many articles and lectures published in journals such as *The Light* of Lahore, *Die Moslemische Revue* of Berlin, and several booklets and books were translated into Albanian and published in the journal of the Albanian Islamic community or as booklets. Albanian readers thus gained access to the works of the Indian Muslim thinkers Muhammad Ali, Sadr-ud-Din[18] and Khwaja Kamaluddin. Translations were based on English and German versions of their works. The first translators were Omer Sharra for the English and Junuz Bulej (or Buliqi) for the German language. After 1929, students of the General Madrasa in Tirana were trained to translate such texts, as English replaced French as the Western foreign language taught at this institution.[19]

Other bounds between the Albanian Islamic institutions and the Lahori-Ahmadis were created through the sending of students to

Lahore. The Indian missionaries had proposed grants for students. As a result, in 1934 two of the first graduates of the General Madrasa, Sherif Putra and Ejup Fasli Kraja, went there, with a third young Albanian Muslim from Shkodër—Halil Repishti, a friend of one of them, also from Shkodër. From Lahore, they tried to contribute to a greater diffusion of the Ahmadi thought in their home country through the editing of a small journal in Albanian, conceived as a supplement of the Ahmadi journal *The Light*. At the end of 1935, three new graduates of the Tirana General Madrasa—Xhelal Hajredini, Adem Rakipi, and Abdurrahman Shahini, all from the southwest of the country—were supposed to join them in Lahore. However, for unknown reasons, they remained in Cairo where they had gone and registered at al-Azhar. Three and a half years later, the Lahore students came back home, but two of them quickly went to Cairo, apparently the new attraction center for Islamic higher studies. A few months later, however, they were expelled from al-Azhar because of their Ahmadi beliefs. They remained in Cairo for a while, studying at the American University and publishing in 1940 a declaration in an Egyptian newspaper in which they retracted their previous beliefs and distanced themselves from the Ahmadi doctrine they were obliged to publicly criticize.[20]

With this, the connection with the Lahori *Ahmadiyya* was certainly weakened. However, the influence of the latter in Albania did not completely come to an end. After 1939, and especially after 1943, the new journal of the Islamic Community, *Kultura Islame*, went on publishing translations of Ahmadi texts. Reflecting this continuing influence, a letter of the secretary of the *Anjuman* was published in the issue of September–October 1940 thanking the head of the Albanian Islamic Community for his telegram.[21] Such contact between the Albanian Islamic institutions and the Lahori-Ahmadi society persisted over the following years, only coming to an end with the communist takeover in 1945.[22]

This reorientation of Albanian Islamic institutions toward the Lahori-Ahmadi network stood for a reorientation toward Europe corresponding to the wish to create a European Islam, even if the center of the *Anjuman* was in India. The networks provided for direct, be they personal or impersonal, contacts with the Lahori-Ahmadis based in Europe, mainly in Berlin and England. The leaders of the Islamic community were receiving Ahmadi publications published there, while in 1935, for example, the baron Omar Rolf von Ehrenfels, an Austrian convert to Islam linked to the Berlin mosque, personally visited Albania.[23]

If we look at the themes developed in the translated literature, we also see that these connections provided resources to facilitate the legitimization of Islam in a European and "modern" country and more generally to enhance the prestige of Islam. Many texts dealt with the place of the women in society or the compatibility of Islam with science and progress; others were about the prominent role of Islam in medieval Europe, and particularly in Spain; others gave an important place to positive views of Islam expressed by Europeans, converts or not, as well as to the dynamical presence of Islam in Europe and America, notably through the activity of the *Ahmadiyya*, whereas other publications aimed at fighting materialism and atheism. In the introduction of the biography of the Prophet Muhammad written by Muhammad Ali (Muhamet Ali, 1929), the founder of the Ahmadi movement—a book translated by Omer Sharra, professor at the technical school in Tirana—Salih Vuçitërni stated that the book was for those who were ignorant of the true knowledge of the Islamic principles. For him, the refutation of ideas expressed by some English writers about Islam and its Prophet could be useful for Albanians Muslims and non-Muslims, to make them understand the importance of Muhammad for humanity and to revalorize Islam in the Albanian context.

The translation of other books written by Europeans about Islam that were acquired by Albanian Muslims during journeys abroad or provided by local librarians served a similar purpose.[24] These books were considered to be scientific and were used to "prove" the superiority of Islam. Already, in 1926, Hamdi Bushati from Shkodër had translated a booklet of the famous British convert and head of the Islamic Centre in Liverpool, Abdullah William Henry Quilliam.[25] In his foreword, the translator explained that he made this text accessible to the Albanian readership so that it would understand the principles of Islam without requiring knowledge of foreign languages such as Arabic and Turkish. For him, the text was important as it showed how Islam had abrogated previous laws, while Islam itself, as the highest religion based on scientific rules and arguments, could not be abrogated.

The "European oriented" Islamic network of the Lahori-Ahmadis was not the only pole of Albanian Muslim networks. As mentioned above, Cairo also became a new pole of attraction for Albanian Muslim officials. For one, the Sharia Higher Council had subscribed to various Egyptian newspapers and had frequently ordered publications from Cairo. Hafiz Ali Korça, who himself corresponded with the political and religious authorities in Egypt in order to make known the situation of the Albanian Muslims in the Muslim world, was one of the main links between Albania and Egypt.[26] As early as 1925, Cairo had acquired among leaders of Albanian Islamic institutions the reputation as an important place for Albanian Muslims for higher theological studies (*Zani i naltë*, II/4, qershor–korrik 1925, 487). The connection with Egypt further deepened in 1933, when five students were sent by the Community to study at al-Azhar.[27] Others students followed, and in 1940 around 20 Albanian Muslims studied either at al-Azhar or Cairo University. Sadik Bega, for instance, the future director of the Islamic Community's journal, graduated at the Faculty of Letters of Cairo University.

Interestingly, this intensified connection with Egypt also furthered the influence of secular works of Egyptian reformist authors such as Taha Husayn and Muhammad Haykal, as we can see through texts published in the journal of the Albanian Islamic Community. It also fostered intra-Balkan links between Muslim students from Albania and Yugoslavia, especially with Albanians from what was called at that time "Southern Serbia" (i.e., present Kosovo and Macedonia), such as Hasan Nahi, who went there in 1930; Bedri Hamidi from Skopje; Mumin efendi from Kumanovo. Like Hasan Nahi, they could also have met in Cairo Mehmet Akif Ersöy—the famous Turkish Islamist of Albanian origin—who was living there.[28]

The connection with Cairo is not illustrated in many book translations to Albanian, probably because using texts written in Europe was of greater value in order to built a European Islam. However, the need to form intellectuals and *ulamas* with a higher Islamic education and the contacts to Egypt in this field seriously limited the previous influence of the Ahmadi connection, widely considered as heretical by Egyptian Muslim institutions.

III. CONNECTIONS WITH NEW TRENDS IN TURKEY

If Islamic networks were reoriented primarily toward the Ahmadi networks and toward Cairo, contacts to Ottoman/Turkish networks persisted as well. After 1925, the journal *Zani i naltë* published several texts that were translated from, or inspired by Turkish sources. Islamic journals were not published in Turkey after 1925, but the leaders of the Albanian Islamic institutions, such as Hafiz Ali Korça, as many other Albanian intellectuals and officials, went on reading the Turkish press, sometimes even engaging in polemics against positions expressed here. However, more important were the more or less indirect ties that emerged between Albanian Islamic institutions and

Turkish Islamic circles around the *Diyanet*, the new Islamic institutions in Republican Turkey on one hand, and a Turkish intellectual Ömer Rıza, on the other. These connections were impersonal and unofficial, and were created through the translation of publications circulating in the Turkish market. They were due to the Ottoman culture of the leaders of the Albanian Islamic institutions and to their knowledge of Ottoman-Turkish. As in the case of the networking with the Lahori-Ahmadis, they reflected the search for a national and scientific Islam, as the desire for arguments legitimizing Islam vis-à-vis its Christian or materialist detractors.

At the end of the 1920s, the main translator of Turkish writings was Jonuz Tafili, who, already in 1925, had proposed to the Higher Sharia Council the publication of three articles a month based on translations of famous authors such as Muhammad Abduh and Mehmed Akif (Ersöy), in the journal of the Islamic institutions.[29] This project was not accepted, and he dedicated himself to the translation of books. The first book[30] was a work containing a new kind of religious instruction, published as the third part of a book under the title *Dini dersler* (1920, *Mësime Feje* in Albanian, i.e. "Religious courses") by Akseki Ahmet Hamdi, a leading figure of the Muslim reformist trend at the end of the Ottoman Empire and later a member of the *Diyanet*.[31] The foreword to the book by Salih Vuçitërni, the Waqfs general director, again tells us why the leaders of the Albanian Islamic institutions were eager to make such a work accessible to the Albanian readers. The presentation of the principles of Islam was supposed to be scientifically founded, "with reason and knowledge," so that no doubts could remain in the mind of believers, as well as in the mind of opponents. Indeed, the lessons conceived by Ahmet Hamdi for the students of the Ottoman School of Maritime Engineering were aimed at eliminating any doubts caused by the diffusion of materialism and atheism among people who might be studying (or had studied) in Europe. The text, that is the third part of the book of Hamdi Hamdi, translated by Jonuz Tafili was more directly dedicated to the significance of religion and the refutation of atheist ideas, with arguments inspired by the famous reformist authors Jamaladdin al-Afghani, Muhammad Abduh, and Ferid Vejdi.[32]

A second book translated by Jonuz Tafili was a collection of Friday prayers (*hutbes*) prepared by the same Ahmet Hamdi, in the framework of the Kemalist policy of turkification of Islam.[33] As soon as it was published in 1927 by the *Diyanet*, the Albanian embassy in Ankara sent it to the Albanian Islamic institutions in Tirana, who found it valuable for translation as, for them, the sermons were corresponding to the needs of the time (*Këshillet e së Premtës* 1928).[34] Again, this illustrates the role of diplomats in the networking with Muslims in other countries. The book even served as model for a second volume of *hutbes* published four years later (*Këshillet e së Premtës* 1932).[35]

Interestingly, a third book translated by Jonuz Tafili leads us to the interest that the Albanian Islamic Community had in the 1930s for Islamic works that were published in Turkey, but were inspired by Lahori-Ahmadis. In 1931, the Sharia High Council published the book of Muhammad Ali, the founder of the *Ahmadiyya* movement, titled *Muhammed, Our Prophet*.[36] The book was originally written in Urdu, but was later translated into English by Muhammad Ali's disciples in England and Germany. This work was translated into Turkish between 1922 and 1924 by Ömer Rıza Doğrul, a Turkish intellectual who was the main advocate of the *Ahmadiyya* thought in Turkey. He wrote, for example, a commentary of the Qur'an inspired by the works of Muhammad Ali, published under the title *Tanrı Buyruğu*.[37]

It is from the works of Ömer Rıza Doğrul that, later on, one of the most famous Albanian *ulamas*, Hafiz Ibrahim Dalliu, who was officially in charge of the translation and commentary of the Qur'an in Albanian,[38] and Shefqet Daiu, a former member of the Parliament, decided, each of them separately, to produce two additional translations. The first was a booklet about Islam, addressed to the youth, in the form of questions and answers.[39] According to Ömer Rıza, the author, the explanations he gave on the beliefs and basis of Islam were simple and expressed in the new way used by contemporary Muslim scholars who were trying—with success—to spread Islam in Europe. This clearly refers to the Ahmadi network. The second was a publication, accredited by the Albanian community, on the Qur'an and its translations, that took inspiration from Ömer Rıza and the Indian Muslim thinker Muhammed Abdullah Menhasi.[40]

IV. A DECENTERED APPROACH: HAFIZ ABDULLAH ZËMBLAKU AND HIS NETWORKS

Let us now look at the networking activities of an *alim* who refused to join the Albanian Islamic institutions—Hafiz Abdullah Zëmblaku (1892–1960). Born in the region of Bilisht, not far from Korçë in today's southeastern Albania, he had first studied in the new type of Ottoman state schools called *rüştiye* in different places where his father was a teacher, especially in Durrës (in present central Albania).[41] Later, he became an assistant to his father and taught calligraphy and writing. After the Young Turk Revolution, he began religious studies in the *madrasa* of Prilep (today Macedonia), where his father was a teacher. Then he carried on his studies in a lyceum, and finally went to the Ottoman capital and attended courses, at the same time, in the *madrasa* of Fatih called *Dar ül-Hilafe* and at the religious studies department of the Istanbul University. In addition to this quite common mixed secular and religious instruction, he received a Sufi initiation and entered Naqshbandi Sufi circles. Apparently, he was also initiated into the Halwatiyya-Hayatiyya, the order of his own grandfather. After having been enlisted for two years into the Ottoman army during World War I, he returned to the region of Korçë, probably around 1918, where he served as a voluntary teacher and *imam-hatib* in the village of Belorta. Just after the integration of the region into the Albanian state in 1921, he was appointed by the Ministry of Instruction as a teacher in the school of Kuç-Belorta. But, in 1924, probably as a result of the political changes and the reorganization of education, he resigned and became imam-hatib in Zëmblak, his family's village. From this time on, he dedicated himself to the translation and the publication of books and booklets, as well as to the teaching of both Albanian language and Islam, especially to girls who, at that time, were not frequenting schools. He refused several times the position of mufti, preferring not to be integrated into the official Albanian Islamic institutions he was very critical of. For that and for his criticism of local governmental institutions, he was even sentenced several times in the 1930s to internal exile.[42]

Hafiz Abdullah was one of the most prolific Islamic entrepreneurs in interwar Albania, not only through his publications—some 30 titles that were widely distributed—but also through teaching and preaching activities all around Albania. In his publications, which came to be conceived as kinds of periodicals, he presented himself as a translator. These booklets contain religious texts and teachings translated mainly from Turkish and Arabic; however they also include many original writings: poems and texts of his own composition, reproduction of documents and letters received and sent by him. These publications allow reconstruction of his network. One of his poems about his spiritual world even draws a picture of this network at the beginning of the 1930s: outside Albania and the neighboring regions of Çamëria (in Greece) and Kosovo (in Yugoslavia), it extended as far as Turkey and Bosnia, Egypt, and also Australia and the Americas (United States, South America and Canada), as well as France and India.[43]

Sure enough, Hafiz Abdullah Zëmblaku maintained his Ottoman/Turkish network that he had forged when he was a student in Istanbul.

In 1936, he was still corresponding with his spiritual master, Hacı Süleyman, *vaiz* (preacher) at the Fatih mosque.[44] The basis of his religious production into Albanian was formed by the literature he had access to at this time through religious schools and other circles. Particularly important in the shaping of his conception of Islam and of Islamic entrepreneurship was the reading of the press, and especially of the Istanbul-based journals *Beyanülhak* and *Sebilürreşad*. According to him, these periodicals that provided religious, geographical, historical, and philosophical knowledge, and also informed their readership about the situation in the Muslim world were so useful for him that he intended to publish a similar journal in Albanian himself. In the 1920s and 1930s, he continued to follow the development of Islam in Turkey. In order to legitimize himself as an *alim* vis-à-vis the Albanian official Islamic institutions, he compared himself to Akseki Ahmet Hamdi, with whom he had studied in Istanbul and who had become a member of the new Islamic institutions in Turkey. Yet, it seems that he rejected part of the Turkish policies toward Islam, accusing some official Turkish circles of being "masons."[45]

On the other hand, like his adversaries within the Albanian official institutions, Hafiz Abdullah Zëmblaku came also to be connected to other networks, in particular to the Lahori-Ahmadi network. Several articles published in his works attest to the connection, at least from 1930 onward, through the exchange of letters and writings and the publication of reports about their respective activities. According to his own declaration, Hafiz Abdullah Zëmblaku had sent his book with part of the Qur'an in Albanian script (i.e., in Arabic and in Latin script) to the *Anjuman*, and the Ahmadi Society answered by providing him around 50 books and journals in different languages. He thus began to give details to his readers about the presence of the Indian missionaries in Berlin, London, and New York; about the *tafsir* of Muhammad Ali from which he had acquired a copy in English; and about the Lahori-Ahmadis' beliefs, aims, and actions. In a publication from 1934, he used a book published by the Ahmadi Society in English and in Arabic (using probably the Arabic version) to elaborate a kind of catechism in the form of questions and answers. To make the *tafsir* of Muhammad Ali accessible to a broader audience, he made his personal copy available to the library of Korçë. He used this connection to legitimate his own work and to renounce attacks by official Albanian Islamic institutions. Similar to the Lahori-Ahmadis, he claimed to be a true "missionary of Islam," and based his activities on the translation and diffusion of Islam in the vernacular language.[46]

This latter link was so important for him, Hafiz Abdullah Zëmblaku also engaged in connections with other individuals and groups. For instance, he was in correspondence with Džemaluddin Čaušević, the *reisululema* of Bosnia-Herzegovina, with whom he exchanged books and discussed matters of translation. In addition, he closely followed the writings of the newspaper *Al-Islam*, published in 1930 in France by an Egyptian in Arabic and French.[47] His networking activities were also turned toward Muslim believers in the whole of Albania and abroad. In particular, his connections—through the exchange of letters, books, and money—even extended to Albanian emigrant communities in the Americas and Australia.[48] These communities were mostly originating from the same region as himself, the region of Korçë. One of his correspondents had a peculiar profile, since he was also an Islamic entrepreneur: Muhammed Naji efendi Revani, a member of the American Islamic Society and resident of Mansfield (Ohio), who would have published several books in English, including a translation of 303 *hadiths*. Interestingly enough, he himself had some connection with the Ahmadi network. At least he was a reader of the Chicago-based journal of Dr. Mufti Muhammed Sadiq, *The Muslim Sunrise*, and was eager to transmit to Hafiz Abdullah Zëmblaku in Albania the names of American converts to Islam published in this periodical, a list that Hafiz Abdullah even published in order to illustrate the impact of Islam in the West and on Westerners.[49]

CONCLUSION

Transnational networking activities played an important role in the building process of a "national," "European," and "modern" Islam in interwar Albania—even though institutional contacts were prevented by state authorities. They were much sought after, as they allowed the elaboration of a new corpus of religious texts and, more broadly, of texts about Islam. They provided resources and ideas for the grammar of action (i.e., the publication of books with the help of believers; the use of the vernacular language; the development of a missionary spirit; and the use of apologetic narratives of Islam as compatible with science, progress, education, reason, and as such compatible with "Europeanness"). They also provided opportunities for the formation of new religious leaders and thinkers.

As we have seen, these transnational connections mainly linked Muslims in Albania with the Lahori-Ahmadi network in Europe and in India, with Cairo and with some reformist circles in Turkey, which were themselves partly connected to the Lahori-Ahmadi, and also with Muslims in Yugoslavia, in America and in Australia. The connection with the Lahori-Ahmadi network—a network that was fluctuating and was not always distinct from other networks or groups of Muslim in western Europe—is the result of a strong proselytism from the part of this group in Europe, in the west as well as in its eastern part, including in Turkey.

However, in the second half of the 1930s, Cairo increasingly emerged as a new point of reference for Albanian Muslim thinking and its drive for reform, principally because it was the main centre for higher Islamic education at that time. New forms of activities, such as youth and charity associations that appeared from 1938 onward at the local level in cities like Shkodër and Durrës, were modeled on the activism of the Egyptian Association of Muslim Youth.[50] Networking with the Arab world—for instance as a result of the hajj and the stays at Egyptian institutions of higher education—was not unusual for individual Albanian Muslims, particularly within traditionalist circles,[51] but it had never been before, for the Albanian Muslims, the main place to go to become a qualified specialist of religion. The "excommunication" of the Ahmadis further added to the prominent place of Cairo as a major centre of Islamic reformism among Albanian Muslims, even if the Lahori-Ahmadi production remained one of the most important sources for the creation for a "modern" Albanian Islam in Europe. These reorientations of the Albanian Islamic networks did not completely marginalize links with Turkey. Beside the persistence of some ancient networks originating from the Ottoman period, new ties appeared with Muslims in the republic of Turkey. The Albanian official Islamic leaders were particularly interested in some aspects of the new Islam proposed by the official Islamic circles in Turkey and by the Islam forged by the intellectual Ömer Rıza Doğrul himself also influenced by the Lahori-Ahmadi.[52]

During the period under study, some transnational networking activities remained confined to personal networks whose origins often went back to the last years of the Ottoman period and which functioned through mobility of individuals or correspondence. But others had an institutional dimension. Diplomatic networks were sometimes involved; in addition, the new official national Islamic institutions played a central role in establishing these netwroks. Remarkably enough, be they individual or institutional, the connections had often during the interwar period an impersonal dimension, as they were due to the diffusion of periodicals and books. Even if, as we have seen both in the case of the official Islamic institutions and of Hafız Abdullah Zëmblaku, these impersonal connections could be reinforced through correspondence and mobility, and thus become more personalized connections, the circulation of periodicals and monographs from outside Albania had a clear impact on Muslim intellectual discourses in the country. References to Muslim scholars—notably European converts—from other parts of the Muslim world, and above all from Europe, provided sources of inspiration for reform and modernization, and arguments during local controversies over power and legitimacy.

Notes

1. See Nathalie Clayer, "Adapting Islam To Europe: The Albanian Example," in *Islam und Muslime in (Südost)Europa im Kontext von Transformation und EU-Erweiterung*, ed. Christian Voss and Jordanka Telbizova-Sack (München-Berlin: Verlag Otto Sagner, 2010), 53–69.
2. I will not consider here all exchanges, in particular I will not examine Sufi networks. For this, cp. Nathalie Clayer, "The Tijaniyya. Islamic Reformism and Islamic Revival in Inter-War Albania," *Journal of Muslim Minority Affairs* 29.4 (2009): 483–493.
3. See Thomas Eich, "Islamic Networks," *European History Online (EGO)*, Mainz 2011–02–07, accessed October 31, 2013, http://www.ieg-ego.eu/eicht-2010-en.
4. I would like to thank the director of the Albanian National library in Tirana, Aurel Plasari, as well as Maks Gjinaj and all the staff of the library for their help while I was conducting this research.
5. Compare Helmut Schwanke, "Zur Geschichte der österreichisch-ungarischen Militärverwaltung in Albanien (1916–1918)" (Phd dissertation, Wien University, 1982); Alexandre Popovic, *L'islam balkanique* (Wiesbaden: Otto Harrassowitz, 1986); and Ali M. Basha, *Rrugëtimi i fesë Islame në Shqipëri (1912–1967)* (Tiranë: n.p., 2011).
6. See Clayer, "Adapting Islam."
7. Clayer, "Adapting Islam."
8. Qazim Xhelili, *Vehbi Dibra* (Tirana: Albin, 1998).
9. Ismail Ahmedi, *Hafiz Ali Korça: Jeta dhe vepra* (Shkup: Logos-A, 2006).
10. Sadik Albayrak, *Son Devir Osmanlı Uleması*, vol. 4 (Istanbul: İstanbul Büyükşehir Belediyesi, 1996), 344–345.
11. The younger and fewer ulemas who had studied in Cairo, such as Hafiz Ali Kraja or Shyqri Myftija, did not belong to the first circle of the Albanian Islamic leaders, see Faik Luli, Islam Dizdari, and Nexhmi Bushati. *Në Kujtim të brezave* (Shkodër: Rozafat, 1997).
12. Ahmedi, *Hafiz Ali Korça*, 45.
13. Hafiz Ali Korça, *Bolshevizma. Çkatërimi i njerëzimit* (Tirana: "Mbrothësia" Kristo P. Luarasi, 1925). In the booklet, there are references to the journal *Yeni Kafkasia* and to the account of the

Muslim traveler Abdürreşid published in *Sebilürreşad's* columns at the end of 1923–beginning of 1924, before it was closed down in March 1925.

14. See, for example, the translation of articles on missionaries (*Zani i naltë*, 1924: 218 sq.), on Indian Muslims (*Zani i naltë*, 1924: 304 sq., 328 sq., and 350 sq.) by Hafiz Ali Korça himself. On *Sebilürreşâd* see Esther Debus, *Sebilürreşad. Eine vergleichende Untersuchung zur islamischen Opposition der vor- und nachkemalistischen Ära* (Frankfurt: Peter Lang, 1991).

15. See Nathalie Clayer, "Behind the Veil. The Reform of Islam in Inter-War Albania or the Search for a 'Modern' and 'European' Islam," in *Islam in Inter-War Europe*, ed. Nathalie Clayer and Eric Germain (London: Hurst, 2008), 153–155 and Basha, *Rrugëtimi*, 129–133.

16. Eric Germain, "The First Muslim Missions on a European Scale: Ahmadi-Lahori Networks in the Inter-war Period," in *Islam in Inter-War Europe*, ed. Nathalie Clayer and Eric Germain (London: Hurst, 2008), 89–118.

17. The Qadiyani Ahmadis also tried during the interwar to extend their network to Albania, but contrary to the Lahoris, unsuccessfully. In 1927, just when the Lahoris had contacted the editors of the Tirana-based Islamic journal, the imam of the London mosque, Rahim Bakhsh Dard, expressed to the Albanian ambassador in Great Britain, Ekrem bey Vlora, his desire to come and visit Albania. The ambassador wrote to the Islamic leaders to welcome this man who had been recommended to him. See Nathalie Clayer, "La Ahmadiyya lahori et la réforme de l'islam albanais dans l'entre-deux-guerres," in *De l'Arabie à l'Himalaya. Chemins croisés en hommage à Marc Gaborieau*, ed. Véronique Bouillier and Catherine Servan-Schreiber (Paris: Maisonneuve et Larose, 2004), 211–228. We do not know if he really came to Albania. However, some ten years later a Qadiyani missionary effectively came to Tirana. On that occasion, maybe because they had suspicions, the leaders of the Islamic community asked to the students in Lahore (see below) if they knew him. They answered that before going to Albania, he had come to them to learn things about the country and about the possibility of opening a mission there. After having tried in vain to discourage him, they warned the Islamic leaders about the danger represented by this rival missionary network, which would endanger the relations not only between Muslims and Christians, but also between Muslims themselves, with false arguments that he would only progressively unveil (Basha, *Rrugëtimi*, 135–136). As a matter of fact, the Qadiyanis had no success in Albania at that time. The Lahoris largely won the competition, even if their network was itself surpassed by the Egyptian power of attraction as demonstrated below.

18. *Der Islamische Mensch,* written by Sadr-ud-Din and published by the Berlin mosque in 1924, was translated this way.

19. Their translations were published in the Islamic Community's journal, particularly in the 1930s. See Clayer, "La Ahmadiyya lahori."

20. See Clayer, "La Ahmadiyya lahori" and Basha, Rrugëtimi, 134–137 and 417–418.

21. We do not know the exact content of the telegram, but, from the letter of the secretary of the Anjuman, one understands that the head of the Albanian Community had explained to the Ahmadis that there will be an important celebration in Albania for the Prophet's birth and that he will make a speech on radio (Kultura Islame II.13–14, September–October 1940, 50).

22. Among Albanian Muslim ulemas exiled in America, Ahmadi influence even continued in the postwar period (Clayer, "La Ahmadiyya lahori").

23. Clayer, "La Ahmadiyya lahori," 214–215.

24. Fehmi Kazazi explains that he had come across the book he translated in a shop-window of a bookshop in Italy. See Fehmi Kazazi, Jeta e Hazretit Muhammed Mustafajt si mbas gojdhanave dhe shkrimtarve të mdhaj arab (Shkodër: Ora e Shkodrës, 1929), 3. We also know that the famous Albanian librarian Lumo Skëndo / Midhat Frashëri was selling books about the history of Islam and the Muslim world. (Basha, Rrugëtimi, 133)

25. See Abdullah Wiljam Gjuiliam, Nji pyetje dijetarve mysliman e përgjegja e A. Gjuiliamit (Shkodër: Ora e Shkodrës, 1926).

26. Cp. Ali Korça, Shtat ëndrat e Shqipërisë (Tirana: Shtyp. i shtetit, 1944).

27. Basha, Rrugëtimi, 134.

28. Ramadan Shkodra, "Myderriz Hasan Efendi Nahi—Arsimdashës e Patriot i Shquar." accessed May 4, 2012, http://shkodrar.wordpress .com/2011/07/04/myderriz-hasan-efendi-nahi-arsimdashes-e -patriot-i-shquar/.

29. Basha, Rrugëtimi, 110.

30. In fact it may not have been the first book translated for the Albanian Islamic institutions and published by it. Indeed, the first six books published by the Sharia Higher Council, under the title Dijeni besimtare pratike (Practical religious knowledge)—which were catechisms (ilmihal) for the six classes of elementary schools—might have been translations as well.

31. Ahmet Hamdi Akseki (1887–1951) became a prominent Ottoman religious thinker after 1908. He was of the main authors publishing in the journal Sebiülreşşad. After 1924, he was a member of the council of the Diyanet. He was the vice-head of the Diyanet between 1941 and 1947 and its head between 1947 and 1951, when he died.

32. Ahmet Hamdi, Mësime feje (Shkodër: Ora e Shkodrës, 1928), "Dy fjalë," I–VII.

33. Umut Azak, Islam and Secularism in Turkey: Kemalism, Religion and The Nation State (London: IB Tauris, 2010), 51.

34. It seems that one *hutbe* asking for the mobilization in favor of the Aviation Society was not translated, as this referred to the particular case of Turkish society.
35. I could not verify if these new *hutbes* could have been translated from the material published in Turkey in the specific journal of the Diyanet, *Hutbe mecmuası*.
36. Muhamet Ali, *Muhamedi profeti i ynë* (Shkodra: Ora e Shkodrës, 1931).
37. See Ali Akpınar, "Ömer Rıza Doğrul (1893–1952) ve Tefsîre Katkısı," accessed May 4, 2012, http://eskidergi.cumhuriyet.edu.tr /makale/330.pdf and Hadiye Ünsal; *Mevlana Muhammed Ali'nin 'The Holy Qur'an' Adlı Meal tefsiri üzerine bir inceleme*, MA dissertation (Adana: Çukurova Üniversitesi, 2010).
38. See Ismail Bardhi, *Hafiz Ibrahim Dalliu dhe ekzegjeza e tij kur'anore* (Shkup: Logos-A, 1998).
39. Ymer Riza [Ömer Rıza], *Ç'asht Islamizma* (Tirana: Shtyp. Tirana, 1935).
40. See Ymer Riza [Ömer Rıza], *Ç'asht Kurani* (Elbasan: Stamles, 1938) and Ömer Rıza, *Kur'an nedir?* (Istanbul: Amedi, 1927). The transmission of the Ahmadi way of thinking by Ömer Rıza also had an impact in Yugoslavia. The first translation of the Qur'an in Serbo-Croatian, published in Sarajevo in 1937, by Muhammad Pandža and Džemaluddin Čaušević, had largely as a basis the work of Ömer Rıza, *Tanrı Buyruğu*, itself largely inspired by the translation and commentary made by Muhammad Ali, see Alexandra Popovic, "Sur une 'nouvelle' traduction du Coran en serbo-croate," *Arabica* XX.1 (1973): 82–84.
41. His father (born in Zëmblak in 1275/1859, died on September 15, 1936) was the son of a shaykh who was the *halife* of the Halwati Hayati *tekke* in Ohrid. He was called Salih Hulusi and had studied in a *mekteb* and a *rüştiye* in Korçë, then several years in the famous Süleymaniye *madrasa* in Istanbul, as well as in a teacher-school. As a teacher, he taught religious and nonreligious topics in different *rüshtiye*-schools in Durrës, Krujë, Bilisht, Kolonjë, Prilep, Alasonja, and Ankara. He knew Turkish, Arabic, and Persian. See Abdullah Sëmlaku, *Bilbil-i shpirtnor ose Misionarët Mysliman* (Korçë: Peppo & Marko, 1936), 10 and 15.
42. See Abdullah Sëmlaku, *Bilbil i gjashtë. Kanarja* (Korçë: Peppo & Marko, 1930), 41–43; and Abdullah Sëmlaku, *Kanar i ri dhe bilbili faqe bardhë* (Korçë: Peppo & Marko, 1938), title page and 3–5.
43. See Abdulla Sëmlaku, *Bilbil i tetë fëllëza* (Korçë: Peppo & Marko, 1931), 5–6.
44. Abdullah Sëmlaku, *Bilbil i gjashtë*, 9; and Abdullah Sëmlaku, *Bilbil-i shpirtnor*, 33.
45. See Abdullah Sëmlaku, *Bilbil i fesë, Sheri-ati Muhamedija* (Korçë: Peppo & Marko, 1930), 2; Abdullah Sëmlaku, *Mevlùdi Pàq. "Nuri*

Ahmedija" (Korçë: Peppo & Marko, 1931), 80; Abdullah Sëmlaku, *Bilbil-i shtatë. Shqiponja. "Besare"* (Korçë: Peppo & Marko, 1933), 27–31; and Abdullah Sëmlaku, *Kanar,* title page and 3–5.

46. Abdullah Sëmlaku, *Bilbil i gjashtë,* 9; Abdullah Sëmlaku, *Bilbil i fesë,* 47–49, 50–52, and 80–83; Abdullah Sëmlaku, *Bilbil i tetë fëllëza,* 15–16; Abdullah Sëmlaku, *Trëndafil i 1* (Korçë: Peppo & Marko, 1932), 138–139; Abdullah Sëmlaku, *Bilbil i ri i Hazreti Kuranit* (Korçë: Peppo & Marko, 1934), 67; Abdullah Sëmlaku, *Kanar,* 9. Zëmblaku stressed the fact that the Ahmadis mentioned his activities and published some of his works, including some poems in Arabic that he had sent to them, in their publications.

47. See Abdullah Sëmlaku, *Bilbil i gjashtë,* 52 and Abdullah Sëmlaku, *Bilbil i fesë,* 83.

48. Abdullah Sëmlaku, *Trëndafil i 1,* 116 and 149; Sëmlaku, *Bilbil-i shtatë,* 25–27; Abdullah Sëmlaku, *Bilbili besëtar* (Korçë: Peppo & Marko, 1935), 56–59; Abdullah Sëmlaku, *Bilbil-i shpirtnor,* 40; Abdullah Sëmlaku, *Bilbili shqiptar* (Korçë: Peppo & Marko, 1936), 24.

49. Abdullah Sëmlaku, *Bilbil i historisë ose Histori e shenjtë* (Korçë: Peppo & Marko, 1930), 128; Abdullah Sëmlaku, *Bilbil i Hadithit. 1001dritë. Fjalët e shenjta e të madhit Pejgamber* (Korçë: Peppo & Marko, 1930), 116 and 121; Abdullah Sëmlaku, *Mevlùdi Pàq,* 67; Abdullah Sëmlaku, *Trëndafil i 1,* 172; Sëmlaku, *Bilbil-i shtatë,* 32–44.

50. The Egyptian Association of Muslim Youth was also imitated by the *Mladi Muslimani* in Bosnia-Herzegovina, see Xavier Bougarel, "L'islam bosniaque, entre identité culturelle et idéologie politique," in *Le nouvel islam balkanique. Les musulmans, acteurs du post-communisme (1990–2000),* ed. Xavier Bougarel and Nathalie Clayer, (Paris: Maisonneuve & Larose, 2001), 79–132.

51. There were even migration cases, such as that of the family of the future *shaykh.* Nasiruddin al-Albani fled from Shkodër to Damascus in the 1920s, supposedly because of the secular nature of the Albanian state.

52. However, the new underground movement of the Nurcus, still developing with difficulty through the diffusion of manuscript works in Anatolia, had no echo in Albania at that time, nor that of the Süleymancıs.

References

Ahmedi, Ismail. *Hafiz Ali Korça: Jeta dhe vepra.* Shkup: Logos-A, 2006.
Ahmet Hamdi. *Mësime feje.* Shkodër: Ora e Shkodrës, 1928.
Akpınar, Ali. "Ömer Rıza Doğrul (1893–1952) ve Tefsire Katkısı." Accessed May 4, 2012. http://eskidergi.cumhuriyet.edu.tr/makale/330.pdf.
Albayrak, Sadik. *Son Devir Osmanlı Uleması,* vol. 4. Istanbul: İstanbul Büyükşehir Belediyesi, 1996.

Azak, Umut. *Islam and Secularism in Turkey: Kemalism, Religion and the Nation State*. London: IB Tauris, 2010.

Bardhi, Ismail. *Hafiz Ibrahim Dalliu dhe ekzegjeza e tij kur'anore*. Shkup: Logos-A, 1998.

Basha, Ali M. *Rrugëtimi i fesë Islame në Shqipëri (1912–1967)*. Tirana: n.p., 2011.

Bougarel, Xavier. "L'islam bosniaque, entre identité culturelle et idéologie politique." In *Le nouvel islam balkanique. Les musulmans, acteurs du post-communisme (1990–2000)*, edited by Xavier Bougarel and Nathalie Clayer, 79–132. Paris: Maisonneuve & Larose, 2001.

Clayer, Nathalie. "Adapting Islam to Europe: The Albanian Example." In *Islam und Muslime in (Südost)Europa im Kontext von Transformation und EU-Erweiterung*, edited by Christian Voss and Jordanka Telbizova-Sack, 53–69. München-Berlin: Verlag Otto Sagner, 2010.

———. "Behind the Veil. the Reform of Islam in Inter-war Albania or the Search for a 'Modern' and 'European' Islam." In *Islam in Inter-War Europe*, edited by Nathalie Clayer and Eric Germain, 128–155. London: Hurst, 2008.

———. "La Ahmadiyya lahori et la réforme de l'islam albanais dans l'entre-deux-guerres." In *De l'Arabie à l'Himalaya. Chemins croisés en hommage à Marc Gaborieau*, edited by Véronique Bouillier and Catherine Servan-Schreiber, 211–228. Paris: Maisonneuve et Larose, 2004.

———. "The Tijaniyya. Islamic Reformism and Islamic Revival in Inter-war Albania." *Journal of Muslim Minority Affairs* 29.4 (2009): 483–493.

Debus, Esther. *Sebilürreşad. Eine vergleichende Untersuchung zur islamischen Opposition der vor- und nachkemalistischen Ära*. Frankfurt: Peter Lang, 1991.

Eich, Thomas. "Islamic Networks." *European History Online (EGO)*. Mainz: Institute of European History (IEG). Accessed June 4, 2012. http://www.ieg-ego.eu/eicht-2010.

Germain, Eric. "The first Muslim Missions on a European Scale: Ahmadi-Lahori Networks in the Inter-war Period." In *Islam in Inter-war Europe*, edited by Nathalie Clayer and Eric Germain, 89–118. London: Hurst, 2008.

Gjuiliam, Abdullah Wiljam. *Nji pyetje dijetarve mysliman e përgjegja e A. Gjuiliamit*. Shkodër: Ora e Shkodrës, 1926.

Kazazi, Fehmi. *Jeta e Hazretit Muhammed Mustafajt si mbas gojdhanave dhe shkrimtarve të mdhaj arab*. Shkodër: Ora e Shkodrës, 1929.

Këshillet e së Premtës. Shkodër: Ora e Shkodrës, 1928.

Këshillet e së Premtës. Shkodër: Ora e Shkodrës, 1932.

[Korça,] Hafiz Ali. *Bolshevizma a çkatërimi i njerëzimit*. Tirana, Albania: "Mbrothësia" Kristo P. Luarasi, 1925.

Korça, Ali. *Shtat ëndrat e Shqipërisë*. Tirana, Albania: Shtyp. i shtetit, 1944 (Shkup: Logos-A, 2006).

Luli, Faik, Islam Dizdari, and Nexhmi Bushati. *Në Kujtim të brezave*. Shkodër: Rozafat, 1997.

Muhamet Ali. *Muhamedi profeti i ynë.* Shkodra: Ora e Shkodrës, 1931.

———. *Një përshkrim i shkurtër i jetës së profitit t'islamizmës. Paraqitun prej Muhamet Ali.* Shkodra: Ora e Shkodrës, 1929.

Ömer Rıza. *Kur'an nedir?* Istanbul: Amedi, 1927.

Popovic, Alexandre. *L'islam balkanique.* Wiesbaden, Germany: Otto Harrassowitz, 1986.

———. "Sur une 'nouvelle' traduction du Coran en serbo-croate." *Arabica* XX.1 (1973): 82–84.

Schwanke, Helmut. "Zur Geschichte der österreichisch-ungarischen Militärverwaltung in Albanien (1916–1918)." Phd dissertation, Wien University, Austria, 1982.

Sëmlaku, Abdullah. *Bilbili besëtar.* Korçë: Peppo & Marko, 1935.

———. *Bilbil i fesë, Sheri-ati Muhamedija.* Korçë: Peppo & Marko, 1930.

———. *Bilbil i gjashtë. Kanarja.* Korçë: Peppo & Marko, 1930.

———. *Bilbil i Hadithit. 1001dritë. Fjalët e shenjta e të madhit Pejgamber.* Korçë: Peppo & Marko, 1930.

———. *Bilbil i ri i Hazreti Kuranit.* Korçë: Peppo & Marko, 1934.

———. *Bilbil i historisë ose Histori e shenjtë.* Korçë: Peppo & Marko, 1930.

———. *Bilbil-i shpirtnor ose Misionarët Mysliman.* Korçë: Peppo & Marko, 1936.

———. *Bilbili shqiptar.* Korçë: Peppo & Marko, 1936.

———. *Bilbil-i shtatë. Shqiponja. "Besare."* Korçë: Peppo & Marko, 1933.

———. *Bilbil i tetë fëllëza.* Korçë: Peppo & Marko, 1931.

———. *Kanar i ri dhe bilbili faqe bardhë.* Korçë: Peppo & Marko, 1938.

———. *Mevlùdi Pàq. "Nuri Ahmedija."* Korçë: Peppo & Marko, 1931.

———. *Trëndafil i 1.* Korçë: Peppo & Marko, 1932.

Shkodra, Ramadan. "Myderriz Hasan Efendi Nahi—Arsimdashës e Patriot i Shquar." Accessed May 4, 2012. http://shkodrar.wordpress.com/2011/07/04/myderriz-hasan-efendi-nahi-arsimdashes-e-patriot-i-shquar/.

Ünsal, Hadiye. "Mevlana Muhammed Ali'nin 'The Holy Qur'an' Adlı Meal tefsiri üzerine bir inceleme." MA dissertation, Çukurova Üniversitesi, Adana, 2010.

Xhelili, Qazim. *Vehbi Dibra.* Tirana, Albania: Albin, 1998.

Ymer Riza. *Ç'asht Islamizma.* Tirana, Albania: Shtyp. Tirana, 1935.

———. *Ç'asht Kurani.* Elbasan, Albania: Stamles, 1938.

CHAPTER 3

Two *Ulama* Traveling to Europe in the Beginning of the Twentieth Century: Muhammad al-Wartatani and Muhammad al-Sa'ih

Richard van Leeuwen

After French administration was established in Algeria and Tunisia in the course of the nineteenth century, a policy was initiated to radically reform Maghribian societies with the aim to conform these societies to colonial interests and to the ideals of the European "mission civilisa-trice." The societies were rapidly transformed into dependencies of the motherland by tightening economic connections, facilitating immigration, and reforming the administrative and social institutions to accommodate the new rulers. An important consequence was the increased mobility between France and north Africa, resulting in the formation of migrant communities on both shores of the Mediterranean, increased cultural exchange through travel, and the emergence of transnational networks of various kinds covering the European metropolises and the urban centers of the Maghreb.[1]

These developments greatly affected the role and social position of a particular group in Maghribian society, namely the body of religious scholars, or "*ulama.*" As guardians of the religious tradition, the *ulama* were naturally inclined to critically scrutinize all tendencies of reorganization and reform. Apart from this, they were usually an integral part of the administrative systems and social institutions, which, under colonial rule, became the object of reform. In this chapter, I would like to concentrate on two examples of *ulama* who were incorporated into the processes summarized above and whose attitudes show the complexities of the role of the *ulama* in the new configuration of French-Maghribian relations. Both scholars traveled to Europe in the first decades of the twentieth century and laid down their experiences in interesting accounts that reveal not only their religious sensitivities, but also their appreciation of the European economic, social, and cultural achievements. They show how the formation of new networks affected the *ulama* in the French Maghreb, and also how the migrants in France were considered part of the Maghribian religious realm.

The first scholar to be discussed is Muhammad al-Wartatani from Qayrawan, Tunisia, who visited France in 1913 and who, as we will see, represented the secular-oriented scholars who were prepared to cooperate with the French authorities. The second scholar is Muhammad Ibn al-Salam al-Sa'ih from Morocco, who traveled to Paris in 1922 as a member of a delegation of religious scholars to supervise the establishment of the *qibla* for the new mosque that the French intended to build in Paris. The accounts of their journeys will be discussed in the light of the important themes of the age: religious versus secular attitudes, and responses to the challenges of colonial relationships.

I. Reform in Tunisia and Morocco

Developments in Tunisia during the nineteenth century were marked by a process of reforms initiated by the *Tanzimat* decrees issued by Istanbul and by the growing influence of European thought and practices. The efforts at reform were mainly the responsibility of local leaders. As elsewhere, the *ulama*, as a group, were directly affected by the reform measures, which involved a revision of the status of citizens; a reform of the judicial apparatus, legislation, and courts; and a reorganization of educational institutions replacing or supplementing traditional curricula and allowing European influences.

The milestones of the reform process were the revision of the educational charter of the Zaytuna mosque in Tunis, which became the most important centre of religious learning (1842), the reform of the Sharia court (1856) and constitutional reforms (1857; 1861–1866).[2] There is no indication that the *ulama*, as a group, resisted reform measures as such. They limited their resistance to the domains that they considered their prerogative, like the legal and educational institutions. As Arnold Green observes, this did not mean that the Tunisian *ulama* rejected all efforts at reform; they rejected measures that would reduce their professional prospects and influence, and supported reforms that widened their job opportunities. Moreover, responses varied according to the social background of the scholars, for instance between members of the vested Tunisian *ulama* families and scholars from provincial towns. Especially the latter saw their opportunities for positions increase by the creation of new institutions.

The reform period in Tunisia cannot be discussed without referring to the great figure of Khayr al-Din al-Tunisi, who was Prime Minister from 1873–1877. During his office, he initiated an ambitious program of reform, including the establishment of a central administration of *waqf* possessions, the revision of the curriculum of the Zaytuna Mosque and the improvement of government supervision of education, and, especially, the foundation of the Sadiqiyya College, a school for continued education following the model of the French *lycée*, providing courses in religious and modern secular disciplines. Khayr al-Din secured the cooperation of the reformist *ulama* by integrating them into the new institutions and creating new positions. The college thus had the effect of strengthening the position of the reformist scholars and creating space for the emergence of a new intellectual elite with a modern education. An effort by Khayr al-Din to reform the curriculum of the Zaytuna was less successful, due to the resistance of conservative *ulama*.

After the confirmation of French rule in Tunisia by the Convention of La Marsa in 1883, a campaign was launched to modernize the Tunisian society in the domains of public works, finance, defense, administration, and judiciary (1883), with the argument that "implanting in Tunisia French institutions and culture would at once facilitate European colonization and raise up generations of loyal, French-speaking Tunisians."[3] One of the measures was the enhanced government control of educational institutions, the *kuttab*s, the *madrasa*s, the Sadiqiyya and the Zaytuna. These interventions strengthened antireformist tendencies among the *ulama* and weakened the partisans of Khayr al-Din, some of whom left the country. In 1885, a revolt broke out after a decision of the Municipal Council of Tunis concerning certain taxes and levies. Some prominent *ulama* who were involved in the protests were punished harshly by the French authorities. However, in the following decades a tendency prevailed to accommodate to the French administration, especially in the 1890s, when the French residents-general were inclined to support Islamic modernism and assimilate it into modern European values, in order to co-opt progressive-minded scholars.

An important event within the process of reform was the establishment in 1896 of the Khalduniyya, by a combined effort of the French authorities and reformist *ulama*. The aim of the new school was the "re-introduction of the universal sciences in the Islamic culture."[4] The responsibility of the institution was mainly entrusted to graduates of the Sadiqiyya, in order to strengthen the roots of the new intellectual elite and reformist thought, against the more conservative *ulama* of the Zaytuna. The reformist coalition that coalesced around the Khalduniyya initiative consolidated itself in the next decades. Increasingly, *ulama* legitimated French measures and participated in institutions sponsored by the French authorities.[5]

Still, the *ulama* were not uniform in their reformist stand, since a large segment, especially in and around the Zaytuna, kept resisting reform measures, and there was a growing concern—even among reformists—that the reformist tendencies were turning into outright secularism. There were discussions among the *ulama* about what religion and societal reform implied, particularly after the emergence of the reformist periodical *al-Manar* of Muhammad Rashid Rida (1865–1935) in Cairo, which was widely read in Tunisia, and the visit of the celebrated Egyptian reformist thinker Muhammad 'Abduh to Tunis in 1903. In 1907, the Party of Young Tunisians was formed, a new alliance of forces aimed at Tunisian emancipation, which can be seen as a regrouping of previous coalitions and which originated from the reformist and Khalduniyya factions.[6] Perhaps paradoxically, the emergence of the movement strengthened the ties between the French authorities and the conservative and traditionalist *ulama*.[7] Thus, in the first decade of the twentieth century the configuration of forces became more diffuse: there was no natural alliance between the Young Tunisians and the *ulama*; the conservative scholars consolidated their position with the help of the French; and the reform movement became divided between religious and secular factions.[8]

The background of the development of reformism in nineteenth-century Morocco and the attitudes of the *ulama* are structurally different from the Tunisian case, although some general tendencies were similar. The differences were caused, first, by the specific administrative tradition and the place of religion in it, which had developed in Morocco from the fifteenth century; and, second, by the relatively late direct intervention in Moroccan affairs by the French, who established a protectorate in Morocco in 1912. The similarities related mainly to the general characteristics of the process of reform, involving centralization of the administration, the interference from abroad and the effects of measures on the career opportunities of the *ulama*. The *ulama* were forced to determine their position within these processes, while at the same time formulating visions of religion that would combine the preservation of tradition and the transformations required by modernity.[9]

The relationship between the *ulama* and the state as it grew between the fifteenth and nineteenth centuries consisted of the mutual acceptance of each other's domains, the *ulama* providing each new sultan with a *bay'a* or investiture, while the sultan, himself a leader with a religious status, respected the privileges which the *ulama* enjoyed as scholars, *shurafa'*, and Sufi leaders. It became a custom that the sultan incorporated the *ulama* into the administrative apparatus, appointing them in various positions that required certain skills or intellectual expediency. These arrangements secured a usually harmonious interrelationship, guarding the autonomy and privileges of both parties and providing ideological legitimacy for the sultan and sources of income for the *ulama*. Another result was that there was no centralized leadership or internal hierarchy among the *ulama* that prevented them from acting "corporately" vis-à-vis processes of change.

This setup became unsettled during the reign of 'Abd al-'Aziz (1894–1908), who, in an effort to centralize the administration, took a number of measures to diminish the power of the *ulama*. In particular, he transformed the office of the chief qadi to enhance his grip on the judiciary. In addition, he took control of appointments in the Qarawiyyin University and limited the right of sanctuary in mosques and convents.[10] Moreover, he and his successor increasingly patronized those scholars known for their reformist ideas, such as 'Abdallah Ibn Idris al-Sanusi and, under 'Abd al-Hafiz, Abu Shu'ayb al-Dukkali. In general, the reform measures that affected the position of the *ulama*, in the judiciary and education, were not severe enough to arouse a general opposition in their ranks, as some of them did not effectively change accepted practices.

Part of the opposition of the *ulama* to reform measures was neutralized by the increase in job opportunities in the state apparatus, the *makhzan*. Reforms, centralization, and especially the intensified trade contacts with Europe necessitated the expansion of the state bureaucracy, which traditionally implied an increased appeal on the intellectual abilities of the *ulama*. This not only afforded them a source of income from their office, but also enabled them and their families to profit from the expansion of trade and its revenues. In this way the *ulama* were integrated into the policies of reform, giving shape to the modernization of the *makhzan* and thereby identifying the interests of the central authorities as their own. However, this support was not unconditional. It was especially the increased economic dependency on foreign loans and the concessions made by the sultan to foreign companies that were seen as contrary to the interests of the commercial bourgeoisie, to which many *ulama* belonged, and which aroused their protests as a relatively coherent group. The *ulama* quite rapidly became the spokesmen of the nationalist cause.

After the takeover by the French, the real process of reforming the administration, the educational institutions and the judiciary began. The whole bureaucratic apparatus of the *makhzan* was reorganized in 1915, and the following year two Muslim colleges were founded by Lyautey, the first resident general of Morocco from 1912 to1925: the Collège Musulman Moulay Idris in Fez and the Collège Musulman Moulay Youssef in Rabat. These institutions were founded with a clear purpose: to meet the need for officials with a "French" attitude, who could act as intermediaries between the French and the Moroccan people.[11] In 1914–1915, an effort was made in cooperation with reform-minded scholars to limit the autonomy of the Qarawiyyin in Fez, efforts that were repeated in 1930.[12] In 1920, a new Institut des Hautes Études was founded in Rabat (Ma'had al-Dirasat al-'Ulya).

As in Tunis, reform measures were directed especially at the administration, education, the judiciary and the control of *'awqaf*. In Morocco, too, these reforms required the incorporation of intellectuals into the governmental institutions and the support of scholars who were not only willing to cooperate, but who also provided the new setup with a religious legitimization. In this way, a new group of scholars emerged who were in principle of a nationalist inclination but who supported French rule as a means to reorganize and strengthen the *makhzan* and reinforce their position as scholars and, in some cases, as members of prominent merchant families. They saw the reform policies as a means to modernize the country and a necessary step toward independence. Thus, as in Tunisia, in Morocco too we can see that the attitude of the scholars toward modernization and foreign intervention was not only motivated by religious or ideological concerns, but also, at least partly, by economic interests connected to their social backgrounds.

II. Muhammad al-Miqdad al-Wartatani

The developments briefly outlined above were the backdrop of the career of Muhammad al-Miqdad al-Wartatani, the author of the travel account that we will discuss here. The information we have about al-Wartatani is mainly found in the introduction of his travel account. He was probably born in 1881 in Ubba, a village between

Tunis and Qayrawan. He studied at the Zaytuna and Khalduniyya and followed courses in history and geography, *usul al-fiqh*, Arabic literature, and logic under prominent reformist scholars. As we have seen above, this educational trajectory would have qualified him as a distinctly "modern" scholar, combining knowledge of religious and secular disciplines. He was well-acquainted with the French language and French history. After his studies he became head of the *waqf* administration in Qayrawan, teacher in the Great Mosque and member of the administrative board of a hospital in Qayrawan. This combination of functions is also typical of a modern style scholar involved in tasks directly related to new and modern institutions, but also to traditional religious scholarship. His works include, especially, historical studies.[13]

It is significant that al-Wartatani stresses that his great-grandfather and grandfather were known for their piety and knowledge. Although he mentions him by name only once, as his "relative," his grandfather was presumably the well-known scholar Ahmad al-Wartatani, who figured prominently among the ranks of the reformist *ulama*.[14] He belonged to the category of Maliki scholars from a rural—even tribal—background, who profited from the career opportunities provided by the reforms by Khayr al-Din.[15] In 1875 he was a member of the committee fostering the foundation of the Sadiqiyya College and he became an assistant of the reformist scholar Muhammad Bayram V, who was put in charge of the government printing house specifically to publish the reformist journal *al-Ra'id al-Tunisi*.[16] Al-Wartatani acted as vice president and later president (1878) of the *waqf* administration set up by Khayr al-Din, under the supervision of Muhammad Bayram V.[17] In 1885, he was dismissed from his post because of his involvement in the revolt against the French authorities.[18]

The career of Ahmad al-Wartatani clearly illustrates the struggles of the early phase of reform, not only in the pragmatic sense of fulfilling roles in the new institutions, but also with regard to the promulgation of reformist ideas. He explicitly endorsed the ideas of Khayr al-Din and apparently belonged to a group who supported Muhammad 'Abduh. He is mentioned as a member of a cell of the society of *al-'Urwa al-wuthqa* in Tunis, which the reformist shaykh Muhammad al-Sanusi claimed to have founded with Muhammad Bayram V when he was in exile in Syria in 1882. More likely, this "cell" was a rather loose group of adherents of the ideas of 'Abduh, who visited Tunis in 1884 to discuss reform with his fellow-*ulama*.[19] Although Muhammad al-Wartatani would hardly have known his grandfather, it is plausible that he served as an model within the family and that his career fostered Muhammad's attitudes as a "modern" scholar. As we will see, whereas Ahmad al-Wartatani's career typifies the position of a certain category of reformist *ulama* in the first phase of reform, Muhammad personifies the "modern scholar" in the third phase.

The Journey

According to his account, Muhammad al-Wartatani traveled to Europe on the invitation of friends in France and Switzerland. The journey lasted from June 5 to July 7, 1913. The text of the account was published on the instigation of some friends by the official Tunisian press in 1914.

The journey took al-Wartatani from Qayrawan to Tunis and by ship to Marseille. From there he traveled to Grenoble and through the Alps to Genève and back to Lyon. From Lyon he took the train to Paris. On the return journey he passed through Toulouse, Nimes, and again Marseille. Al-Wartatani had some distinguished predecessors such as, of course, Khayr al-Din al-Tunisi (1867); Muhammadibn al-Khudja (1895), whose account he apparently edited; and Muhammad al-Sanusi (1892). The texts published by these travelers were no mere accounts of journeys; they contained extensive contemplation on and description of the situation in Europe, as well as historical and geographical information. Moreover, they were steeped in the discourse of reform, comparing the conditions in Europe with those in north Africa, and advocating modernizing reforms of various kinds.

As we will see, al-Wartatani's account is to a large extent dedicated to the summarizing of historical and geographical knowledge. This is not to say that it is basically a compendium or reference work; it contains a clear element of experience, consisting of personal observations and meetings and conversations with other people. His display of knowledge is usually put at the service of some argument, for instance for explaining differences between the French and Tunisian historical situations, or comparing economic conditions of both countries. Since comparison is an important aim, the text contains at first sight a surprising amount of information about Tunisia itself, as if the traveler has left his country only to better describe and evaluate its condition. The account of al-Wartatani begins with an elaborate discussion of the admissible "reasons for traveling" as they are given in the Islamic tradition. The author reiterates the three well-known accepted reasons: science and knowledge, trade and livelihood, and religion (especially pilgrimage and *hijra*). He adds two more reasons: political requirements such as diplomacy and the exchange of royal gifts, and social reasons such as visiting family members or friends. For each category he mentions various examples of famous Tunisians or, preferably, Qayrawanis who traveled for similar purposes.

This introduction shows that al-Wartatani embedded his account firmly in the religious and historical tradition by connecting it to these general "paradigms" of the travelogue. The references are not limited to the introductory parts, however, but are also spread through the text itself to remind the reader of its generic framework. In the next sections we will analyze al-Wartatani's account in a more detailed way, using the two sub-frameworks of secular and religious discourses to reveal potential tensions, and to evaluate al-Wartatani's judgments against his background as a religious scholar.

The Religious Framework

In his discussion of the legitimate purposes for traveling, al-Wartatani starts with the famous triad—trade, knowledge, pilgrimage—which is sustained by the Prophetic *Sunna*. After this, he dedicates a small paragraph to the question of whether a Muslim is allowed to travel to a non-Islamic country. He argues that there is no objection to do so, on condition that the safety of a person's body, religion, and possessions is guaranteed. It is even recommended in some cases, when such a journey entails profit or supports worldly or religious interests and well-being. There are many examples of *ulama* who have traveled for these purposes or for the conveying of knowledge. Al-Wartatani acquiesces his readers that a trip to France meets these requirements. He continues to say that the issue of Muslims traveling to the *Dar al-Harb* (i.e., non-Muslim countries) was already discussed by early Muslim jurists. However, later scholars have misinterpreted their statements without proper scrutiny and absolutely forbade travel to non-Islamic countries, overlooking the meaning of the term *Dar al-Harb*. Some Qayrawani scholars maintained that it was reprehensible (*makruh*) on the basis of Malik's *al-Muwatta*. However, al-Wartatani argued that the true definition of the concept of *Dar al-Harb* does not lead to a total prohibition: "The Dar al-Harb is a country of a hostile people with whom we are at war (*qital*), that is, when one of them vanquishes one of us and the safety of his person and his wealth will not be secured. Some *'ulama'* have widened this argument and said that the traveler to a non-Islamic land is subject to non-Islamic laws, and it is not allowed that a Muslim should expose himself to these laws."[20] Al-Wartatani concludes by referring to the scholar Ibn Muhriz that traveling is "reprehensible" only when the traveler is subjected to humiliation.

It is interesting to see how al-Wartatani deals with these arguments. He criticizes more conservative scholars who base their prohibition on a haphazard interpretation of the early scholars, but his own reasoning does not itself seem very solid. He accepts the more flexible interpretation of the early scholars without presenting much additional proof. This would mean that his discussion of this subject is *pro forma* only and that he takes a pragmatic position while still evaluating a religious justification for his journey; or that he takes the side of a less legalistic reformist group of scholars. Apart from this, his reasoning is rather ambiguous as regards the status of France as part of the *Dar al-Harb*. Does he think that the definition of the concept by the ancient scholars applies to France? Do the treaties of 1881 and 1883, establishing French rule in Tunisia, dissociate France from the *Dar al-Harb*, turning it into a mere "non-Islamic" country?

The importance of religion is emphasized in the discussion of general "reasons for traveling" when the following hierarchy is given of matters "near to the soul": religion, honor (*ird*, dignity), honor/nobility (*sharaf*), life, money (*mal*), fatherland (*watan*). This ranking implies that the fatherland may be sacrificed in the pursuit of wealth, wealth in the pursuit of life, life in the pursuit of honor, and so on. What is remarkable is, of course, not that religion is on top, but rather that the *watan* is at the bottom of the list. This once again stresses the importance of religion, not only as a value, but also as a framework of al-Wartatani's text.

After these remarks about religion in the introductory sections, there are few references to religion in the account itself. Al-Wartatani does not embark upon discussions of religious differences, Islamic and Christian doctrines or their effect on society. Religion remains implicit, and only incidentally comes to the surface. For example, when the author praises the beauty of French women, he adds that according to Islam he is not allowed to look at them. Islamic customs are also an issue of debate as far as the position of women in society is concerned. People ask al-Wartatani regularly about the position of women in Tunisian society and their lack of liberty. They mean, al-Wartatani thinks, the liberty to marry the man who they themselves choose and to go out without a veil, and customs with regard to polygamy and divorce. Al-Wartatani's answer does not satisfy his interlocutors, since they consider the seclusion of women and the legal predominance of men as bereaving women of the liberty to which the Europeans are accustomed.[21] Al-Wartatani adds that in France "women are everything," because they "own everything" from "luxury goods to respect, progress, authority and freedom."[22]

As in the case of the social position of women, al-Wartatani also refers to Islam in his discussion of the system of religious endowments, or *awqaf,* in his country. Apparently, many Europeans asked him about this practice, probably because he mentioned it as his field of work, and he answered by calling it one of the "beautiful things" (*mahasin*) of Islamic Law. He praises the organization that was established by Khayr al-Din to manage and protect the many *waqf* possessions: the Djam'iyyat al-Awqaf (Association of Endowments) was connected with the state, which is thus responsible for the economic exploitation of the properties and the preservation of their religious component, according to the law and the stipulations of the founder.[23] Apparently, as in the case of women's rights, al-Wartatani suggests that he only dwells on this subject because he is asked about it, but he seems not reluctant to give his—positive—opinion.

There is one more instance in which al-Wartatani shows some religious reflection, qualifying his overwhelming elaboration on the non-religious world: "I saw what I saw and wrote what I wrote about the aspects of the earth and the externalities of the world, while knowing that all these beauties are only seen by the eye and not by the heart." However, the eye is deceptive and reality is different: "All mountains, water, forests are not worth a moth's wing or a mustard seed compared to the bliss of life in the Hereafter."[24] The embellishments of life in this world, the bliss of riches and the serenity of appearances are only a trivial illusion. A more thorough consciousness of the value of life would reveal the importance of simplicity, sympathy, and help for poor and unfortunate fellow men.[25]

The Secular Framework

As mentioned above, in the introductory sections of al-Wartatani's account, the religious discursive paradigm is quite explicit and predominant, although it allows some room for more secular considerations such as politics, trade, and social communication. Still, it is surprising to see that the discursive paradigm of the account itself is overwhelmingly dedicated to secular interests. One of the main concerns of al-Wartatani is agriculture, on the one hand to describe products and production methods, but especially as the material basis of social life. A productive agriculture and a good organization of the distribution of cereals and other products will prevent the spread of diseases and will lead to an increase in population. This will in turn result in safety, good administration, respect for the law, the spread of industry, the flourishing of sciences, and the rise of capable men in every social class and generation. It will thus not only lead to prosperity, but also to a refined civilization and fertile thought and arts.[26]

This view of agriculture combines al-Wartatani's idealism with his pragmatism, but it especially reveals a view of history and society that is inspired by the great scholar and historian Ibn Khaldun (1332–1406). Ibn Khaldun is mentioned in several places, especially his model of history, which is based on a cyclic development of civilizations and societies, influenced by the interaction of desert and town, and forces of ascendancy and decay. The basic model of Ibn Khaldun, as interpreted by al-Wartatani, is especially the interrelatedness of the diverse components of a civilization, such as economy, industry, health, morality, science, freedom, and so on. All these sectors flourish simultaneously when civilization is ascending in its life cycle and at the same time contribute to its rise. In this model the development of urban societies and the rise of cities as centers of power are of crucial importance. At one point, al-Wartatani relates this model to Paris, comparing the French capital with the other urban centers such as Cairo in the eighth century and in ancient Babylon. Here, too, the population was industrious, healthy, attached to honor and freedom, dressing elegantly, and working hard.

Within the historical cycle, modern Europe, according to al-Wartatani, has reached a state of equilibrium, not being threatened by weakness, lack of defense, or devotion to passion and pleasures. All emotions are turned toward the common welfare, and this unity is the best protection against catastrophe. This human civilization (*tamaddun*) and political sophistication has been reached after centuries of trials. Europeans strove to develop the sciences and education in order to provide the people with knowledge of their world and with a strongly rooted "identity." However, they only occupied themselves with matters of the created world, acquainted with the useful externalities of worldly life.[27] This has made European society strong enough to recover quickly from wars, but at present an equilibrium pervades everything and this is the cause of the long period of peace in Europe. Ironically, al-Wartatani apparently perceived no signs of the coming catastrophe of the Great War.[28]

The cyclic vision of history is also related to Tunisia and especially to the new era inaugurated by the French Protectorate. Remarkably, al-Wartatani here refers to the time when the Arabs came to the Maghreb from Egypt in the fifth century, marking the beginning of devastation, repression, and impoverishment. Now a new phase in the history of Tunisia has commenced, based on science, mutual knowledge among nations, freedom of expression, the recording of events, easy travel, the protection of health and the codification of laws. Thus a generation seeks protection under the cover of safety reaching the summit of progress. Clear proofs of this progress (*ruqy*) are the zeal of the French in conquering all obstacles in the way of progress (*taqaddum*), subduing the forces of poverty and ignorance. Full of admiration, al-Wartatani mentions the construction of the telegraph and the railroad between Souss and Qayrawan as an example.[29]

The references to Ibn Khaldun show al-Wartatani's interest in history, geography, and economic organization as founding factors of civilization. Within this framework it is especially science, education, and art that are the signs of a blossoming society.[30] Al-Wartatani praises the eagerness of the French to learn and to start teaching their children at an early age. He advocates the reorganization of education in Tunisia by "reviving" the Arabic language and rhetoric and spreading the interest in sciences and, more specifically, the same persistence in scientific inquisitiveness as he perceives among the French and which is the basis of their scientific progress. In the same spirit, al-Wartatani visits the School of Oriental languages and the Bibliothèque Nationale, where he inspects a manuscript of al-Hariri's *Maqamat*. Finally, he visits two Parisian hospitals, which are of special interest to him since he is a member of the board of the hospital of Qayrawan, as mentioned above.[31]

Al-Wartatani is especially positive about the Louvre—where he admires a painting by David and regrets the absence of the Mona Lisa, which had been stolen in 1911—and the performances he attended in the Opéra. His admiration for the theatre, which, according to him, visualizes history, spreads morality, and revives language, is remarkable, since it is a topos in Maghribian travel literature of this period and earlier to denounce European theatre performances as tasteless and decadent. Even the "revue" in the Moulin Rouge and the Folies Bergières are deemed useful and interesting by al-Wartatani as comments on Parisian life, love, politics, and current affairs.[32]

III. Muhammad Ibn 'Abd al-Salam al-Sa'ih and His Journey

Muhammad Ibn 'Abd al-Salam al-Sa'ih was born in Rabat in 1891/1892 and after his studies became a teacher in the Yusufiyya College and the Institute for Advanced Studies (*Ma'had al-Dirasat al-'Ulya*) in Rabat, both institutions founded by the French authorities to modernize the educational system. He studied under several scholars in disciplines such as Islamic jurisprudence, Arabic grammar, theological doctrines, logic, and so on, next to arithmetic and *tawqit*, or time measurement. Subsequently, he entered the magistrature as judge of the *Majlis Isti'naf al-Ahkam al-Shar'iyya* in the Royal Palace, and as qadi in several towns, including Fez and Meknes, where he died in 1948. He was also a member of the examination committee of the Qarawiyyin. Probably not only because of his status as a judge, but also for his expertise in *tawqit* he was added to a delegation that was sent off to Paris in 1922 to attend the official determination of the *qibla* for the Islamic Institute in Paris, the first official mosque in the French capital. Shortly before his death in 1948 he was appointed as head of the Moroccan delegation of pilgrims to Mecca. As a religious scholar, he also wrote a number of legal treatises.[33]

Al-Sa'ih left from Casablanca in 1922 on a French ship to Bordeaux as a member of the Moroccan "scientific delegation" to the ceremonies in Paris. After a short stay in Bordeaux, the group traveled by train to Paris. Here he especially admired the technical ingenuities that symbolize modern progress, such as telephone, warm and cold running water, elevators, electric light, heating, the metro, electric stairs, and so on. He visited the Louvre, and more specifically the departments of precious stones, Coptic art, and Syrian and Phoenician archaeology. He drank a cup of coffee on the second store of the Eiffel Tower and was impressed by the clever ways in which the French advertised their merchandise, using images outside the buildings to show what is sold inside.[34]

The ceremony itself was held at the site where the Islamic Institute was going to be built. Delegations from Algeria, Tunisia, and Morocco gathered around a big compass on a wooden table, far from any interfering metal objects. Al-Sa'ih gave extensive calculations for establishing the right direction for the future *mihrab*, conceding that the French engineers were capable of the task. The ceremony was attended by several Muslims from Afghanistan, Egypt, Iran, and the Maghreb. The future centre would consist of a mosque and several provisions for Muslims living in Paris, such as a library, a *hammam*, and a restaurant serving Arabic food. Al-Sa'ih especially appreciated the symbolic value of the institute, as a monument for the cooperation of the Muslims with France during the Great War, and hoped that it would help the cause of learning. For him, the construction of the mosque was the implementation of the agreement between Sidi Muhammad Ibn 'Abdallah, the Moroccan sultan, and Louis XV in 1767, sealing the friendship between France and the Muslims.

After the ceremony, the delegation traveled by train to Marseille and by *paquet* boat back to Casablanca.

The Secular Framework

As al-Wartatani's account, al-Sa'ih's, too, mixes religious and nonreligious elements to mark the embedding of his text in the Maghribian Arabic-Islamic tradition. The secular component is first of all based on the personal experiences of the author, such as his seasickness, his amazement by the strange objects and technical inventions that he encounters, and his admiration for certain customs of the Europeans. His evaluation of these experiences is not very elaborate and not related to religion or even morality. Referring to his attendance to a performance in the theatre of Bordeaux he cannot hide his astonishment, remarking: "I felt like I was on the throne of Bilqis in a world of devils."[35] To counter the avalanche of strangeness, al-Sa'ih regularly referred to the Arabic literary tradition, for instance to al-Tha'alibi and al-Suyuti, but also, remarkably, to the account of al-Wartatani,[36] which perhaps served him as a guide. Like al-Wartatani's account, al-Sa'ih's text, too, contains information about Paris and France and the places of interest, although al-Sa'ih is much less elaborate.

As has been said above, al-Sa'ih does not give an extensive evaluation or assessment of French society, but he takes the opportunity of the journey to present a long plea for the importance of science for modern society, taken from a speech he had given for the club of the Institute of Advanced Studies in Rabat. According to al-Sa'ih, Morocco is now different than in the past. A new spirit and a program for the future are necessary, a future which "does not consist of desires built from waking dreams," but in which "all previous efforts are incorporated, with a single aim," and which "comprises all the available means." This, in short, is science. Everyone must strive to foster and acquire science, in order to be strong enough to preserve one's existence, religion, language, honor, morality, and material wealth. Science, al-Sa'ih argues, protects religion, and religion is the common bond of the *umma*, and its life. If the *umma* is in some way defective or threatened by decline, one should act according to the requirements of science.[37]

Clearly, the realms of science and religion are connected in a mutually supportive sense. Science keeps the language alive, and language is the medium of solidarity within the *umma*. Al-Sa'ih quotes a Qur'anic verse to say that science is also a condition of natural welfare. Science means penetrating into the enigmas, not only observing their surface or contemplating their beauty "from behind the glass of words," but penetrating into them to understand them. Al-Sa'ih proceeds by stressing that Morocco is not deprived of all scientific knowledge. It has inherited the sciences from previous civilizations and taken care of them, but it should develop the most important sciences according to the requirements of the present circumstances and the future.[38]

Al-Sa'ih adds that many people think that Morocco is incurably prone to ignorance. However, Morocco is endowed with great knowledge in the fields of *fiqh*, *hadith*, *tafsir*, Arabic, history, time measurement, and arithmetic. It is moreover sufficiently versed in various kinds of artisanship and technical occupations. What it needs is attention for the sciences of the age, such as medicine, engineering, the study of law and technology, although these disciplines may be of limited scope. Al-Sa'ih stresses that Morocco should share its knowledge with the rest of the world and profit from the knowledge of others. Science is not strange to or intruding into its tradition, because Islam has known many outstanding scholars in these fields; it has absorbed Greek knowledge and has transmitted it to the Europeans. The Qarawiyyin should become, once again, a university attracting students from the Arabic world and Europe.[39]

This passionate call for the pursuit of modern science is of course remarkable for a scholar who was steeped in traditional Islamic knowledge. It is noteworthy that al-Sa'ih does not enter into the intricacies of reconciling modern sciences with theology, exegesis, religious law, and similar disciplines, but carefully distinguishes the two domains and accentuates the importance of science for the practical purpose of strengthening the *umma*. Science is imagined as a phenomenon that is already inherent in the Islamic tradition and thus can be incorporated once again. There is no way into the future for Muslims or Moroccans except when they assimilate modern science and technology. Still, while appropriating modern science, the Muslims should offer their religious sciences to the world to enlighten it.

The Religious Framework

The aim of the Parisian mission of which al-Sa'ih was a member was overtly religious and it is not surprising that in spite of the prominent place awarded to secular science, the main discursive framework of the travelogue is religion. This framework is anchored, first of all, by the report on the ceremony of establishing the *qibla* as a symbol of good Muslim-French relations and of intra-Muslim solidarity. The whole project of the Islamic Institute is seen as the result of a historical development that in the end will not only serve Muslims living in Europe, but also strengthen Islam as a world religion and facilitate the spreading of the Islamic faith.[40] The account of the ceremony is accompanied by an elaborate instruction for determining the *qibla*.[41]

After the ceremony the delegation returns to Morocco almost instantaneously and the actual travel account comes to an end. However, a long section is added by al-Sa'ih in which he discusses some legal issues connected with the residence of Muslims in non-Muslim countries. It was not unusual that traveling *ulama* gave *fatwa*s to migrant communities that they visited and it is clear that there was a need for knowledge about the juridical consequences of migration in the modern era of globalization. It seems that al-Sa'ih, too, gave his opinion at least partly as a response to questions from Muslims living in France. It is also clear, however, that the section about legal issues should in no way be seen as a compendium of cases with which Muslim migrants were confronted. The subjects seem rather haphazard and are not discussed in their full practical and theoretical implications.

Among the subjects that al-Sa'ih discusses are, first, the question whether a Muslim is allowed to eat meat that is not *halal*, referring to the Qur'anic verse in *al-Ma'ida* that reads: "And the food of those who received the Scripture is lawful for you," implying that Muslims are allowed to eat the food of Christians. Several opinions about these issues are cited, especially from Ibn 'Arabi, Malik and al-Shatibi, some cases leading to a conclusive opinion (prohibition of pig fat), other cases to a rather diffuse judgment (meat and fish prepared by a Christian are allowed, but not game). A second, in the circumstances quite appropriate, question, is whether non-Muslims are allowed to enter a mosque, since they are considered "impure" by religious law. The question is of course relevant because it is Christians who are constructing the Parisian mosque. Al-Sa'ih again enumerates various opinions, for instance of Malik (only allowed when unavoidable) and Abu Hanifa (not prohibited). In the end, he prefers the Shafi'i's opinion that holds that a Christian may enter a mosque with permission of a Muslim.

Other questions are whether a Muslim is allowed to use European *eau-de-cologne*, since it contains alcohol (allowed, since it is not meant to intoxicate); and whether alcohol may be used as a medicine (only in the case of fear of death). In general, al-Sa'ih juxtaposes several opinions, invokes the Qur'an, the *hadith*, and various *mujtahid*s to support his judgment. It is beyond the scope of this chapter to discuss the legal reasoning and juridical methods that al-Sa'ih applies in his answers. It is remarkable that he does not refer to more recent authorities of Islamic law and does not explicitly treat the issues in a "modern," reformist context. There is no indication that al-Sa'ih thought that new circumstances required new kinds of reasoning or new legal methods.

CONCLUSION

The travelogues discussed above show that the two authors were aware of the far-reaching geopolitical change and societal transformation caused by the shifts in political and cultural boundaries that had occurred during their lifetimes. These changes affected their lives as scholars and opened up opportunities within the newly developing networks. This background probably in turn influenced their attitude toward the new circumstances, inducing a positive evaluation of the French administration in the Maghreb. Al-Wartatani analyzed French and Tunisian societies as part of historical cycles inspired by the theories of Ibn Khaldun and praised the positive effects of the French administration within this process. He saw the French influence as contributing to a "natural" historical evolution, seen from an autochthonous perspective. Al-Sa'ih, too, judged French influence as a source of strength for Morocco, especially in the fields of science and education. These attitudes reveal to what extent the two authors were incorporated, as scholars, in the newly created institutions and intellectual networks that had been formed through the reform programs. They represent a specific group of *ulama* who welcomed change and who, in spite of their love for their homelands, did not combine their "modern" views with an outspoken nationalist fervor.

If we balance the secular and religious components in the two travelogues, we can see how the shifting geopolitical and societal boundaries result in discussions about religious demarcations. Al-Wartatani explicitly refers to the crossing of the religious boundaries invoking the justifications of leaving the *Dar al-Islam*, but in his account religion plays only a secondary role. For him, religion is confined to individual codes of behavior and social institutions and apparently it is not a predominant marker of identity. In al-Sa'ih's account, religion is much more prominent and the *umma* is inferred as a concept of religious identity. Al-Sa'ih sees interaction with the French as a possibility to strengthen the faith, enabling the Muslims to adopt the secular sciences and use new networks to spread religious scholarship. The mosque in Paris will support the transnational spreading of Islam.

Neither al-Sa'ih, nor al-Wartatani considers the penetration of the French into their societies as a threat to Islam or the Islamic nature of society. The differences between French society on the one hand, and Tunisian and Moroccan societies on the other are not seen as deriving from religious differences, and religious doctrines are neither discussed nor evaluated. This enables the authors to construct the French presence in the Maghreb not as an intrusion of Christianity into the Muslim domain, but rather as a new balance of power between religious and secular forces, from which Islam could ultimately profit. For both, religious boundaries have shifted, even within their own societies, but especially for al-Sa'ih the new porosity of boundaries works both ways: Islam will take root in France through the Muslim migrant community, and as long as the Sharia is applied, inside and outside Morocco, the faith will prosper. The creation of new networks will ultimately be to the advantage of Islam, on condition that the boundaries between the religious and the secular domains are preserved.

The formation of new boundaries between Europe and the Muslim Maghreb and new networks results in a new vision of differentiation and incorporation, but an approach based either on an internal perspective (al-Wartatani) or on a normative view of the faith (al-Sa'ih) legitimates a positive attitude toward the far-reaching transformation.

NOTES

1. For more, see, O. Moreau, ed., *Réforme de l'État et reformismes au Maghreb (XIXe-XX siècles)* (Paris: L'Harmattan, 2009).
2. A. H. Green, *The Tunisian Ulama 1873–1915; Social Structure and Response to Ideological Currents* (Leiden, Netherlands: E. J. Brill, 1978), 103–105. See also, K. Arfaoui, "Les modernistes tunisiens et la justice (1881–1909). Quels projets de réforme?" in *Réforme*, ed. Moreau, 211–222; H. Belaïd, "La diffusion des associations à but culturel en Tunisie (1888–1951)," in *Réforme*, ed. Moreau, 261–277; J. Clancy-Smith, "Passages: Khayr al-Din al-Tunisi et une communauté méditerranéenne de pensée (1800–1890)," in *Réforme*, ed. Moreau, 161–196; D. Newman, "Sulayman al-Hariri: an early Tunisian reformer in Europe," *Les cahiers de Tunisie; revue de sciences humaines* 207–208 (2008–2009), 13–58.
3. Green, *The Tunisian*, 134–135.
4. Green, *The Tunisian*, 167.
5. Green, *The Tunisian*, 169.
6. See, M. Sayadi, *Al-Jam'iyya al-Khaldūniyya, 1896–1958* (Tunis: Maison Tunisienne de l'Éducation, 1974).
7. Green, *The Tunisian*, 197.
8. Green, *The Tunisian*, 206, 208–209, 219.

9. E. Burke III, "The Moroccan Ulama, 1860–1912; an Introduction," in *Scholars, Saints and Sufis, Muslim Religious Institutions in the Middle East since* 1500, ed. N. Keddie (Berkeley: University of California Press, 1972), 93–125.
10. Burke III, "The Moroccan Ulama," 107–109.
11. F. Kogelmann, *Islamische Stiftungen und Staat; der Wandel in den Beziehungen zwischen einer religiösen Institution und dem marokkanischen Staat seit dem 19. Jahrhundert bis 1937* (Würzburg: Ergon Verlag, 1999), 158.
12. Kogelmann, *Islamische Stiftungen*, 258–259.
13. Muhammadal-Miqdad al-Wartatani, *al-Burnus fi Baris: Rihla ila Fransa wa-Suwisra, 1913* (Abu Dhabi and Beirut: Dar al-Suwaydi li-al-Nashr wa-al-Tawzi'—al-Mu'assasa al-'Arabiyya li-al-Dirasat wa-al-Nashr, 2004), 11–13.
14. al-Wartatani, *al-Burnus*, 11.
15. Green, *The Tunisian*, 72, 90, 119.
16. Green, *The Tunisian*, 115–116.
17. Green, *The Tunisian*, 86, 112.
18. Green, *The Tunisian*, 152.
19. Green, *The Tunisian*, 149.
20. al-Wartatani, *al-Burnus*, 87–88.
21. al-Wartatani, *al-Burnus*, 321.
22. al-Wartatani, *al-Burnus*, 234.
23. al-Wartatani, *al-Burnus*, 321–322.
24. al-Wartatani, *al-Burnus*, 163.
25. al-Wartatani, *al-Burnus*, 163–164.
26. al-Wartatani, *al-Burnus*, 319.
27. al-Wartatani, *al-Burnus*, 179–180.
28. al-Wartatani, *al-Burnus*, 179–181.
29. al-Wartatani, *al-Burnus*, 39, 58–59.
30. al-Wartatani, *al-Burnus*, 319.
31. al-Wartatani, *al-Burnus*, 198–200, 312–313.
32. al-Wartatani, *al-Burnus*, 231–235.
33. Muhammad Ibn 'Abd al-Salam al-Sa'ih, *Usbu' fi Baris: 1922*, S. al-Qurashi, ed., (Abu Dhabi and Beirut: Dar al-Suwaydi li-al-Nashr wa-al-Tawzi'—al-Mu'assasa al-'Arabiyya li-al-Dirasat wa-al-Nashr, 2004), 13–17.
34. al-Sa'ih, *Usbu'*, 35–38, 44–56.
35. al-Sa'ih, *Usbu'*, 34.
36. al-Sa'ih, *Usbu'*, 39.
37. al-Sa'ih, *Usbu'*, 41.
38. al-Sa'ih, *Usbu'*, 42–43.
39. al-Sa'ih, *Usbu'*, 43–44.
40. al-Sa'ih, *Usbu'*, 62–64.
41. al-Sa'ih, *Usbu'*, 66.

REFERENCES

al-Sa'ih, Muhammad Ibn 'Abd al-Salam. *Usbu' fi Baris; 1922*, edited by S. al-Qirshi. Abu Dhabi and Beirut: Dar al-Suwaydi li-al-Nashr wa-al-Tawzi'; al-Mu'assasa al-'Arabiyya li-al-Dirasat wa-al-Nashr, 2004.

Arfaoui, K. "Les modernistes tunisiens et la justice (1881–1909). Quels projets de réforme?" In *Réforme de l'État et reformismes au Maghreb (XIXe–XX siècles)*, edited by O. Moreau, 211–222. Paris: L'Harmattan, 2009.

Belaïd, H. "La diffusion des associations à but culturel en Tunisie (1888–1951)." In *Réforme de l'État et reformismes au Maghreb (XIXe-XX siècles)*, edited by O. Moreau, 261–277. Paris: L'Harmattan, 2009.

Burke III, E. "The Moroccan Ulama, 1860–1912; an Introduction." In *Scholars, Saints and Sufis, Muslim Religious Institutions in the Middle East Since 1500*, edited by N. Keddie, 93–125. Berkeley: University of California Press: 1972.

Clancy-Smith, J. "Passages: Khayr al-Din al-Tunisi et une communauté méditerranéenne de pensée (1800–1890)." In *Réforme de l'État et reformismes au Maghreb (XIXe-XX siècles)*, edited by O. Moreau, 161–196. Paris: L'Harmattan, 2009.

Green, A. H. *The Tunisian Ulama 1873–1915; Social Structure and Response to Ideological Currents*. Leiden, Netherlands: E. J. Brill, 1978.

Kogelmann, F. *Islamische Stiftungen und Staat. Der Wandel in den Beziehungen zwischen einer religiösen Institution und dem marokkanischen Staat seit dem 19. Jahrhundert bis 1937.* Würzburg, Germany: Ergon Verlag, 1999.

Moreau, O. *Réforme de l'État et reformismes au Maghreb (XIXe-XX siècles)*. Paris: L'Harmattan, 2009.

Newman, D. "Sulayman Al-Hariri: An Early Tunisian Reformer in Europe." *Les cahiers de Tunisie; revue de sciences humaines* 207–208 (2008–2009): 13–58. Université de Tunis.

Sayadi, M. *Al-Jam'iyya al-Khalduniyya, 1896–1958.* Tunis, Tunisia: Maison Tunisienne de l'Éducation, 1974.

Souissi, M. "Science européenne et enjeux éducatifs de 1850 à l'Indépendance." *Modernités arabes et torque: maitres et ingénieurs, Revue du Monde Musulman et de la Méditerranée* 72.2 (1994): 53–59.

Sraïeb, N. "Le college Sadiki de Tunis et les nouvelles elites," *Modernités arabes et torque: maitres et ingénieurs, Revue du Monde Musulman et de la Méditerranée* 72.2 (1994): 37–52.

Wartatani, Muhammad al-Miqdad. *al-Burnus fi Baris: rihla ila Fransa wa-Suwisra, 1913.* Abu Dhabi and Beirut: Dar al-Suwaydi li-al-Nashr wa-al-Tawzi'; al-Mu'assasa al-'Arabiyya li-al-Dirasat wa-al-Nashr, 2004.

CHAPTER 4

Arab Scholars at the Institut de Droit Comparé in Lyon—Rereading the History of Arab-European Intellectual Encounters in the Interwar Period

Götz Nordbruch

I. INTRODUCTION

The period of the interwar years was marked by profound social and political transformations, affecting both Europe and the countries of the eastern Mediterranean. These transformations resounded in a quest for new ideational signposts that would provide guidance for future political changes and reforms. Arab thinkers actively engaged in this search for orientation, drawing on various intellectual sources and traditions; in this context, Arab intellectuals living in Europe had a strong impact on debates developing among Arab audiences.

This chapter discusses the intellectual production of Arab legal scholars at the Institut de Droit Comparé in Lyon during the interwar years and uses this case study for a rereading of the history of Arab-European intellectual encounters. As a study of a small but influential group of thinkers, it sheds light at an important facet of Arab-Islamic intellectual networks and exchanges across the Mediterranean and highlights the role of comparative law studies, and the place of Arab scholars within it, as a means to create "an international juridical consciousness..., a corpus of positive law that is based on the shared consciousness or will of the peoples."[1] In doing so, my aim is to contribute new perspectives to the ongoing academic discussion on cultural encounters and transfer in the context of European colonial rule in the Middle East.

The main argument that I will make is that leading Arab legal scholars of the interwar years actively contributed to international legal debates; these contributions were characterized by attempts to formulate a "perfect law" that would reflect universal conditions of humankind on the one hand, and that would meet the particularities of national cultures and societies on the other. While European and North American scholars of comparative law had long ignored non-Western legal traditions,[2] since the early 1900s Arab and Muslim scholars have gradually joined in academic debates and provided insights and perspectives from Islamic legal traditions. Although colonial rule closely framed intellectual debates in Middle Eastern societies, Middle Eastern intellectuals and their intellectual production were no mere products of Western domination. Nationalism and the quest for religious reform and their expressions in local discourses aimed at legitimizing the quest for an authentic culture that would reflect local religious traditions, social structures, and political order; yet, many intellectuals vehemently defended a universal idea of thought, science, and human development. While laws and legal traditions have in legal scholarship long been considered as a mirror of particular cultures, a growing number of scholars had, since the middle of the nineteenth century, interpreted legal history as an outcome of social conditions and political struggles. Laws were not considered as immediate products of certain national spirits anymore, but as *faits sociaux*. This also coincided with Orientalist debates on the nature of Islamic law. As Léon Buskens and Baudouin Dupret have shown in a recent study, Orientalist scholarship of the late nineteenth and early twentieth century greatly contributed to an understanding of Islamic law along the lines of Western notions of positive law.[3] Yet, such "invention" of Islamic law as a systematic set of codes and norms was no arbitrary Western imposition; it met the requirements of the emerging Arab and Muslim states and the need to institutionalize legal norms and procedures. Arab legal scholars increasingly joined in these debates and translated these debates' concepts and perspectives to local contexts.

The circles of Arab scholars at the Institut de Droit Comparé in Lyon echoed an approach to law and jurisprudence that was strongly inspired by the institute's founder, Édouard Lambert (1866–1947). For the students at Lambert's institute and the Lyon faculty of law, laws and legal traditions were not fixed by cultural and religious legacies, but remained subject to sociological and historical change and transformation. This was true for the legal foundations of the political order—as with regard to the caliphate—but no less so with regard to personal status, fiscal law, or economic regulations. Intellectuals such as 'Abd al-Razzaq al-Sanhuri or Muhammad 'Abd al-Jawad, who covered various fields of private and public law, consequently highlighted the adaptability of legal structures and norms to changing social realities. Their contributions to the work of the institute, and their later works in the domain of law clearly echoed an approach to legal traditions that was described by Lambert as a comparative historical and sociological investigation into the "accidental products of diverse national histories."[4]

In the light of the particular histories of the southern and eastern Mediterranean, the Muslim world provided exceptional insights into the emergence of legal concepts and principles. Not only did it offer new perspectives to European debates about law and justice; Muslim societies themselves were marked by a pluralism of legal traditions, rendering their histories into important case studies that could advance the discipline of comparative law. Egypt, for Lambert, was "one of the first testing grounds for comparative law and will for long remain one of the most fertile fields of demonstration."[5] Its mixed courts, for instance, were "models for practical investigations of comparative law."[6] This approach was supported by Arab scholars who were engaged in a quest to establish comparative law as a relevant academic discipline that would help advance the development of local political culture. Speaking to a mainly European audience at the Congress of Comparative Law that was organized by Lambert in 1932, Egyptian law professor 'Ali M. Badawi highlighted the historical character of Muslim legal traditions. For him, it was crucial to understand that Islam had changed over time, and that it was impossible to assess today's Muslim societies through the ancient past alone. While legal scholars had long ignored the linkage between religion and law in Europe, they consistently overestimated it in the Islamic context.[7] Islamic law was not static, but flexible, and had thus to be read in the light of changing social conditions. This "plasticity" of Islamic legal tradition made it into a crucial field of comparative legal inquiry.

II. Beyond Particularities: Global "Rhythms of Change"

The study of these endeavors is situated in recent research that has challenged existing approaches to Middle Eastern–European encounters.

Any history of ideas of the Middle East—as of any other region—is closely tied to the region's relations and interactions with its neighboring societies and cultures. Instead of focusing on comparisons and differences between national or cultural entities, recent debates on cultural and intellectual encounters have increasingly turned to the conditions under which certain ideas and concepts are received and appropriated.

Looking into the particular conditions and expressions of attempts to "domesticate knowledge,"[8] this research has questioned established notions of transfer and reception in the context of colonial rule. While the groundbreaking studies of Timothy Mitchell and Omnia El Shakry have investigated the impact of encounters in the fields of administration, education, and science,[9] others have shed new light on the echoes and appropriation of Western discourses in architecture, painting, and music. Yet, academic discussions of Middle Eastern intellectual history continue to resound claims of a supposedly exceptional and unique character of Arab and Islamic societies. Even following the debates triggered by Edward Said's *Orientalism* (1978), the image of the Middle East and Islam as a "paradigmatic alternative to Europe"[10] persisted in major works on Arab and/or Islamic history. In this sense, Antony Black insists on the distinctiveness of Islamic intellectual traditions: "Islamic political thought forms a significant part of the intellectual history of homo sapiens. It comprises a coherent, ongoing tradition, separate from the West and with a logic of its own."[11]

A similar understanding—although significantly less rigid—of distinct intellectual traditions also resounds in a recent study on the emergence of modern social sciences in the late Ottoman Empire. Tracing the evolving controversies between proponents of Islamic *fiqh* on the one hand and of social sciences and scientific methodologies on the other, Recep Senturk reconstructs the increasingly varied intellectual responses to questions of religion, science, and the future of society. Senturk explicitly focuses on intellectual attempts to synthesize social sciences and *fiqh*; yet he identifies the respective intellectual approaches with particular cultural traditions: while *fiqh* is Islamic, social sciences are Western and, in consequence, nonlocal. Social sciences are implicitly described here as an imposition from the outside, as they gradually "conquered the space traditionally occupied by *fiqh*, and its professional representatives (such as academicians, jurists, educationists, and writers) replaced the *fuqaha*."[12] In consequence, the synthesis of both, which many intellectuals longed for, is not perceived as one of the various possible local responses to a society in change; instead, the synthesis is interpreted as an imposition of one culturally distinct intellectual tradition over another.

Recent studies have challenged such understanding. The gradual shift of perspective from outside origins to local contexts is made explicit in Albert Hourani's scholarship on Middle Eastern intellectual history. Hourani's classic *Arabic Thought in the Liberal Age, 1798–1939* (1962) had a profound impact on the writing of Arab intellectual history in the following decades. His book, he summarized in a preface to a later edition, was meant to describe the reaction "of those (Arab intellectuals), who saw the growth of European power and the spread of new ideas as a challenge to which they had to respond by changing their own societies, and the systems of beliefs and values which gave them legitimacy, in a certain direction, through acceptance of some ideas and some institutions of modern Europe."[13]

Hourani critically rethought the perspective he had adopted in his previous work 30 years later. Echoing the growing importance of social history in the writing of the history of the Middle East, he now questioned a narrow reading of Arab liberal thought as an adaptation of European intellectual traditions. Instead, Hourani called for a stronger consideration of "two interlocking rhythms of change"[14] that were shaping the developments in the region: rhythms imposed by external powers and local elites on the one hand, and those produced by local traditions, and these traditions' continuities and discontinuities on the other.

This focus on local transformations and "rhythms of changes" against which intellectual history should be read was fostered by a growing awareness for the fragmented character of contemporary Arab societies, and the needs of state formation processes in the region that were not limited to local particularities. Increasing social and geographic mobility was one of the effects provoked by the Ottoman reforms of the mid-nineteenth century, leading to a gradual diversification of social realities, and in consequence of intellectual and political frameworks and visions. James L. Gelvin has highlighted the importance of these transformations for the emergence of a "multiplicity of analogues ideologies"[15] among the educated elite. While these ideologies—Arabism, Ottomanism, Syrian nationalism, and so on—differed in their specific contents, they shared an underlying approach to society that "cohered with or duplicated those enjoined by the dominant culture within the métropole."[16] Mirroring the social realities in Europe and the urban centers of the eastern Mediterranean, these ideologies of communal identity, whether formulated in the Middle East or in Europe, echoed the longing for new identities and a reconceptualization of society. Gelvin thus concludes that the "fundamental ideological divide within Middle Eastern society during the late nineteenth and early twentieth century did not separate Ottomanists from Arabists; rather, the fundamental ideological divide separated Ottomanists, Arabists and their ilk from the remainder of society, whose transformation and integration had been less thoroughly accomplished or whose encounter with the transformation was less agreeable."[17] Despite being elaborated in a particular national and religious setting, the basic premises of theses ideologies were not specific to the national-religious, but to the socioeconomic context in which they evolved; as such, these ideologies had a double character, they were at once a reflection of local conditions while being, at the same time, potentially universal.

This perspective has also been adopted in recent research that has focused on the evolution of legal concept and laws. In a study of 'Abd al-Razzaq al-Sanhuri, one of the leading Egyptian scholars of the first half of the twentieth century, Enid Hill has argued that "those nations which adopted bodies of law from foreign sources have added to them legislation based on conditions and considerations unique to those nations. The changes which a law undergoes when introduced into or received by a different culture are of considerable significance in comparative law."[18] Law—and the reception of law—is basically a historical phenomenon that was inseparably linked to local challenges and concerns: "Reception is, by its nature, a historical phenomenon. It is law in a condition of becoming."[19]

III. Law and Legal Traditions as an Œuvre Humaine

The Institut du Droit Comparé in Lyon was formally established in 1920.[20] It built on the work of Édouard Lambert who had made himself known as a protagonist of French legal scholarship. As a director of the Khedival Law School in Cairo in 1906 and 1907, he had introduced numerous students to recent controversies that have marked legal scholarship over the past decades. The students' interest was not so much based on the particularities of the French legal system but "on a comprehension of the principles of law and of the directions of political science that form the common basis of the Occidental civilization. They wanted me (Lambert) to help them to scrutinize them in view of adapting the particular needs of Oriental and Muslim societies."[21] Following his return from Egypt to France, Lambert created the Séminaire oriental d'études juridiques et sociales that provided the institutional basis for the formal establishment of the Institut de Droit Comparé at the University of Lyon in the following years. Its aim was not limited to a study of Muslim societies as such, but consisted in "developing the scientific research in the field of law, understood both as a social and international science."[22] While the topics that were taught at this seminar included a course on History and Sources of Islamic Law, Political Economy, and Roman Law and the History of Law, the seminar explicitly aimed at preparing Egyptian students for a career not in France, but in Egypt. Already in the first years following Lambert's return from Cairo, some ten Egyptian students had inscribed at the Faculty of Law in Lyon.[23] Such interest, Lambert argued, was due to an "intellectual renaissance of Oriental Islam" on the one hand, and an "awakening of the national spirit in Egypt"[24] on the other. A remark made in the mid-1920s by Lambert about the growing number of Egyptian students at the institute illustrates the considerable appeal of this institution among young Egyptian scholars. Referring to the number of publications by Egyptian students in the seminary's series *Travaux du Séminaire oriental d'études juridiques et sociales*, Lambert claimed to have "slowed down" the efforts of these students as the number of their "works risked to destroy the balance that we are trying to maintain among the contributions of the various groups of foreigners who work at our institute."[25]

The outreach of the institute consisted to a large part in the publication of research and the organization of international conferences; perhaps more importantly, its director actively worked for the establishment of institutions outside France that would provide the basis for academic networks focused on comparative inquiries into the development of legal traditions. The close bonds created by Lambert with his students are reflected in the various contacts that continued even following the return of his former students to Cairo, Beirut, or Damascus. The founding of the Institut de Droit Comparé in 1936/1937 as part of the Faculty of Law at the Egyptian University in Cairo took inspiration from these efforts. Going back to an initiative of the Lyon alumnus 'Abd al-Razzaq al-Sanhuri, the dean of the faculty, the programmatic outlook of this institute strongly echoed the aims and approaches previously formulated by Lambert.

Despite the variety of themes and approaches adopted in the theses that were published at the institute or its immediate institutional surrounding of the Faculty of Law, two premises are shared by most authors: first is the historically contingent character of codes and legal traditions, and second an understanding of Islam as one factor among others that have shaped local social history. Such historized understanding of Islam and Islamic history strongly contrasted with the controversial debates in the Arab/Muslim world over the future of the caliphate and about the primacy of the Sharia as the ultimate point of reference for the organization of society.

One author, A. El-Shorbagi, explicitly highlighted the dependency of local social orders on the historical conditions in which they emerged. In his thesis *La Responsabilité Politique des Ministres devant les Sénats et les Chambres Hautes* (1932), Shorbagi discusses one particular element of contemporary constitutional orders in the light of democratic principles and political stability. Taking recent French political history as a starting point, in which the Senate on three occasions caused the downfall of elected governments, Shorbagi raises the question of an appropriate constitutional setting for the rights of ministers in relationship to the parliament. Striking in this context is the comparative nature of his study. Investigating the cases of the United States, Germany, Egypt, England, and France, Shorbagi considered these particular constitutional experiences to allow for a discussion of the question "in a very complete way."[26] While these cases stood for particular national experiences, they potentially hold lessons relevant for other nations as well. In this regard, Shorbagi emphasizes the "double contingency, a contingency at once in time and space" of society: "One should not forget that the constitutional life of nations is, in the first place, an *œuvre humaine*. It is hence, by nature, changing, uncertain; it is constructed and deconstructed at one and the same moment. It makes difficult any prediction of the future."[27] Yet, although contingent, it would be mistaken to strip social orders of the historical contexts in which they evolved: "Drawing quick comparisons (between different societies) under the pretext that this would allow generating general ideas would thus mean to formulate principles of only artificial existence."[28] Reflecting this ambivalence with regard to the potential conclusions that could be drawn from comparative investigations into different social orders, Shorbagi concludes: "Every nation should thus study its institutions in her own context; she can look elsewhere for points of comparison, but it is in their own histories that the states can find the raison d'être of their constitutions."[29] Universal solutions for constitutional questions thus do not exist; the respective solutions for these questions are the "logical consequence of a certain number of particular conditions that frame each national constitutional arrangement."[30]

While Shorbagi stresses the impact of local contexts, it is noteworthy that religion and religious traditions do not play a prominent role in his reasoning. Even for those authors that had turned to explicitly religious research topics, Islam was not perceived as an unchanging trait of Muslim societies. In his thesis *L'Exécution Testamentaire en Droit Musulman—Rite Hanafite* (1926), Muhammad 'Abd al-Jawad studied the evolution of the execution of wills over time, and in comparison to Christian, Roman, German, and Anglo-Saxon legal traditions. In this context, 'Abd al-Jawad challenges common readings of these norms by Islamic jurisprudents as being ultimately based on Qur'anic regulations and sayings of Muhammad.[31] For him, the principles of family organization that have marked Islamic traditions can be traced back to pre-Islamic customs and rules; on the other hand, the various legislative projects of the late nineteenth and early twentieth century have finally eliminated previous Hanafi doctrines regarding the execution of wills. For 'Abd al-Jawad, such evolution does not stand per se for a loss or decline of timeless religious principles; on the contrary, these legislative changes are "an original product of nationalized Muslim law."[32]

Unsurprisingly, similar understandings of Islamic legal traditions as subject to evolution can be found among Christian authors that worked in these circles. Alfred Thabet, then *président de section* at the court of Beirut, in a doctoral thesis submitted to the Faculty of Law in Lyon, extensively covered the historical evolution of regulations governing the role of witnesses in legal proceedings. The starting point of Thabet's thesis *La Preuve Testimoniale en Droit Ottoman* (1927) is the continuing applicability of Ottoman laws in Lebanon and Syria, countries now under French mandate. While the mandate powers had initiated legal reforms, these remained limited in scope and impact: "We are still governed by preceding, outmoded, legal dispositions that had been abandoned by their authors themselves: the Turks. These dispositions do not correspond to the needs of today's social life, nor to the new juridical concepts that are—to the advantage of these societies—respected in those countries where Civilization has made its way."[33] For Thabet, "reform has thus become inevitable."[34]

While Thabet acknowledged that progress had been made in the field of penal law, he considered the persisting application of Ottoman provisions in Lebanon and Syria in the field of civil law a major threat to justice on the one hand, and social and economic progress on the other. Among the required changes, Thabet vehemently argued for a revision of Ottoman and Islamic provisions regarding the status of women as witnesses in civil cases. In today's society, he argued, the gender of a witness was as irrelevant as her social status, her wealth or her profession. "If such provisions regarding the gender of witnesses might have appeared necessary—due to the situation of the women—in the ancient times of Holy Law and the Mejelleh, their preservation cannot be justified in our days, when women take a more and more active role in social life and play already a role of similar importance as the one of man—despite some insignificant exceptions whose number is gradually decreasing."[35]

A very similar approach was adopted by Emile Tayyan, a lecturer at the École Française de Droit in Beirut, in his thesis *Histoire de l'Organisation Judiciaire en Pays d'Islam* (1938). Tayyan challenged the interpretation forwarded by medieval Muslim scholars with regard to the Islamic origin of legal provisions governing civil affairs. According to him, these scholars actively attempted to camouflage the diverse historic origins of respective regulations and principles, hence fostering, "as a knowledgeable Orientalist has observed, 'the impression of unity and even originality'"[36] of these principles.

For several of these authors, the origins of legal uncertainties and obstacles to social and economic stability and progress were not limited to outmoded forms of Islamic jurisprudence; no less relevant were the politics of European colonial powers as they limited social and intellectual progress. For scholars like Joseph Achcar, local resistance against French mandate power in Syria and Lebanon was thus not a reflection of fundamental opposition to France or other European powers as such; they were the result of a growing self-consciousness of local political actors that called for independence from regional and international players. Independent rule, he insisted in his study *L'Évolution Politique de la Syrie et du Liban, de la Palestine et de l'Irak* (1934), would not imply a break with long-standing political and cultural links to Europe, but would instead provide the basis for equality with the colonial powers.[37]

Yet, such views were not shared entirely by all scholars who worked at the institute. The idea that intellectual traditions, manners, and mores were subject to change was not inconsistent with notions of timeless communities and culture. In this regard, the thesis submitted by Muhammad al-Salih Mzali under the title *L'Évolution Économique de la Tunisie* (1921) stood for the popularity of concepts such as race in some approaches to changing societies of the Mediterranean. This thesis, it should be noted, was not supervised by Lambert, but by a fellow professor at the faculty. Mzali clearly identified certain mental traits with Jews and Arabs as collective entities; yet, similar to his fellow scholars at the institute, he did not perceive traditions and characteristics of populations as frozen in time: "A people does not change in one day alone, there is no magic wand to change men, and even less masses. Let us repeat this: it is the generations that

change.... Civilisation, moral and social progress, economic progress were imposed ideas, activating ideas that had to be assimilated in
the first place."[38] While he held negative views about contemporary
"Muslim fatalism,"[39] he insisted that Islam by itself was no obstacle to
modernization. Through educational reform—and the help of France
that should work as a medical doctor to improve local population—
Tunisia could expect a promising future.

Among the students at the institute, the Egyptian jurist 'Abd
al-Razzaq al-Sanhuri is without doubt the most prominent. As the
author of the Egyptian Code Civil, Sanhuri had profound impact
on modern Egyptian history. As a cornerstone for the modernization of Egyptian society in the pre-Nasser period, which combined
"modern Occidental legislation" with "Egyptian jurisprudence of the
last fifty years" and "the Shari'a or Muslim law,"[40] the Egyptian code
had echoes across the region. Already during his studies in France,
Sanhuri contributed significant works to the field of comparative
law.[41] His two doctoral theses *Les restrictions contractuelles à la liberté
individuelle de travail dans la Jurisprudence anglaise* (1925) and *Le
Califat: Son évolution vers une Société des Nations Orientale* (1926)
stood for an attempt to combine the "socialisation of modern law and
the modernisation of Islamic law."[42]

Sanhuri summarized the topic of his first thesis as an attempt to
"reconcile contractual liberty with the liberty of labor."[43] As such,
this was a general problem that had to be solved in modern societies that were marked by economic instability and labor struggles.
Discussing the ways this challenge was addressed in English, US, and
French law, Sanhuri acknowledged the universality of this question,
while at the same time recognizing the particular settings in which
legislators had to find solutions. The challenge was not only shared by
most societies; it was also one that changed over time: "It is a permanent and never-ending effort of adaptation and harmonization that
has to be achieved by reflecting the evolution of social life."[44]

No less important was his work on the caliphate as a modern
institutional setting for the emerging nations in the Muslim world.
Drawing on Islamic traditions and on developments in modern political sciences, Sanhuri formulated a vision that would place Middle
Eastern societies on equal footing in global politics, while preserving
their roots in Islamic history. He aimed, in the words of Lambert, at
"a reconstitution (of the unity of the Muslim world) in a form that
would be more flexible and better accommodated to the requirements
of the emerging nationalisms."[45] In a later work of the late 1930s that
was related to his project of the Egyptian Civil Code, Sanhuri clearly

described this approach to Muslim law: "The rules of Muslim law are in need of a scientific *retouche* that would revitalise their primitive energy that would update their principles that are today forgotten under the dust (of time). It would liberate them from the ties in which the jurists of the intermediate period have immobilized them."[46]

Conclusion

While Sanhuri was one of the most prolific and prominent students that had passed through the Institut de Droit Comparé in Lyon, many of his peers from Egypt, Lebanon, or Syria who had registered at the Faculty of Law in Lyon shared his interest in modern Western legal scholarship as an instrument to modernize Middle Eastern societies. The quest for a modernization of society had marked public debates in many of these countries during the interwar years. While debates about social and political reforms are often described as confronting "Westernizers" with nationalists and Islamic revivalists, a considerable number of Arab scholars challenged such perspectives of social change and transformation.

The works conducted at the Lyon institute echoed a shared desire to preserve local traditions that were seen as characteristic to Middle Eastern societies. Yet, while most authors agreed upon the need to value national and religious particularities in processes of reform and modernization, they explicitly highlighted the existence of universal principles and standards that could claim validity across religious, cultural, or geographic boundaries.

This challenge, to balance national particularities with claims of universal humanism, was itself not particular to Middle Eastern debates; similar questions had shaped intellectual controversies in Europe during these years. In the light of the global transformations of the early twentieth century, "their" questions increasingly resembled "ours"; it is thus not surprising that "their" answers too often resembled those that were formulated abroad.

Notes

1. Édouard Lambert, "Le droit comparé et la formation d'une conscience juridique internationale," *Revue de l'Université de Lyon* (December 1929), 443.
2. See, for instance, Michaelis on the proceedings of the First International Congress of Comparative Law in Paris in 1900, Ralf Michaelis, "Im Westen nichts Neues? 100 Jahre Pariser Kongress für Rechtsvergleichung. Gedanken anläßlich einer Jubiläumskonferenz

in New Orleans," *Rabels Zeitschrift für ausländisches und internationales Privatrecht* 66.1 (2002), 97–115.

3. Léon Buskens/Baudouin Dupret, "L'invention du droit musulman. Genèse et diffusion du positivisme juridique dans le contexte normatif islamique," in *Après l'Orientalisme. L'Orient créé par l'Orient*, edited by François Pouillon and Jean-Claude Vatin (Paris: Karthala, 2011), 92. See also Raja Sakrani, *Au croisement des cultures de droit occidentale et musulmane. Le pluralisme juridique dans le code tunisien des obligations et des contrats* (Hamburg: EB-Verlag, 2009) and Michael R. Feener, "Cross-Cultural Contexts of Modern Muslim Intellectualism," *Die Welt des Islams* 47.3–4 (2007), 264–282.

4. Édouard Lambert, *L'Institut de droit comparé. Son programme, ses méthodes d'enseignement* (Lyon: A. Rey, 1921), 10.

5. Édouard Lambert, *Le Congrès international de droit comparé de 1932. Les travaux de la section générale. Souvenirs d'un congressiste* (Lyon: A. Rey, 1934), 92.

6. Lambert, *Congrès international*, 92.

7. Lambert, *Congrès international*, 93.

8. Khaled Asfour, "The Domestication of Knowledge: Cairo at the Turn of the Century," *Muqarnas* 10 (1993), 125–137.

9. See Omnia El Shakry, *The Great Social Laboratory: Subjects of Knowledge in Colonial and Postcolonial Egypt* (Stanford: Stanford University Press, 2007) and Timothy Mitchell, *Rule of Experts: Egypt, Techno-Politics, Modernity* (Berkeley: University of California Press, 2002).

10. Antony Black, *The History of Islamic Political Thought. From the Prophet to the Present* (Edinburgh: Edinburgh University Press), 3.

11. Black, *History*, 1.

12. Recep Senturk, "Intellectual Dependency: Late Ottoman Intellectuals between Fiqh and Social Science," *Die Welt des Islams* 47.3–4 (2007), 283. This quote is taken from the abstract of the article; it appears in a slightly varied form in the article itself. In the article, the connotation of a "Western conquest" is less explicit: "Western social science challenged the space traditionally occupied by fiqh." (Senturk, "Intellectual dependency," 294). For a different reading of these interactions and encounters see Dietrich Jung, *Orientalists, Islamists, and the Global Public Sphere: A Genealogy of the Modern Essentialist Image of Islam* (Sheffield: Equinox, 2011) and François Siino, "Sciences, savoirs modernes et évolutions des modèles politiques," *Revue des Mondes Musulmans et de la Méditerranée* 9.28 (2003), 9–28.

13. Albert Hourani, *Arabic Thought in the Liberal Age, 1798–1939* (Cambridge: Cambridge University Press, 1983), iv.

14. Albert Hourani, "How Should We Write the History of the Middle East?" *International Journal of Middle East Studies* 23.2 (May 1991), 129.

15. James L. Gelvin, "The Other Arab Nationalism. Syrian/Arab Populism in Its Historical and International Context," in *Rethinking*

Nationalism in the Arab Middle East, ed. James Jankowski and Israel Gershoni (New York: Columbia University Press, 1997), 235.

16. Gelvin, "Other Arab Nationalism," 235.

17. Gelvin, "Other Arab Nationalism," 235.

18. Enid Hill, "Comparative and Historical Study of Modern Middle Eastern Law," *The American Journal of Comparative Law* 26.2 (Spring 1978), 285.

19. Hill, "Comparative and Historical Study," 287.

20. See Édouard Lambert, *L'Institut de droit comparé*; and Édouard Lambert, *Conférences de M. le Professeur Édouard Lambert. Extrait de la Revue al Qanoun wal Iqtisad—3/1937* (Cairo: F. E. Noury et Fils, 1937).

21. Lambert, *Conférences*, 174.

22. Lambert quoted in Suzanne Basdevant-Bastid, "L'Institut de droit comparé de Lyon," *Introduction à l'Étude du droit comparé. Recueils d'Études en l'honneur d'Édouard Lambert* (Paris: Librairie de la Société Anonyme du Recueil Sirey, 1938), 12.

23. For a discussion of the trajectories of Arab students in France during the twentieth century, see Caroline Barrera, *Étudiants d'ailleurs. Histoire des étudiants étrangers, coloniaux et français de l'étranger de la Faculté de droit de Toulouse (XIXème siècle—1944)* (Toulouse: Presses du Centre Universitaire Champollion, 2007); Thomas Brisson, *Les intellectuels arabes en France* (Paris: La Dispute, 2008); Ian Coller, "Arab France: Mobility and Community in Early-Nineteenth-Century Paris and Marseille," *French Historical Studies* 29.3 (2006), 433–456; Kais Ezzerelli, "Les étudiants arabes dans l'Hexagone, entre apolitisme et engagement militant (1918–1939)," in *Histoire de l'immigration et question coloniale en France,* ed. Nancy L. Green and Marie Poinsot (Paris: La documentation française, 2008), 159–165; and Ed De Moor, "Egyptian Love in a Cold Climate. Egyptian Students in Paris at the Beginning of the 20th Century," in *The Middle East & Europe: Encounters and Exchanges*, ed. Geert Jan van Gelder and Ed de Moor (Amsterdam: Radopi, 1992), 147–166. Important insights can also be drawn from the memoirs of these students; see, for instance, Zaki Mubarak, *Zikriyyat Baris. Suwar lima fi madinat-il-nur min sira' bayna al-hawa wa-l-ʿaql wa-l-huda wa-l-dalal* (Cairo: al-Mataba'at al-Rahmaniyya, 1931); and Nadiyya al-Sanhuri/Tawfiq al-Shawi, eds., *Al-Sanhuri min khilal awraqihi al-shakhsiyya* (Cairo: Dar al-Shuruq, 2008).

24. Édouard Lambert, *Rapport sur un projet d'organisation de cours spéciaux aux étudiants égyptiens présenté à la Faculté de droit de Lyon* (Lyon: A. Rey et Cie, 1908), 2.

25. Édouard Lambert, *Préface au tome 10 de la Bibliothèque de l'Institut de droit comparé de Lyon* (Paris: Marcel Giard, 1925), 1.

26. A. El Shorbagi, *La Responsabilité Politique des Ministres devant les Sénats et les Chambres Hautes* (Lyon: Bosc Frères et Riou 1932), 5.

27. El Shorbagi, *La Responsabilité Politique*, 146.
28. El Shorbagi, *La Responsabilité Politique*, 146.
29. El Shorbagi, *La Responsabilité Politique*, 157.
30. El Shorbagi, *La Responsabilité Politique*, 157.
31. Mohamed Abdel Gawad ('Abd al-Jawad, Muhammad), *L'Exécution Testamentaire en Droit Musulman—Rite Hanafite* (Lyon: Bosc Frères et Riou, 1926), 9.
32. Gawad, *L'Exécution Testamentaire*, 154.
33. Alfred Tabet (Alfred Thabit), *La Preuve Testimoniale en Droit Ottoman* (Lyon: Bosc Frères et Riou, 1927), 7.
34. Tabet, *La Preuve Testimoniale*, 9.
35. Tabet, *La Preuve Testimoniale*, 117–118.
36. Emile Tyan, (Emil Tayyan), *Histoire de l'Organisation Judiciaire en Pays d'Islam* (Paris: Libraire du Recueil Sirey, 1938), 14.
37. Joseph Achcar, *L'Évolution Politique de la Syrie et du Liban, de la Palestine et de l'Irak* (Lyon: Imprimerie M. Martin, 1934), 117.
38. M.-S. Mzali (Muhammad al-Salih Mzali), *Évolution Économique de la Tunisie* (Tunis: Société anonyme de l'imprimerie rapide de Tunis, 1921), 147.
39. Mzali, *Évolution Économique*, 56.
40. Abd el-Razzak Sanhoury ('Abd al-Razzaq al-Sanhuri), "Le Droit musulman comme élément de refonte du Code Civil Egyptien," in *Introduction à l'Étude du droit comparé. Recueils d'Études en l'honneur d'Édouard Lambert* (Paris: Librairie de la Société Anonyme du Recueil Sirey, 1938), 621
41. The works of Sanhuri have been studied in detail by Amr Shalakany and Enid Hill. Both authors have covered various aspects of his career as a legal scholar and as a comparativist. See for instance Amr Shalakany, "Sanhuri and the Historical Origins of Comparative Law in the Arab World (or How Sometimes Losing Your Asalah Can Be Good for You)," in *Rethinking the Masters of Comparative Law*, ed. Annelise Riles (Oxford: Hart Publishing 2001), 152–188; Enid Hill, "Al-Sanhuri and Islamic Law. the Place and Significance of Islamic Law in the Life and Work of 'Abd Al-Razzaq Ahmad Al-Sanhuri, Egyptian Jurist and Scholar, 1895–1971," *Arab Law Quarterly* 3.1 (1988); and Hill, "Comparative and Historical Study."
42. Shalakany, "Sanhuri," 178.
43. Abd el-Razzak Al-Sanhoury ('Abd al-Razzaq al-Sanhuri), *Les restrictions contractuelles à la liberté individuelle de travail dans la jurisprudence anglaise* (Paris: Marcel Giard, 1925), 5. See also Abd el-Razzak Sanhoury ('Abd al-Razzaq al-Sanhuri), *Le Califat: Son évolution vers une Société des Nations Orientale* (Paris: Librairie orientaliste Paul Geuthner, 1926).
44. Sanhoury, *Les restrictions contractuelles*, 9.
45. Édouard Lambert, introduction to *Le Califat*, by Sanhoury, vii.
46. Sanhoury," Le Droit musulman," 623.

References

Achcar, Joseph. *L'Évolution Politique de la Syrie et du Liban, de la Palestine et de l'Irak*. Lyon, France: Imprimerie M. Martin, 1934.

Asfour, Khaled. "The Domestication of Knowledge: Cairo at the Turn of the Century." *Muqarnas* 10 (1993): 125–137.

Barrera, Caroline. *Étudiants d'ailleurs. Histoire des étudiants étrangers, coloniaux et français de l'étranger de la Faculté de droit de Toulouse (XIXème siècle—1944)*. Toulouse, France: Presses du Centre Universitaire Champollion, 2007.

Basdevant-Bastid, Suzanne. "L'Institut de droit comparé de Lyon." In *Introduction à l'Étude du droit comparé. Recueils d'Études en l'honneur d'Édouard Lambert*. Paris: Librairie de la Société Anonyme du Recueil Sirey, 1938.

Black, Antony. *The History of Islamic Political Thought. From the Prophet to the Present*. Edinburgh: Edinburgh University Press.

Brisson, Thomas. *Les intellectuels arabes en France*. Paris: La Dispute, 2008.

Buskens, Léon / Baduouin Dupret. "L'invention du droit musulman. Genèse et diffusion du positivisme juridique dans le contexte normatif islamique." In *Après l'Orientalisme. L'Orient créé par l'Orient*, edited by François Pouillon and Jean-Claude Vatin. Paris: Karthala, 2011.

Coller, Ian. "Arab France: Mobility and Community in Early-Nineteenth-Century Paris and Marseille." *French Historical Studies* 29.3 (2006): 433–456.

Ezzerelli, Kais. "Les étudiants arabes dans l'Hexagone, entre apolitisme et engagement militant (1918–1939)." In *Histoire de l'immigration et question coloniale en France*, edited by Nancy L. Green and Marie Poinsot. Paris: La documentation française, 2008, 159–165.

Feener, Michael R. "Cross-Cultural Contexts of Modern Muslim Intellectualism." *Die Welt des Islams* 47.3–4 (2007): 264–282.

Gawad Mohamed Abdel. ('Abd al-Jawad, Muhammad), *L'Exécution Testamentaire en Droit Musulman—Rite Hanafite*. Lyon, France: Bosc Frères et Riou, 1926.

Gelvin, James L. "The Other Arab Nationalism. Syrian/Arab Populism in Its Historical and International Context." In *Rethinking Nationalism in the Arab Middle East*, edited by James Jankowski and Israel Gershoni, 231–248. New York: Columbia University Press, 1997.

Hill, Enid. "Al-Sanhuri and Islamic Law. the Place and Significance of Islamic Law in the Life and Work of 'Abd Al-Razzaq Ahmad Al-Sanhuri, Egyptian Jurist and Scholar, 1895–1971." *Arab Law Quarterly* 3.1 (1988): 182–218.

———. "Comparative and Historical Study of Modern Middle Eastern Law," *The American Journal of Comparative Law* 26.2 (Spring 1978): 279–304.

Hourani, Albert. *Arabic Thought in the Liberal Age, 1798–1939*. Cambridge: Cambridge University Press, 1983.

————. "How Should We Write the History of the Middle East?" *International Journal of Middle East Studies* 23.2 (May 1991): 125–136.

Jung, Dietrich. *Orientalists, Islamists, and the Global Public Sphere: A Genealogy of the Modern Essentialist Image of Islam.* Sheffield, UK: Equinox, 2011.

Lambert, Édouard. *Conférences de M. le Professeur Édouard Lambert. Extrait de la Revue al Qanoun wal Iqtisad—3/1937.* Cairo: F. E. Noury et Fils, 1937.

————. *Le Congrès international de droit comparé de 1932. Les travaux de la section générale. Souvenirs d'un congressiste.* Lyon, France: A. Rey, 1934.

————. "Le droit comparé et la formation d'une conscience juridique internationale." *Revue de l'Université de Lyon* (December 1929): 441–463.

————. *L'Institut de droit comparé. Son programme, ses méthodes d'enseignement.* Lyon, France: A. Rey, 1921.

————. *Préface au tome 10 de la Bibliothèque de l'Institut de droit comparé de Lyon.* Paris: Marcel Giard, 1925.

————. *Rapport sur un projet d'organisation de cours spéciaux aux étudiants égyptiens présenté à la Faculté de droit de Lyon.* Lyon, France: A. Rey et Cie, 1908.

Michaelis, Ralf. "Im Westen nichts Neues? 100 Jahre Pariser Kongress für Rechtsvergleichung. Gedanken anläßlich einer Jubiläumskonferenz in New Orleans." *Rabels Zeitschrift für ausländisches und internationales Privatrecht* 66.1 (2002): 97–115.

Mitchell, Timothy. *Rule of Experts: Egypt, Techno-Politics, Modernity.* Berkeley: University of California Press, 2002.

Moor, Ed De. "Egyptian Love in a Cold Climate. Egyptian Students in Paris at the Beginning of the 20th Century." In *The Middle East & Europe: Encounters and Exchanges*, edited by Geert Jan van Gelder and Ed de Moor, 147–166. Amsterdam: Radopi, 1992.

Mubarak, Zaki. *Zikriyyat Baris. Suwar lima fi madinat-il-nur min sira' bayna al-hawa wa-l-ʿaql wa-l-huda wa-l-dalal.* Cairo: al-Mataba'at al-Rahmaniyya, 1931.

Mzali M.-S. (Muhammad al-Salih Mzali), *Évolution Économique de la Tunisie.* Tunis, Tunisia: Société anonyme de l'imprimerie rapide de Tunis, 1921.

Sakrani, Raja. *Au croisement des cultures de droit occidentale et musulmane. Le pluralisme juridique dans le code tunisien des obligations et des contrats.* Hamburg: EB-Verlag, 2009.

Sanhoury, Abd el-Razzak ('Abd al-Razzaq al-Sanhuri). *Le Califat: Son évolution vers une Société des Nations Orientale.* Paris: Librairie orientaliste Paul Geuthner, 1926.

————. "Le Droit musulman comme élément de refonte du Code Civil Egyptien." In *Introduction à l'Étude du droit comparé. Recueils d'Études en l'honneur d'Édouard Lambert.* Paris: Librairie de la Société Anonyme du Recueil Sirey, 1938.

————. *Les restrictions contractuelles à la liberté individuelle de travail dans la jurisprudence anglaise.* (Paris: Marcel Giard, 1925).

Sanhuri, Nadiyya al- and Tawfiq al-Shawi, eds. *Al-Sanhuri min khilal awraqihi al-shakhsiyya*. Cairo: Dar al-Shuruq, 2008.

Senturk, Recep. "Intellectual Dependency: Late Ottoman Intellectuals between Fiqh and Social Science." *Die Welt des Islams* 47.3–4 (2007): 283–318.

Shakry, Omnia El. *The Great Social Laboratory: Subjects of Knowledge in Colonial and Postcolonial Egypt*. Stanford: Stanford University Press, 2007.

Shalakany, Amr. "Sanhuri and the Historical Origins of Comparative Law in the Arab World (or How Sometimes Losing Your Asalah Can Be Good for You)." In *Rethinking the Masters of Comparative Law*, edited by Annelise Riles, 152–188. Oxford: Hart Publishing, 2001.

Shorbagi, A. El. *La Responsabilité Politique des Ministres devant les Sénats et les Chambres Hautes*. Lyon, France: Bosc Frères et Riou, 1932.

Siino, François. "Sciences, savoirs modernes et évolutions des modèles politiques." *Revue des Mondes Musulmans et de la Méditerranée* 9.28 (2003): 9–28.

Tabet, Alfred (Alfred Thabit). *La Preuve Testimoniale en Droit Ottoman*. Lyon, France: Bosc Frères et Riou, 1927.

Tyan, Emile (Emil Tayyan), *Histoire de l'Organisation Judiciaire en Pays d'Islam*. Paris: Libraire du Recueil Sirey, 1938.

CHAPTER 5

A *Salafi* Student, Orientalist Scholarship, and Radio Berlin in Nazi Germany: Taqi al-Din al-Hilali and His Experiences in the West

Umar Ryad

In recent years, two methods of research have been developed for the study of Arab-Nazi encounters.[1] A group of historians try to "contextualize authoritarian and totalitarian trends in the Arab world within a broad political spectrum, choosing subaltern perspectives and privileging the analysis of local voices in the press over colonial archives and the voices of grand theoreticians."[2] Such relations should be seen within the scope of the interaction between memory, politics, and the history of Arab-Nazi encounters and experiences.[3] On the other side, some people argue for an inherent and structural affinity between Arab nationalism and Pan-Islamism on the one hand, and Nazi racist ideologies and anti-Semitism against the Jews on the other.[4]

In the Nazi period, Germany hosted a significant number of foreign students, including many Arabs. Arab students were exposed to implications of the incentives and pressures of their exile in Germany before and during World War II.[5] In general, many Arab and Muslim students in interwar Europe joined a great Muslim transnational reformist network that called for the unity of Islam against the colonial encroachment in the Muslim world.[6]

The present chapter argues that Muslim actors within these networks played their transnational role as part of European transcultural history. In what follows, we shall focus on the figure of the Moroccan prominent *Salafi* scholar Taqi al-Din al-Hilali (1894–1987) as a case study with a special focus on his cross-national and cross-cultural role in Nazi Germany before and during World War II. It was the peak time, when many Arab Christian and Muslim nationalists assumed leftist, Fascist, and Nazi coalitions as natural allies in their struggle against Western imperialism and the domination of the post–World War I international order by France and Great Britain.[7]

After Hilali's arrival in interwar Germany, the country had already witnessed a lengthy history of Muslim émigré activism, boasting numerous Muslim publications and institutions.[8] The study of his engagement in Nazi Germany presents a unique figure between two different worlds, his being a subject under National Socialism who was also strongly involved in making anticolonial and populist *Salafi* propaganda in the Muslim world. Particularly, Hilali belonged to the network of the Druze prince Shakib Arslan (d. 1946) and Hajj Amin al-Husayni (1897–1974) in interwar Europe. His place in the Arab-German encounters of that time should be seen within the broader context that Peter Wien has called "culpability of exile," which is "a moral dilemma that affects foreigners who take up residence in a villainous country such as Nazi Germany."[9]

At first sight we might assume that Hilali's collaboration with the Nazis was based entirely on ideological considerations while our rereading of the context of his activities reveals other paradoxical factors. As far as we can observe and analyze the problem on the basis of his writings and remaining documents, we can define a clear dichotomy between both strands of action. First of all, we sketch here a remarkable story of collaboration between a *Salafi* Muslim student and lecturer and his German mentor, the well-known German Orientalist Paul Kahle (1875–1964) at the Oriental Seminar at the University of Bonn. As World War II was approaching, Kahle and his wife fled Germany because of their opposition to the Nazi oppression and their support to the Jews. This chapter emphasizes the seeming contradiction of Hilali's close cooperation and friendship with Kahle before the war, and Hilali's later collaboration with the Nazis.

We shall also witness many paradoxes in Hilali's German period and afterward. On many levels, his experience in Germany expressed a certain intellectual interaction between purist-minded *Salafism* and the West.[10] His thoughts in the Nazi period were inherently connected to an increasingly growing movement of "*Salafi* populism," which sternly aspired for creating a nostalgic early Islamic history. This populist discourse claimed to participate in recovering the deteriorating state of the Muslim world, and in combating what they perceived as non-Muslim "enemies" of Islam. It moreover intended to raise the awareness of Muslim masses of the significance of action in various religious, political, and social matters.

As a matter of fact, Hilali was a "globetrotter."[11] His life is multi-faceted and a full biography of all his trips and contacts in the Muslim world and Europe falls beyond the scope of the present chapter. As we shall see, Hilali insisted that his agenda in Germany was to defend Islam. Nevertheless, he sometimes pursued his ultimate goal by accepting the methods and approaches of the Orientalist prevalent scholarship of his time, which he tried to reconcile with his *Salafi* frame of thinking. Hilali's stay in Nazi Germany molded his ideas on such various topics as race, Jews, Western society and women, religiosity, imperialism, and colonialism. This chapter specifically deals with his academic, cultural, religious, and political encounters in Nazi Germany. How did Hilali, a staunchly conservative Muslim scholar, experience his tutorship with German Orientalists? How did he interact with the German people and culture in the Nazi period? How did an Arab student and activist writer act inside Europe when the war was ravaging Germany and Europe?

Hilali's work in Bonn reveals that the interaction between Orientalists and Arab intellectuals was not confined to students who later became well-known for their modernist, secularist, and sometimes liberal affiliations, but included students who later developed reformist and traditionalist conservative viewpoints of Islam as well. At another level, many decisive factors shaped the course of his nationalist action in Nazi Germany. As we shall see, his sojourn in Nazi Germany best exemplifies that his sense of transnationalism as a Muslim activist was not detached from the spirit of nationalism widespread in that period. Thus, the study tries to reconstruct a story of a significant *Salafi*-oriented scholar, who, like many other Muslim nationalists, estab-lished a view of European supremacy as the "ugly colonizer," while he took Europe itself as his basis of settlement. Besides his position in the Oriental Seminar in Bonn and cooperation with German Orientalists, Hilali played later a role in the Arabic propaganda for the Nazi regime through Radio Berlin—Zeesen. We shall also see that even before his joining the Arab staff in Berlin, Hilali was impressed by the radio as a significant instrument in the dissemination of religious reform and anti-imperialism. This might support Götz Nordbruch's argument that the German Radio Berlin—Zeesen "was just one foreign station touting for attention. British, Italian and French stations were others engaged in this *'guerre des ondes'* during World War II, with Soviet print propaganda adding to the mix of foreign sources available to the broad public in Cairo, Jerusalem and Damascus."[12]

Hilali was born in 1894 in Sijilmasa (in the Tafilalt region of south-east Morocco). He arrived in Germany at the age of 42 after more than 20 years of living in various regions in the Muslim world. He received his religious education from his father, who was a jurist and a deputy judge in their village.[13] In 1915, he left for Algeria to make a living, where he became a follower of the Sufi Tijani brotherhood. By 1921, Hilali converted to the *Salafiyya* trend in Fez after a debate with the well-known Moroccan reformist Muhammad Ibn al-'Arabi al-'Alawi (d. 1964) on the core elements of the Tijani mystical knowledge and superiority as *Khatam al-Awliya* (Seal of Sainthood) within this order. Following his conversion to the *Salafiyya*, Hilali arrived in Egypt in 1922, where became a close student of the famous Muslim reformist Muhammad Rashid Rida (1865–1935), the founder of *Al-Manar* magazine in Cairo. During his years in Egypt, Hilali traveled throughout the country in order to propagate *Salafi* ideas, and had several debates and confrontations with mystical scholars in southern Egypt and Alexandria. His close contact with Rida enabled him to take up a prominent role in a huge transnational Pan-Islamic reformist network of that time. In the interwar period, he traveled, lived, and taught in several countries, such as Saudi Arabia, India, Afghanistan, Iraq, and finally Europe. His popularity remarkably increased in the Muslim world due to his numerous articles in the Islamic press in various countries about his travels and thoughts on many Islamic topics, especially in the *Salafiyya*-oriented magazine *Al-Fath*, founded by the Syro-Egyptian publicist Muhhib al-Din al-Khatib (1886–1969).

I. Hilali's Life in Germany in Previous Studies

In his published autobiography, Hilali did not record his life in chronological order. There is no special section directly dealing with his stay in Germany, but succinct information can be found in different places throughout the book.[14] In his study on the reception of National-Socialist ideologies in the Arab Near East, Stefan Wild briefly mentioned the name of Hilali by referring to an anticommunist article by Hilali in the above-mentioned *Al-Fath* during his stay in Bonn.[15] In a biography of al-Hilali, Henri Lauzière studied him as part of the evolution of *Salafism* and its epistemological underpinnings over the course of the twentieth century. In a separate chapter, the author saw Hilali's Nazi period as continuation of the struggle of Islamic nationalism for cohesion and standardization. He argued that in a period marked by the celebration of strong nationalist ideologies in Europe,

Muslim *Salafi* thinkers tried to standardize Islamic tenets under a unifying process by looking for analogies to the concept of the *umma* as a nation rather than an aggregate of various Muslim subgroups with their own cultures and histories.[16] Lauzière pinpointed many aspects of Hilali's assumed position within the interwar Pan-Islamic network established by the above-mentioned Shakib Arslan from his exile in Switzerland. However, due to the lack of direct contemporaneous sources on Hilali's thoughts and activities, Lauzière indirectly repeated the history of Arslan instead of highlighting a new history of Hilali's role within that network.[17]

It is true that Hilali was impressed by the Druze prince to the extent that he named his eldest son Shakib after him.[18] But one might get the impression that Lauzière in that work lacked data regarding Hilali's close contacts with Arslan before the former's trip to Europe. He maintained that although Hilali was 25 years younger than Arslan, he nevertheless espoused the same anticolonial cause. However, they came from different generations and were not exactly of equal standing.[19] He moreover assumed that Hilali's "close personal association with Arslan had intellectual repercussions that are attested by much textual evidence."[20] As a matter of fact, the sources at hand stressed Hilali's direct contacts with Arslan, and the fact that both were most prolific writers in common Muslim journals. A difference of opinion regarding the Arabic grammar between Arslan and the above-mentioned Rashid Rida, for example, was sometimes solved by the young scholar al-Hilali.[21]

Another critical remark to Lauzière's chapter on Hilali's Nazi period is that the author reached specific conclusions on the basis of biographical information and anecdotes, which Hilali himself gave in his later works. Yet the reader gets only a scanty image of Hilali's religious, intellectual, and political thinking in a period of turmoil in world politics during his stay on German soil. On the basis of Hilali's writings from this period and the collection of his remaining private papers in the possession of his grandson in Morocco, the present study highlights his interaction with German Orientalists against the background of his transnational activities and later collaboration with the Nazis.

II. In Germany for a "Scholarly Passport": Experience with Orientalism

Hilali's encounter with Western Orientalists was, like that of many Arab students in the first half of the twentieth century, not an ahistorical phenomenon and not without mutual experiences. The historical treatment of such students as part of the structure of Western Orientalism is useful to understand what Edward Said had called "overlapping experience."[22] While European scholars traveled to the Near East and taught in Arab/Muslim universities, the coming of those students to study their own culture in the West shows the significance of the meeting of "foreign knowledge" and "self-knowledge" in the history of ideas.[23]

Hilali's studentship in German scholarship of Oriental Studies in the late 1930s should be also seen as part of the encounter of Islamic reformism with Orientalism in the interwar period, especially within the circle of Rashid Rida and his journal *Al-Manar*. Muslim writers were aware of the Orientalist challenges that touched on specific sensitivities in Islam. In addition, they opposed westernized intellectuals and rejected many of their perspectives.[24] This period also witnessed growing influence of Orientalism on local ideas, and an increasing public debate among different groups about Orientalists, their intentions, and the quality of their scholarship.[25]

Since his youth in Morocco, Hilali always dreamt of earning an internationally recognized diploma from a Western university and of studying foreign languages. By such a "scholarly passport," he would gain authority in the Muslim world.[26] After learning English in India, he wanted to travel to England to finish his studies, but, as he claimed, he could not afford the study costs there.[27] Hilali finally decided to travel to Germany, which was cheaper and an attractive destination for many Arab students, especially in engineering and exact sciences.

Hilali's central position in the Rida-Arslan transnational Muslim network and enormous articles in the Muslim press enabled him to realize his ambitions. In an unpublished diary, Hilali described his trip from Iraq to Europe via Syria and Egypt. In Syria, he became a guest of the well-known reformist scholar Muhammad Bahjat al-Baitar (d. 1976), one of Rida's associates. Some Syrian Muslim newspapers welcomed Hilali's coming to the country as a renowned writer; and many notables and Arab diplomats in Damascus came to meet him. In Baitar's house, he met the Palestinian journalist Ihsan Sami Haqqi, one of the main organizers, and the assistant secretary general, of the Muslim European Congress held in Geneva in 1935 under Arslan's supervision.[28] On his part, Haqqi wrote a recommendation letter to the Swiss ambassador in Damascus regarding Hilali's plan to visit Switzerland, and helped him in his preparations for his European trip. In the meantime, Hilali approached the Italian embassy in order to get a permit to enter Italy, which was also easily arranged.[29]

STUDENT, SCHOLARSHIP, AND RADIO IN NAZI GERMANY ❖ 113

From Alexandria he left for Italy on an Italian ship and from there he arrived in Switzerland. In the fall of 1936, Hilali had finally arrived in Geneva, where he became the guest of Arslan for one month looking for a suitable opportunity to undertake his graduate studies in Europe.[30]

In the same year, he left for Bonn, where he first obtained a diploma of proficiency in the German language. In the winter of 1936–1937, he became a lecturer of Arabic at the University of Bonn. Consequently he embarked upon his academic research under the supervision of Paul Kahle, the head of the Oriental Seminar at the University of Bonn.[31] In that period, Oriental studies at German universities underwent many changes and became overdriven by the new political Nazi force. Many students and teachers were dismissed from the university on the grounds of "race," religion, or/and political convictions.[32]

As Arslan had a very high opinion of the abilities of Hilali, he wrote to the German Arabist and diplomat Curt Prüfer (1881–1959), then director of the ministry's personnel division in the German Foreign Office,[33] to inquire whether it was possible to send a qualified and prominent Arab scholar to Germany for a few years to get acquainted with Western scholarship. This Arabic scholar was Hilali. Prüfer passed the letter on to Kahle in case he wished to make particular use of his knowledge. Kahle welcomed Hilali to join the seminar in Bonn where other Orientals had been already studying and teaching.[34] Hilali himself felt the need to get in touch with European colleagues.[35] After his arrival in Bonn, Kahle convinced Hilali to commence a doctoral thesis on *al-Jamahir fi al-Jawahir* by the encyclopedic Persian scholar and philosopher Abu al-Rayhan Muhammad Ibn Ahmad al-Biruni (973–1048).

Collaboration with Paul Kahle

Hilali's scientific cooperation with Paul Kahle was a remarkable experience in which Orientalism and *Salafism* successfully complemented each other. The reason behind this successful cooperation was surely the philological and historical character of the work itself. Lauzière argues that Hilali had intentionally chosen al-Biruni as a research subject instead of another medieval puritan scholar such as Ibn Taymiyya because it was compatible with Arslan's understanding of Islamic modernism at this time. Hilali might have intended to present Islam in the most positive light possible in the realm of natural sciences.[36] Yet, Hilali presented a rather different picture; the reason for his research choice was that such a highly esteemed Muslim scholar was unfortunately unknown among Muslims. His interest in the work of this great philosopher was originally suggested by Kahle, who stressed the importance of producing a German edition of Biruni's book or parts of it. During Hilali's initial preparation for a German translation of Biruni's introduction, the German Orientalist F. Krenkow (1872–1953), a convert to Islam under the Muslim name Salim al-Krinawki, had already edited Biruni's *Jamahir* in Haydarabad.[37]

Hilali had always a high esteem for Paul Kahle as a scholar and Orientalist. However, his active role in the German scholarship in Bonn did not inhibit him from severely attacking other German Orientalists such as Eduard Sachau (1845–1930), another German Orientalist who showed great interest in Biruni's works as well.[38] In *Al-Fath*, Hilali openly accused Sachau of "inventing lies" about Biruni. He argued that Sachau ascribed unsound accounts to Biruni in order to prove the latter's aversion to the Arabs because of their destruction of the civilization of his Sasanian ancestors. In his violent apologetics, Hilali was also upset about the prominent German scholar Carl Brockelmann (1868–1956) who followed Sachau's view in this regard and "blackened his pages of his works with similar allegations."[39] Hilali studied Biruni in order to defend the Persian scholar's sincere religiosity and love toward the Arabs. He was also worried that many "charlatans" in the Muslim world were keen on collaborating with the "enemies of Islam" among influential European "devils" living in the East and propagating "lies" about Islam. Their views consequently caused great damage, which Muslim scholars might find hard to correct and remove from the minds of ignorant people.[40]

Hilali was not the only Oriental student in Kahle's seminar in Bonn. Kahle also supported the well-known Coptic scholar Aziz Suryal Atiyya (1898–1988) for the position of honorary professor in medieval history in Bonn. The prominent Bashkir nationalist activist Ahmed Zeki Validov (sometimes Validi or Walidi) Togan (1890–1970) was also a staff member and colleague of Hilali.[41] It might be relevant to note that Validi himself described his experience and the dialogue with Orientalists as "a self-conscious activity for Arab and other Eastern intellectuals and for their Orientalist interlocutor"[42]

Kahle described the academic sphere of his seminar: "Every member of the staff, every assistant and research student had his special working place. If a book was not in the seminar, it was borrowed from the University Library or ordered from another library. . . . Manuscripts sent to the seminar from other Libraries were carefully kept in one of the three safes."[43] Before the Nazification of the university, differences of political, confessional, and racial character did not play any role in Kahle's seminar. "Germans and foreigners, Christians and Muhammedans, Jews and non-Jews, Protestants and Catholics, Chinese and Japanese, worked peacefully together: whoever intended to work was welcome."[44]

Despite Hilali's harsh critique of several German Orientalists, it seems that he was integrated in Kahle's seminar. In his later memoirs about the Nazification of the University of Bonn, Kahle did not mention Hilali by name, but alluded to him by saying: "There were, however, several prominent Orientals as scholars in Bonn besides these two; for instance, an excellent expert in the Arabic language and literature."[45] Elsewhere, Kahle praised Hilali by name, saying that he had "fitted well into such company."[46] Kahle was impressed by Hilali's knowledge of Arabic literature, and expressed gratitude for his assistance in Bonn. They used to come together for some hours almost every day in order to work on the edition of difficult Arabic texts, such as *Kitab al-Futuwwa* by Muhammad Ibn al-'Ammar al-Baghdadi and *Tayf al-Khayal (Shadow Plays)* by the fourteenth-century Mosul-born Egyptian oculist and poet Muhammad Ibn Daniyal.[47] As for the first text, Kahle wrote that:

> It was also possible to discuss through this text with Takieddin al-Hilali, the old friend from the Bonn period. A [certain] *Futuwwa* text had been the first Arabic text with which we were occupied, when Hilali came to Bonn in the spring of 1936, namely the *Futuwwa* chapter from the introduction to Biruni's Book of Stone.[48]

Kahle described their 14-day work together on *Kitab al-Futuwwa* as "unforgettable."[49] He also maintained that their cooperation was also significant for Hilali, as it finally resulted in a PhD thesis in Berlin, which he described as "an outstanding academic achievement."[50]

As for the second text *Tayf al-Khayal*, Kahle embarked on translating it after the death of his friend Georg Jacob (d. 1937), who had already made a start in editing this work. However, Kahle believed that he was more fortunate than Jacob, who had tried to understand these texts with the occasional assistance of eminent Orientalists such as Noeldeke, Goldziher, de Goeje, Snouck Hurgronje, and others, whose comments were carefully noted in the translation. Kahle's work with Hilali on that text was finished in spring 1939 by when Kahle had to leave Germany. Writing from England in 1940, Kahle commented:

> I, on the other hand, was able to enjoy the co-operation of an outstanding Arab scholar, professor Taqieddin al-Hilali, who was born in Morocco, studied in Fez, lived for some time in Egypt, and for

several years in al-Hijaz....He is a truly critical scholar, particularly conversant with Arabic literature, and I think that with his help I have come to a considerably better understanding of these difficult texts than Jacob.[51]

Hilali had never heard of Ibn Daniyal and his poetry before coming to Bonn. Before starting the work, he took some time to get acquainted with the text through copies and photographs. Hilali grew enthusiastic over the text, stressing that he had never read an Arabic text so full of humor like the *Tayf.* Ibn Daniyal's *Shadow Plays* are a satiric portrayal of the social, moral, and political situation in Mamluk Cairo.[52] At the end of 1937 they started to work systematically on the whole text, but much remained unclear for both of them on the first reading. The second time it was much better, since Ibn Daniyal repeated himself and that helped toward an understanding of his style. On the third reading, everything became quite clear, apart from the places where Ibn Daniyal used special argot, the so-called *lughat bani Sasan.* Over time, Hilali became very familiar with the work of Ibn Daniyal. Kahle was proud of their joint work that produced the commentary that Noeldeke missed in Ibn Daniyal's shadow texts.[53] Before the Congress of Orientalists in September 1938 in Brussels, Kahle presented his work on Ibn Daniyal by enthusiastically telling his Orientalist colleagues about his cooperation with his Moroccan student: "A distinguished Arab scholar, Prof Takieddin al-Hilaly, has enjoyed [the time] during the work on this important contribution. He hopes to publish the Arabic text together with a translation soon."[54]

Kahle's Sympathy toward German Jews

Despite Hilali's later cooperation with those conducting Arabic propaganda on Radio Berlin, he was certainly aware of his mentor's sympathy toward German Jews, having been an eyewitness to the events in Berlin. In 1939, Kahle was obliged to escape Nazi Germany after his wife, Marie, had helped her Jewish neighbors clean up their shops after the *Kristallnacht.* When she was condemned by a Nazi court, Kahle lost his job and the couple and their children left for England in March 1939.[55] During this stressful time, Kahle was not able to go to his office. Nevertheless, Hilali and other students regularly visited him at home to assist him and discuss matters of research and study. In her memoirs, Marie Kahle wrote about Hilali's daily visit to their house: "Every morning Professor Taki Hilali, a famous Arab scholar, came to study with my husband."[56]

Strangely, in April 1937, before the escalation of public Nazi violence against the Jews and the complete Nazification of the University of Bonn, Hilali wrote an article in *Al-Fath* on the meaning of religious freedom at a time when Jewish merchants started to lose their business.[57] He did not believe any press report of prosecution against the Jews and Catholics in Germany. He himself had been already "deceived" by such reports before his arrival in Germany. He asserted that any case of harassment had nothing to do with the status of Jews, but was related to politics. Although many Jews were harmed in their business because of the German boycott on their goods, those who avoided politics were free and safe in their religious practices and rights. At this moment, Hilali believed that the German government did not intend to completely tighten its grips on the Jews. It was merely a policy of keeping an eye on the remaining Jews for fear of their collaboration with fellow Jews abroad who collaborated with the Allies and the United States against Germany's interests. Hilali maintained that there were three confessional Jewish students in the same seminar in Bonn, who were not ill-treated. Once he was surprised to see two Jewish students studying at the university during a Christian religious feast, while other students had left to be with their families on a holiday. Besides, he also noted that Jewish students regularly took pride in their faith, and nobody was harassing them.[58]

Nevertheless, Kahle was obliged to leave for England after the harassment of him and his family by the German authorities. His departure had ironically immediate effects on Hilali's personal life. Wilhelm Heffening (1894–1944), Kahle's successor, decided to reject Hilali's dissertation because a scholar in Cambridge had finished his work on a similar topic. Hilali, on the other hand, stated that the real reason behind this refusal was Heffening's personal hostility toward him.[59]

According to Hilali's memoirs, he left Bonn because of several conflicts with Heffening and a Jewish student under the name Jakobi. Hilali claimed that he had admitted Jakobi to his classes of Arabic and Islamic studies, but the latter regularly showed an unsympathetic attitude toward his Arab teacher. Hilali reported that Heffening too had a similar attitude toward him for two reasons: first, due to a conflict regarding the sharing of teaching staff rooms; and second because of his bias toward Jews as a German Catholic lecturer of Hebrew studies. Many years later, Hilali recalled that when he was studying at the university library, Jakobi put a copy of the Qur'an on a table and started to laugh by saying: "This is the word of God," but none of the students paid him any attention. At the end, Hilali stood up and put a copy of the Bible beside the Qur'an harshly rebuked Jakobi:

> You Jew! If this [Bible] were the word of God, the [Qur'an] should be as well. We are neither kids nor ignorant laymen, but university students learning the methods of research and investigation. These two scriptures [Torah and Gospel] were brought by two men as we know. Why these two [holy] scriptures should be considered as the word of God, while the other one [namely the Qur'an] should be a lie upon God?[60]

Dissertation in Berlin

After Heffening's refusal of Hilali's thesis, the latter received an invitation to work in the Arabic program of the German shortwave radio station established by the Ministry of Propaganda in Berlin-Zeesen (see below).[61] In 1940 Hilali therefore moved to Berlin for his new job and to study at the Institut für Arabistik und Islamkunde at the University of Berlin. One year later he defended his doctoral thesis, which had previously been rejected by Heffening, under the supervision of Richard Hartmann (1881–1965).[62] Shortly afterward, he published a short article on the caste-like aspects of tribalism in the Arabian Peninsula in the prominent German journal *Die Welt des Islams*.[63]

Hilali's doctoral defense did not go without problems. The committee consisted of ten scholars, including Carl Brockelmann (1868–1956), who did not like Hilali's dissertation at all.[64] Brockelmann did not agree with Hilali's previous insistence that Biruni was a devout Muslim rather than a free thinker. He found Hilali's propositions inaccurate and defensive, as Biruni's knowledge of science and nature had made him too rational to believe in such a religion as Islam. Other members of the committee did not completely agree with Brockelmann, and Hilali passed the exam. In his comment on this event many years later, Hilali wrote: "Truth, reason and freedom of thought prevailed: the foreign Arab student triumphed over the greatest Orientalist of his time."[65] In contrast, Kahle praised Hilali and his dissertation as "a fine scholar who had obtained a real understanding of al-Biruni."[66]

An Orientalist Vision of the Qur'an

Hilali had close contacts with other German Orientalists. Besides his appreciation of Kahle, he lauded his Berlin supervisor Richard

Hartmann for his support of academic freedom, intellectual standards, and lack of bias, unlike many other contemporary French, British, and Scandinavian Orientalists.[67]

In the beginning, he believed that his study at the Oriental Seminar in Bonn could now enable him to refute Orientalist claims that specific Qur'anic passages were rehashed from the Bible.[68] However, his interaction with Orientalist works made slight temporary changes in his mind. In Berlin, for instance, Hilali had a chance to see the private collection of Arabic manuscripts brought from the Muslim world by the German Arabist Bernhard Moritz (1859–1939), then an employee at the German Foreign Office.[69] One of the manuscripts was a Greek translation of the opening chapter of the Qur'an, *al-Fatiha*, on a papyrus from Egypt. Discussing the contents of manuscript, Moritz was able to convince Hilali that some classical Muslim exegetes did not correctly explain the meanings of *al-Rahim* and *al-Rahman* (merciful)—in contrast to some of the early Muslims at the time of the revelation who understood these terms in different ways. In the traditional Muslim exegesis, *al-Rahim* refers to God's *khass*, that is, "specific," mercy, whereas *al-Rahman* points to His *amm* or "general" mercy. As Hilali was learning Syriac at this time, Moritz explained to him that the root of the two terms *r.h.m*, in Syriac, means "love." And since Arabic and Syriac were originally one language, this last meaning was forgotten in Arabic during the process of writing down lexicons in the classical period. Hilali enthusiastically defended Moritz's new interpretation on the pages of *Al-Fath*.[70]

Hilali's propagation of such views in the *Salafi* circles triggered a reaction from a traditional Muslim scholar in Cairo. Soon, in the same journal, 'Abd al-Latif Abu al-Samh, one of Hilali's old *Salafi* friends in Egypt, objected to Moritz's Orientalist interpretation and Hilali's defense of it.[71] In his answer, Hilali argued that anybody who studied Syriac and Hebrew should be strongly convinced that they are two "full sisters" or "daughters" of Arabic. He was in no doubt that the three languages had the same origin. Hilali accepted Moritz's explanation as it better clarified the question of repetition in the Qur'an than the interpretation of Muslim traditional commentators that focused on the specific and general connotation of mercy. Understanding *al-Rahim* as "loving" was more convincing; and he felt that Muslim researchers should not reject it just because of their fear of opposing the early generations of *Salaf*. Hilali gave the example of the Prophet's companion Zayd Ibn Thabit, who had been able to learn Hebrew in one month. His ability to read Jewish documents to the Prophet suggests that Hebrew as a language was very close to Arabic. It was also narrated that 'Umar Ibn al-Khattab could read some Hebrew. In Hilali's view, the reason why such research and interpretations were not known among early Muslim exegetes was their lack of knowledge of other languages, as learning foreign languages decreased after the time of the Prophet.[72]

III. An Occidentalist Image from within

Hilali's training in Orientalist scholarship made Hilali establish an "Occidentalist" view of Europe from within. His stay in Germany and his role in the Oriental Seminar in Bonn enabled him to create specific images about European culture, society, and religion. His choice of topics was probably deliberate. One should actually read his ideas as implicit reactions to Western critique of Islam, the position of women in the Muslim world, Muslim values, and political and racial issues. His "conservative" acclaim of the proper Muslim behavior vis-à-vis his severe critical ideas about the West was also integrated in the German neoromantic *völkisch* tradition and its national concepts toward the significant meanings of race and nation. Such ideals offered all sorts of inspiration not only to indigenous European nationalists and conservatives, but included Hilali and many Muslim and Arab compatriots in Europe as well.

As we shall see, in explaining Islam to the Germans, Hilali relied on anecdotes, which were often enlightening and characteristic for both Hilali and his interlocutors. It is true that Hilali looked at Islam through the lens of nationalism as a compelling modern term, while the *Salafi* discourse was increasingly modeled after the concept of nationalism in Europe. However such a unifying ideal would keep the community strong in the face of colonialism.[73]

Western Women

The position of women in Muslim tradition was a thorny issue in the Western debates about Islam. In response, Hilali made a counter-campaign by constructing specific images on the life and fate of European women as based on his observations in Germany. His sociological interpretations of the status of family and women in the West reflect a certain feeling of frustration about the European and Orientalist images of Islam and its social norms. They also carry an undertone of the challenging Western questions about such Islamic norms as polygamy and gender equality. These questions were already echoing in Muslim reformist circles as well. But as he was living in the

West, Hilali claimed to have a better authority of understanding the European society and its social concerns from within.

Under the headline "*Laysa 'indi Harim*'" (I have no harem), Hilali made a straightforward value judgment that the position of Muslim women in their indigenous lands was much better (though not ideal) than their European counterparts. In Germany, he observed that people normally used the word "harem" as a word of offence to houses of immoral character because of its connotation to Muslim houses with many slave girls. His unnamed German landlady was unwilling to rent a room to a German student, since he regularly had various girlfriends. She did not tolerate his behavior, and severely rebuked him: "Either you get one girlfriend only, or you leave my house...I have no harem here."[74] She often complained to Hilali about the bad reputation of another German female student, who was said to have changed four boyfriends in a year, all of whom had promised to marry with her, but later backed out. Hilali tried to explain to his landlady that it was the man's guilt, but she insisted that a woman should always protect herself if she wanted that nobody should deceive her.[75]

Such anecdotes made Hilali believe that Europeans, particularly the common people, had inherited unyielding and deeply rooted misconceptions about Muslim households. As per his harsh defense, "the harem—even in the time when it contained more than one wife and more than one slave-girl—was a thousand time purer than any of their purest house."[76] After one and a half years in Germany, Hilali had reached a conclusion that Western women, unlike what westernized easterners propagated about their dignified status, were the victims of "ill-treatment, pain, disrespect, and spinsterhood extreme." It was futile to hope that European men would one day change their ill-treatment toward their women.[77]

Hilali compared four different stages of women's upbringing in the West with the situation in Muslim societies. In the first stage of childhood, Western governments, unlike the Muslim ones, often took care of health, perfect hygiene, and good nutrition for all young girls of all social classes. During the second stage, young girls always got obligatory primary schooling, but in the third stage everything started to change. Girls usually left their parents' house to study at college or university. Rich and middle-class families continued to support their daughters financially, either on campus or in a rented place. Hilali denounced the moral life of many of European girls for their habitual visits to nightclubs and dancing. Day and night they wandered with men across the city and the forests, while their "poor" parents continued to send them money. They were thus exposed to lose what "Arabs and Muslims would call *'ird'* (honour)."[78] In that stage, European girls, for Hilali, were like "feathers" flying in a heavy storm. After finishing their studies, generally at the age of 25, the lucky ones officially married their boyfriend. But most young men and women feared the marriage bond at a young age, as it restricted their freedom and pleasures, and in many cases, girls remained a burden on their families. Besides, European girls were usually obliged to collect their own dowry to be paid to any potential bridegroom, but in most cases they remained spinsters. Hilali assured that any Muslim witnessing the situation of European women should acknowledge God's favor upon Muslim women and the significance of "strict" and "just" Sharia regulations in protecting women.[79] The only way for poor European girls to get a decent life was to finish school and find a suitable job. Even though, Hilali argued, women in Europe suffered under tough work, let alone the forms of debasement in their jobs. In many cases, they would take care of their disabled mothers and would save money for their dowry. In their leisure time, many of them were obliged to look for a suitable man for the future. As dancing was a public custom in Europe, dancing clubs were common places where men and women used to enter relationships that could result into marriage or cohabitation. Hilali informed his readers that men of all classes rarely danced with their own wives, and a wife often chose a man other than her husband to dance with.[80] As for the fourth stage of middle age and old age, Hilali argued that married women usually became too fatigued because of the tedium of housekeeping and looking after children with no support from their husbands. But some good husbands shared the work with them, and their wives normally passed their middle age in a comparatively better state. Alternatively, unmarried middle-aged women continued working till they retired. In old age, they would either depend on social welfare or on their own savings. Hilali pitied elderly women on the streets in Germany doing their shopping without any help from the society.[81]

Hilali used to discuss with some of his German fellows that the situation of Muslim women was better than that of women in Europe. As a result a highly educated lady had even agreed with him on that point although she did not like the idea of a second wife. But Hilali asserted that he was able to convince her that polygamy might protect the rights of women if it is applied properly.[82] However, he admitted, the status of Muslim women was not ideal in practice. Nevertheless, Muslim women were happier, even if they lacked appropriate and useful education. In Hilali's understanding, some Muslim men also displayed their jealousy by tightening the matter of veiling and depriving women of education in contrast to the "tolerant" and "moderate" attitude of Islam and the *Salaf* in that regard.[83]

Another related issue was what Hilali saw as the suffering of women under the bond of Catholic marriage. In Germany, he heard about a Catholic lady who, despite her official divorce and that her husband had abandoned their children, was neither able to get the church's recognition of her divorce, nor to remarry. Having a new unwedded relation with another man, she felt guilty about her "sin." The priest advised her that it was better for her to come every week to confess for her sin than remarry. Since another civil marriage meant, in her case, excommunication from the church, the lady lived her life in a dilemma between her feeling of guilt and being a sincere member of the church community.[84] Hilali considered this as a sign of the church's "ruthless" attitude toward the people's social life. Unlike Islam, he argued, the Catholic Church, due to its corruption, was only concerned about increasing its income by retaining as many members as it could.[85]

White "Race"

Racial policies and the Aryan/non-Aryan binary were specific characteristics of Nazi Germany. Hilali once witnessed a dialogue between an "American lady" and a "German man" concerning the role of the white man in modern history. The German man supported the idea that Germany should retrieve its single "modest" colony as its legitimate possession in East Africa. His American counterpart denounced colonialism and European "aggression" upon weak nations as unjust. In her view, the European struggle on getting colonies resembled two thieves attacking a house in order to steal its possessions, but finally differing in dividing the plunder: both were essentially evil. The German rejected her claim as an "empty" philosophy saying that colonialism persists as long as human beings remain different in colors and powers. Therefore, the white man should carry out his mission in life by rescuing "barbarous" nations from their ignorance and chaos. The American lady was not deluded into believing that France and Great Britain had crossed the sea in order to save and civilize nations, but believed that they, on the contrary, initiated "terrorism" and destruction of weak peoples.[86]

Whether this debate is fictional or real, it perfectly suited Hilali's anticolonial sentiments. He mocked that the term "white man" had become equal to "European" with no regard for one's color. He observed that many Europeans of his time were sometimes astonished when they knew that other non-Europeans were white-skinned, or that snow sometimes falls in north Africa. They even thought that "the whole Africa is boiling because of its hot temperature and that its entire people are black or look like milk mixed with coffee, and are not in need of wearing wool clothes to get warmth."[87]

Hilali himself knew of incidents of European racism in Germany. He praised a Turkish man in Germany (probably his fellow Ahmed Zeki Validov Togan), who severely reacted to some pejorative statements made by a German lady about the low nature of Oriental people. By referring to the superiority of Japanese civilization and progress, he also reproached the lady for her belittling views as if "European heads were made of 'light,' whereas that of other nations was made of 'darkness.'"[88]

Despite Hilali's opposition to racism, we did not come across any writing in which he directly criticized the Aryan ideologies in Nazi Germany in 1930s. Later in 1960s, he recalled his German period by saying that the German idea of the "superiority" of the white race affected all classes, including the German Orientalists Carl Brockelmann and Martin Hartmann.[89] Hilali now argued that Brockelmann's claim that al-Biruni was a Persian who hated the Arabs was nothing but an echo of National Socialist racial theories and superiority of the Aryan race as opposed to their contempt for Semites, that is, Arabs.[90]

Religion and Religiosity in Europe

Before his arrival in Germany, Hilali shared the widespread view in the Arab press regarding the undiminished role of religion in the West in contrast to the increase of biblical critical works doubting the authenticity of the Holy Scriptures. His stay in Europe made him recognize that both facts were actually true. Democracy in Europe means that all governments, including the Nazis, should respect the public feelings of one's traditions, beliefs, and visiting the church. He was impressed by the policy of social nationalist regimes, except Russia, for their "affectionate feelings of unity" as long as they did not disturb internal politics.[91]

As for the sense of religious piety, Hilali observed that many German students were devout Christians. A German student once refused to accompany him to Cologne on Sunday because of his attachment to the "divine law" obliging him to attend the weekly morning sermons in the Church. He admired such a "polite, mature and highly-educated" young man who, despite his good command over Latin and many European languages and also studying Arabic,

Turkish, Persian, Aramaic, and Sanskrit, was not ready to abandon his faith.[92] However, there were other German friends who used to go to the church just out of respect for their parents and for fear due to a certain degree of social control. As he now mixed with diverse social classes in Germany, Hilali noted that people in Europe had a certain degree of religious respect for each other; and nobody could utter any antireligious words that might hurt the feelings of others. Even scholars critical of religion were mostly obliged to preserve the public order by not offending people's beliefs.[93]

As for religiosity at the grassroots level, Hilali narrated a story of two of his German neighbors, a butcher and a postman, who once visited him in hospital. During their conversation, he insisted on discussing with them the invalidity of Christian doctrines, but they preferred to abandon the debate because keeping up one's religion was far better than looseness and immorality.[94] However, Hilali noted that superstitions did not disappear in modern Europe. One of his visiting German neighbors, for example, did not take regular medicine for treating callosity. Rather, he requested any of his friends or family members after the death of anybody in their circle to put water on the callosity saying: "Die, just as he dies." This was seen as a more painless treatment than removing callosity from his body.[95]

This dichotomy between the Christian faith and some members of the community is clearly illustrated in Hilali's anecdotes in the Arab press of Cairo. One of them was a story circulated among the local people of Bonn about the compulsory church tax levied on all members of the church (introduced in Germany during the nineteenth century as a state law).[96] A church collector in Bonn went to collect this tax from a non-practicing Christian shopkeeper, who was hesitant to pay. When the collector warned that he would report him to the municipality, he finally succumbed and paid the tax. Meanwhile, this shopkeeper sent his assistant to the religious leader of the church with an invoice for an unspecified number of wine bottles. Having been told by the clergyman that they had never ordered those things, the assistant conveyed his boss' message: "And we have never observed prayers or listened to any of your sermons in order to pay taxes."[97]

Hilali recalled that an unnamed German university lecturer once invited him for a Christmas dinner at home. Among the guests there were another Muslim student and a Jew, while the others were all Christians.[98] This lecturer was probably Paul Kahle, because it was his habit to invite his staff group for Christmas. For example, his wife Marie, who was a member of the Confessional Church, recorded in her memoirs the Christmas of 1938 before their escape to Britain that there had been two (one Indian and one Arab) students present at their home on the Christmas Eve.[99] While people were waiting for food, the host wife brought the Gospel and placed a copy before all guests, and religious hymns were sung accompanied by piano music. In the midnight everybody was ready to leave, and the "devout" wife of Hilali's teacher prepared herself to go to the church for the Christmas service. She asked whether anybody was interested in accompanying her, but everyone kept silent. Hilali cynically said to her: "None would like to join you, because when you enter into the Kingdom, you shall be alone and will not take anybody of us." All people, including her, laughed. But Hilali knew later that she did not like his joke at all.[100]

The reason why Hilali brought forward such anecdotes was to prove that there was a certain degree of "European fanaticism" in religion not only at the grassroots level, but also at the level of university professors and highly educated youth. Muslims should not be misled by the "camouflage of atheists" in the East, who strongly called for a blind imitation of Europeans in all ways of life including in abandoning religion and traditions.[101]

Debates on Muslim Values in Interwar Europe

As a *Salafi* student in interwar Germany, Hilali's discussions of religiosity in Europe were integrated in his ideas on the uniformity of reformist Islam and its needs for Muslims in the Muslim world and in the West as well. He did not like the existence of "extreme" mystical sects, as they were the direct reason for the degeneration of Muslim societies and creation of disharmony, especially under colonial powers.[102] Hilali regularly lamented that lay and "ignorant" Europeans always looked down at the practices of Oriental people living amongst them. His Oriental fellows in Europe should be therefore well-prepared for debates on such issues as polygamy, male inheritance, women veiling, and segregation between sexes in Islam. Even some of his German friends even saw the concept of dowry in Islam as a symbol for the enslavement of women.[103]

Hilali gave a special reference of two of such typical debates with Europeans. Fellow Muslims in Germany, unlike him, used to eat pork in restaurants. On many occasions, Europeans urged him to taste pork; saying he would never leave it again. A German colleague was surprised he had one day ordered eggs with his meal at work instead of pork. To this, Hilali sarcastically reacted that although the "ugliest insulting" word in the German language is "Schweinehund" (Swine dog), Europeans still insist on eating the first part of the word while avoiding the second. Many of the friends present laughed. Asked by his German counterpart about the Muslim ruling regarding eating dogs, Hilali stated that Muslims do not eat dogs either, but that pork is more strictly forbidden. Hilali added that pork was considered unclean in the Old Testament too; and that Jesus never ate it because he did not come to abolish the laws of the Torah (Matthew 5:17 20).[104]

The life of people in paradise according to the Islamic tradition was another central point of debate. In one of his gatherings with German academic fellows, someone mockingly commented about the beauty of the paradise of Muslims where they will eat, drink, and marry as well. Another man asserted that the idea of marriage in the Muslim picture of paradise was not rational. Hilali reacted that there was no paradox in this notion because people remain human beings with desires even in paradise:

> The Muslim paradise is rational because it will be in accordance with the human nature, unlike your paradise which will only contain playing flutes and harps and singing songs [referring to Revelation 5:8]. After a while, one gets tired and bored when he always plays harp or sings, and will start to seek something else. If they all play, who will listen to them?! To whom will they play?! Human nature and mind get bored of eternal playing and singing.[105]

As for wine drinking among Muslim students in Europe, the well-known Indonesian Muslim reformist writer Muhammad Basyuni b. Muhammad 'Imran (1885–1953) of Sambas, West Borneo, asked Hilali to spell out his views about the ruling about wine drinking in Islam on the basis of his experience in Europe.[106] Some Indonesian students retained their Western teachers' habits of wine drinking even after their return from Europe where it was a custom because of the cold weather. As the Sharia was merciful, it should not prohibit what people in cold countries needed in that weather. 'Imran's questions focused on the following points: Does Islam prohibit useful things that have no harm? Are those Indonesians right in their claim? Is wine drinking useful or necessary for the people of Europe?[107]

In his answer, Hilali stressed that prohibitions in Islam are of two types: (1) purely harmful, such as *shirk* (polytheism) and murder, and (2) things having both benefit and harm, but whose harmful effects are greater, such as wine (Qur'an, 2:219). In his view, not everybody in the West agreed on the unconditional benefits of wine. In the

United States there had been attempts to prohibit wine since 1874. Hilali wrote:

> All wise men and leaders in the United States were unanimous on the prohibition of wine, [since] they became certain that it was a source of corruption whose harm exceeded its probable usefulness; and that its benefit was too small compared to its harmfulness. They exerted great efforts to forbid *umm al-khaba'ith* (the mother of all filthiness)....They had continued for years till Jewish merchants were triumphant in causing strife among them. They finally succumbed to legalize it because of their judicial system.[108]

As for the second assertion that people in cold regions need alcohol, Hilali severely reacted to that as "nonsense." His answer remained rhetoric that the Sharia guarantees happiness in all matters of life. If God knew that wine was useful for the inhabitants of cold areas, he would have never prohibited it. Hilali argued that all physicians agreed that wine drinking is not essential for the health of any human being, but without it health improves and mental and physical diseases decrease. In Germany he observed that wine drinkers usually got headaches, swollen eyes, and uncomfortable sleep.[109]

Hilali found the claim of those "westernized" Indonesian students in Europe as merely an allegation. University teachers in Europe were generally moderate in their habit of drinking, since being excessively drunk would badly affect their academic reputation. He concluded that alcoholism was detested in Europe as well. Unlike wine drinkers among Muslims, Europeans see wine as a superfluous matter, which they drink during festivities without lavishly spoiling their health or money. In contrast, Europeans also looked down on easterners who heavily indulged in wine drinking.[110]

IV. NAZI PROPAGANDA

Hilali's role in the Nazi propaganda is one of the most intriguing parts of his career in Germany. In his recent study on Nazi propaganda for the Arab world, Herf saw common grounds between radical German anti-Semitism and radical anti-Semitism rooted in Qur'anic verses and the traditional commentaries of Islam. Arabs and Nazis were brought together in a shared project of radicalizing their own past traditions.[111] Critics of Herf's arguments insist that his foremost aim was to prove specific similarities of Jew hatred in both cultures at this historical moment, without paying fair attention to the reality of politics and memories specific to this era. Herf's assertion of a joint

German-Arab message of Jew hatred could be supported only if we were able verify the role of Arab exiles in Germany in the choice of thematic priorities and texts, and what were their contributions to the strategic decisions made by the various offices in charge of the radio policy of the German Foreign Ministry.[112]

Like many Arab nationalists, Hilali admired the Third Reich's economic policy, authoritarian and egalitarian ideology, and struggle against the Allies, communism, and Jewry. His collaboration with Nazi Germany was probably a notorious historical moment, but Berlin Arabic Radio offered an unprecedented opportunity to him and other Muslim and Arab nationalists to foster a certain sense of communion in the Arab world. Although it was committed to propagate specific anti-Jewish sentiments, the shortwave played a good role in "enlightening" Arab and Muslim peoples about the French and British injustice in north Africa and Palestine.[113]

As we shall see, Hilali started his job in the radio as a proofreader and linguistic corrector (*musahhih wa muraji' lughawi*). Soon he joined the team as one of the main speakers on air.[114] Hilali was mostly in charge of the broadcasting of issues related to north Africa and the French policies there. The French authorities were concerned with the anti-French sentiments in German propaganda. Among the subjects that Hilali broadcasted were the celebration of the anniversary of the Berber Dhahir (decree), the notion of *jihad* as a religious obligation to combat colonialism, and apolitical matters such as the month of Ramadan.[115]

Power of Radio

By studying the role of Arab nationalists in Nazi propaganda, one should not ignore the fact that the invention of radio had its impact on them just as it did on their Western peers. Hilali's enthusiasm about the radio was not in a vacuum. His Pan-Islamic ideas were actually formed within the circle of great reformers such as Rida and Arslan, who had greatly valued the role of the media in propagating Islam.[116] His later joining of Radio Berlin was also a result of admiration to this new technique and its anticolonial and religious power. As the radio was a token of a nation's progress, Hilali hoped that Muslims could create a space for their anticolonial activities on air by establishing national radio stations for Muslim propaganda.

Hilali had already felt the usefulness of radio as a significant mass communication medium long before his arrival in Germany. In Iraq he was regularly listening to the Italian radio and the English-speaking

Radio Jerusalem.[117] After his arrival in Germany, he bought a radio in order to follow world news.[118] After his daily work, he often avoided public meetings, spending most of his time listening to the radio. The voices of different broadcasters were competing on air in disseminating their countries' political interests. In Nazi Germany, Hilali now recognized the significance of radio propaganda in empowering the state and its extension of diplomacy, since "ear is the messenger to one's heart."[119] He must have had the same feeling as many others in interwar Europe that "listening to foreign stations was a symbol of the right to think for oneself."[120]

In February 1937, Hilali was admitted to a hospital for an eye surgery. While he was listening to music and news, he heard, all of a sudden the voice of an Egyptian reciter of the Qur'an, which was immediately interrupted by a French shortwave. He got excited about listening to the Qur'an on the radio in Europe. Another Muslim patient in a neighboring room wished he would have been with Hilali in his room. In Bonn, there were about 20–30 Muslims, who were, like him, eager to listen to the Qur'an and other Arabic speeches on air. Hilali believed that propagating Islam in Europe by using radio waves was feasible because churches in Europe were already broadcasting the ringing of their bells, organ music, hymns, and prayers. However, there was no single efficient Arab broadcasting wave, like those in Germany, spreading its cultural and political views in different languages.[121]

Hilali was sometimes upset about Arab radio stations broadcasting in foreign languages without using Arabic in their opening speeches. While he was listening to a music concert (March 19, 1937) on the Cairo-based English Nil-Channel, he noticed that the whole program was presented in English and French, except an Arabic greeting phrase. European radio stations normally started their programs in foreign languages with an introduction in their native language. He found that even broadcasting national music could be used for propaganda, and felt that Arab radio stations should propagate Oriental music above Western music, otherwise it would be like "selling a product to its own producers."[122]

Hilali lamented the "ignorance" and "laxity" of Arabs handling radio propaganda. Egypt, which was supposed to take the lead in that matter, was lagging behind, unlike the Japanese on Radio Tokyo or other small European states, such as Luxembourg, on their radios.[123] Although he usually enjoyed the Qur'anic recitation by the well-known Egyptian reciter Muhammad Rif'at (1900–1950), he was not happy about the "archaic" language of Egyptian broadcasters and the British propaganda on it.[124] Hearing "Hello…Hello, this is Tokyo" on the Japanese radio made Hilali believe that the upcoming Japanese propaganda power would be the greatest challenge to the European "obstinate" and "damned" idea that the Orient's nature was intrinsically and unchangeably imperfect.[125] Muslims should take Japan as a model; and Europeans should now confess the greatness of Japan despite its non-Aryan origin.[126]

As the radio had become the speaking "tongue" of nations, Hilali had aspired that the Egyptian radio station would address Arabs and Muslims in Europe by broadcasting Qur'anic recitation and Islamic lectures. Muslim scholars and writers were encouraged to take the example of the Vatican Radio (established in 1931) in its faithful proclaiming of the Catholic message on air.[127]

However, Hilali saw the European rivalry in radio wave techniques as a struggle between the good and evil. In this competition, the Germans were keen on spoiling Radio Moscow, as the Russians created shortwaves of higher quality that were well-received in remote areas. Hilali was informed that Germany had 12 efficient broadcasts, whereas Hitler kept another 12 stations in his "pocket" in order to spoil the enemy's radio broadcasting during the war. But Hilali was aware that in their radio propaganda European governments sometimes exaggerated their minor achievements in order to manipulate their people.[128]

Listening to the radio had changed many of Hilali's views on world politics and reinforced his antipathy toward colonialism. For example, before his arrival in Germany he admired Abba Jofir, the last sultan of the Kingdom of Jimma in Ethiopia. But Jofir's excessive public praise for Italy on Rome Arabic Radio made him change his mind.[129] He was shocked to hear Jofir demanding of Muslims in a radio speech to obey Italy's rule by citing the Qur'anic verse: "Obey God, the Messenger and those in authority among you" (Qur'an 4:59). Hilali found that Jofir committed a grave and evident *kufr* (disbelief), which had already reached a countless number of people on the globe via the radio. In order to erase his "sin" and retrieve his faith, the king had to declare his repentance on air as well.[130]

Radio as an Anticolonial Weapon

During his stay in Nazi Germany, Hilali eagerly searched for French colonial broadcasting stations on his radio device in order to keep updated on the French propaganda in north Africa. He was thrilled when many times a German station tried to disturb Radio Paris.[131]

One day he was disappointed when a certain Ahmed Lihbib, the main speaker on the French radio, *Algeria*, lauded France for its "motherly tenderness" and "generosity" toward her Algerian "children." In his radio speeches, Hilali habitually attacked French colonialism as the most "abominable" and "diabolic" oppression in the world.[132]

Hilali ridiculed such Arab propagandists as "barking dogs." On the French radio *Paris Mondial*, one Arab broadcaster even went further in equating the role of the French radical Prime Minister Édouard Daladier (1884–1970) and his British counterpart Neville Chamberlain (1869–1940) with prophets in history. While prophets had been sent down by God to preserve humanity, Hilali commented, those two leaders were destined to destroy the world despite their claim of democracy.[133] In response, Hilali contrasted the "misdeeds" of Daladier and Chamberlain in their colonies with the Nazi regime and Hitler, who, in his view, was not an absolute tyrant or authoritarian as many people might have thought. Unlike these two leaders, Hitler ruled as a native Catholic leader in his own country, not in the country of others. Hilali also asserted that he also treated the Germans equally with no distinction or bias. Unlike the French and British colonizers, Hitler was keen on preserving his nation's wealth. He neither had a wife or any sons, nor did he appoint any of his family members in office.[134]

Being aware of the notoriety of his defense to Nazism and Fascism, Hilali remarked that Germany and Italy remained, for him, foreign nations. Especially Italian and French authorities were alike in their "brutality" against Muslims. In his view, Italian Fascism in Libya resembled the French "Fascist" behavior in north Africa. For him, neither France nor Italy was a good friend of Islam. For that reason, Islam should never exist under any foreign form of colonialism that explicitly rejects the Qur'an, the Sunna and the good *Salaf* (ancestors).[135]

For Hilali, the emergence of authoritarian or democratic political systems in Europe were the product of freedom. The people in the East, on the contrary, were "dying of thirst" for a "drop of justice."[136] He argued that Germany's political system, good or bad, would benefit or harm only its people. The same held true for France's democracy, which was beautiful only for the French themselves. The so-called democratic regimes were sometimes even worse than authoritarian political systems, as they remained democratic only within their borders, but were tyrant and suppressive in other lands. Hilali found that what Daladier was saying on the radio was completely at variance with the ethics Europeans taught their children at schools.[137]

Hilali attacked *Paris Mondial* for its "pro-Jewish" tone against the Palestinian cause. He harshly labeled it a "devilish Jewish Mondial," which deserved instead to be labeled as "Radio Tel Aviv" for its unconditional defense of the Jewish question more than the Jews themselves did.[138] No less worse was *Radio-Tunis PTT* broadcasting station, which was officially inaugurated by the French PTT minister M. Jules Julien in September 1938 during the celebration of the month of Ramadan. Hilali doubted that such a colonial station was set up as respect to Islam and Muslims.[139] For him, the colonial stamp was obvious on this station, as it regularly broadcasted its inauguration ceremonies in French, besides Arabic. Ironically, the Tunisian station carried the French abbreviation "PTT," and always ended its programs with the French national anthem. He suspected its coverage for the simple reason that it labeled the *mujahidin* in Palestine as "rebellious" and "thieves."[140] Due to his puritan understanding of Islam, Hilali accused the French propagandists of pacifying Muslims by broadcasting musical concerts and mystical gatherings, religious hymns, and poems on radio as the "best" form of Islam in order to entice its listeners against resistance.[141] Also he saw that *Radio-Tunis* propagated the idea that the Berbers were superior to Arabs, as proved by what had happened in Morocco during Berber Dhahir in 1931. They tried to convince people that the French introduced culture, democracy, and liberty to the Berbers, while the Arabs brought them a religion only.[142]

Hilali was thrilled to hear about the establishment of any Muslim or Arab anticolonial radio stations, such as *Radio Ankara* (October 1938). Also the establishment of "moderate" radio waves in Arabic by other colonial states, such as Spain, was sometimes also welcomed.[143] On browsing stations on his radio, Hilali came across the anti-French radio station of *Greater Syria*, which was broadcasted from an anonymous place in order to escape any French interference. Now having gained experience with the radio world, Hilali advised Syrian broadcasters to air their programs in English, French, Italian, and German. In order to escape any foreign interference, they were advised to change the wave from time to time, and to put their radio wave beside *Paris Mondial* in order to guarantee that the French could not interfere with it without spoiling their own station. In *Al-Fath*, Hilali made an announcement for his Arab readers about its broadcasting times; and urged other Arabs and Muslims in Europe to follow its programs.[144] To his mind, the radio of *Greater Syria* was the only anticolonial Arabic Muslim station that the French authorities were trying to spoil.[145] When it returned back on air after a short period of disappearance, Hilali welcomed its return by equaling it with the *adhan* (call of prayer), that drove the "Satan" [referring to colonialism] away.[146]

Due to the lack of Arab anticolonial radios, Hilali was ready to accept Nazi propaganda in serving the Muslim Arab cause in Palestine. Thanks to the Nazi radio propaganda, he believed, Germans from all classes became well-informed about the British disproportionate policies in the Muslim world. The Germans had therefore started to show a certain degree of sympathy toward the people of Palestine.[147] Hilali was sometimes rejoiced by Hitler's challenge to the British imperial policies in Palestine. For example, he talked of the well-known assault of Hitler in his *Reichstag* speech (February 22, 1938) in the British House of Commons for its critique to the German racial policy, in which he said: "I advise the members of the House of Commons to concern themselves with the judgments of British military courts in Jerusalem, and not with the judgments of German courts of justice."[148]

Hilali broadcasted his dismay about the news of the partition of British mandatory Palestine on the Nazi radio.[149] He was impressed by the voices of German masses, men and women, broadcasted on the radio while they were shouting "Heil Hitler" on the streets of Berlin for his annexation of Sudetenland in 1938. This scene on German streets reminded Hilali of the suffering of Muslim prisoners in colonial jails. He bemoaned that Muslims had *no Hitler, no nation, and no hope* to rescue them from the colonial oppression like Hitler did with Sudetenland.[150]

Also the call of German authorities for the Winter relief campaign (*Winterhilfswerk*) in October 1938 for the sake of Sudetenland was of great importance in Hilali's admiration of the German Reich.[151] His landlady in Bonn doubled her contribution that year because of her strong faith in her government's sincerity in helping German fellows in Sudetenland. Had a quarter of the number of Arabs had been like this old German lady in her national faith and work, he wrote, the Arab situation would have drastically changed. Hilali was certain that this German mass charity demonstration (clothes, toys, and huge amounts of money) should improve the status of those annexed fellow Germans by reconstructing their roads, buildings, schools, and public parks.[152]

Political Convictions

As for his political convictions, Hilali shared the Nazi propaganda campaign against communism and Bolshevism as evil for the world.[153] Particularly in 1937, immediately after Hilali's arrival in Germany and before joining the radio, *Reichspropagandaleitung* organized a major anti-Bolshevist exhibit that traveled to big cities. Joseph Goebbels (1897–1945), the Reich Minister of Propaganda in Nazi Germany, promoted a severe anti-Bolshevik campaign by delivering inflammatory speeches, blaming the entire Spanish Civil War on "Jewish Bolshevism."[154] Against this background, Hilali jumped to warn his fellow Moroccan nationalists against the Spanish Bolshevik Party as more hostile to the Islam and the Moroccan people due its blind loyalty to Paris and Moscow.[155] Although Muslims should never expect any good from a European, he wrote, one should try to diminish any French or Russian influence in Spain.[156]

As a Pan-Islamic thinker, Hilali argued that the Islamic state is the most ideal political system. In his view, the social nationalist state system was closer to Islam than democratic, communist, autocratic forms. The social nationalist system, such as the German case, was keen on the unification of a nation under the leadership of a "sincere" and "fair-minded" group cooperating for the sake of the nation's reform, happiness, and welfare in all aspects and for the struggle against anarchists. Following the line of Nazi propaganda, Hilali stressed that the National Socialist regime had saved Germany from disastrous crisis, burglary, corruption, hunger, chaos, enemies of the nation abroad, and the "corrupting" Jews who "inflamed the fire" inside the country.[157]

For him, the Germans had borrowed the welfare system from Islam. He was impressed by the charitable work of the *Winterhilfswerk des Deutschen Volkes* (the National Socialist People's Welfare Organization) and its winter-help collection drive for the sake of needy people.[158] He considered taxation and the social welfare and pension system in Germany as primarily instituted to serve the people with no intention of any propaganda. It was only aimed at supporting poor families, fighting against monopoly and usury, and keeping the social balance in contrast to the "bloody" Bolshevism.[159]

Hilali shared with his Pan-Islamic peers an ambition of liberating all Muslims and Arabs from colonial powers under one nation. But it is noteworthy that he did not agree with the mainstream reformist Muslim political thinking that stressed an Islamic appeal for democracy by comparing it with *Shura*, and gave instead his preference for national socialist regimes as closer to Islam. He argued that democratic systems are based on "beautiful" elections in the first place. However, when a democratic government comes to power, it tries to manipulate votes of weak and naïve people for the following elections. Strikes within democratic systems easily lead to chaos and wasting of national money. In conclusion, democracy is, in his view, contradictory to Islam because of its "chaos and corruption," and the absence of a proper imam leadership in the community.[160] Hilali remarked that communist and autocratic systems, especially the communist Bolshevik model, were the worst type of governments for their "enslaving" of people and depriving them of their religion and money. Hilali seems to agree with the German organized anti-Bolshevik propaganda that Bolshevists lavishly spent their national income on propaganda, while their people were dying of hunger. He also added that the Jews were the force behind the communist system.[161]

Arabic Radio Berlin

Many of Hilali's above-mentioned reflections were later more clearly crystallized during his work in the Berlin Arabic Radio. The proofs for his qualification criteria for the job as a translator at this radio were beforehand examined by his German teachers, namely the above-mentioned Bernhard Moritz, Richard Hartmann, and the Swedish Arabist Walther Björkman, the editor of *Mitteilungen der Auslands-Hochschule an der Universität Berlin*. Together with three other Arab employees, Hilali accepted the position in mid-April 1939 after Kahle had fled to Great Britain due to the Nazi harassment to him and to his family. In the meantime, the propaganda department applied at the *Reichserziehungsministerium* (Reich Ministry of Education) for leave from his post at the University of Bonn.[162] According to his employment dossier in the Bundesarchiv, the monthly salary for this new function in the Wireless Service (*Der Drahtlose Dienst*) as a "translator and language specialist and advisor" was 550Reichsmark (RM). On May 9, 1939, Hilali signed a statement subjecting himself to the regulations of scrupulous performance of duties and commitment to obligations.[163] In the summer of 1939, the Secret State Police (*Geheime Staatpolizei*) screened him and reported that nothing negative was known about his political detriment (*politisch Nachteiliges*).[164] Finally, Hilali received a permit from the Reich Ministry of Education to move to Berlin.[165]

Later he became a broadcaster on the radio. In *Al-Fath*, now as a professional broadcaster in Europe, he continued to tell his readers about the usefulness of the radio power in modern times. He published a few of his speeches that he read on air in Berlin. Some of them were apolitical dealing with such topics as the Prophet's birthday (May 1939) and the significance of Prophet's traditions and ethics in the progress of Muslim life.[166]

Besides his anti-French speeches, Hilali sharply criticized Muslims for their laxity in defending Palestine. In those speeches he made use of Qur'anic citations related to the duty of *jihad* in Islam. His projection of such passages on the modern political state of Muslims was sometimes mixed with anti-Jewish sentiments, which fitted perfectly well in Nazi propaganda campaigns.[167] In one speech, he announced that Muslim collaborators with the French in north Africa were as bad as those who collaborated with the British and Jews in Palestine. "If the Jews had 'murdered' some of their Prophets in the past," he said, "those Muslim 'traitors' murder the divine laws by their acts."[168] Meanwhile, it should be emphasized that Radio Berlin had given Hilali a chance to fulfill his anti-imperial aspirations, due to its strategy of stigmatizing the interests of the Allies in the Middle East as "greedy imperialism," and "robbing the Arabs from their wealth and enslaving them." Allied leaders were mostly presented as "untrustworthy" and "decadent individuals" who were "controlled by the Jews."[169]

In a severely polemical series of speeches in July 1939 under the title "Prophetic Guidance Which Muslims Had Abandoned," Hilali launched a harsh attack on the increasing French, British, and Jewish power in the world. In his words, "the horn of the devil" had grown again, whereas the Prophetic traditions had disappeared in the Muslim life. The state of *Jahiliyya* (pre-Islamic ignorance) had replaced those traditions. Because of their negligence of *jihad*, Muslims had acquired a more miserable life than death. His harsh anti-Jewish words reflect his frustration of Arab and Muslim efforts in defending the Palestinian cause. He found that the Arabs in Palestine supporting the British and the Jews against their brethren by helping Jewish commissioners to sell Muslim lands and houses were as evil as the Jews themselves. In contrast, a contemporary Jew would neither kill his fellow Jew, nor confiscate his land.[170] In another radio speech, Hilali repeated that the Jews were able to confiscate a great part of the Holy Land not because of their military power, but due to their expenditure of huge amounts money in support of their common cause. If Muslims "had spent half of the money amounts they often lavishly spent on smoking and...own pleasures, the Jews would have never been able to buy a span of land in Palestine."[171]

Regretting or Justifying?

Hilali worked for Radio Berlin for almost three years. In early 1942, he left Germany and arrived in Spanish Morocco in March. Based on Hilali's published autobiography, Henri Lauzière maintained that his departure to his fatherland was rather secretive. For reasons that are not entirely clear, life in Berlin became more difficult for him after the outbreak of the war. Hilali admitted that he was on a mission at a request of Hajj Amin al-Husayni, who requested him to deliver an "oral message" to the Moroccan nationalist and leader of the National Reform Party 'Abd al-Khalik al-Turrays regarding their common anticolonial cause.[172] As Hilali was an Iraqi by nationality, and had no Moroccan passport at that time, Turrays provided him with a doctored document that had enabled him to enter his fatherland again. The Spanish authorities were alarmed by his arrival and put him under surveillance fearing his role in any secret contacts between the Germans and Moroccan nationalists.[173]

Hilali did not reveal what kind of message it was. However, a German political document suggested that this "message" had something to do with Husayni's plan to establish a center for Arab legions by establishing a German-Arab *Lehrabteilung* in north Africa after any German march to the region.[174] Turrays had been in contact with Husayni before Hilali's departure to Morocco. In a letter (November 14, 1941), Turrays assured the mufti that his National Reform Party and all nationalist organizations would be under Husayni's command and were "ready for any sacrifice."[175]

After his departure from Germany, Hilali had been keeping contact with Husayni, who was still active in Berlin during the war, through the German consul in Tetuán Herbert Georg Richter, who channeled money and propaganda to Moroccan nationalists in the French zone.[176] Hilali was said to have given information to German officials about the size of American and British propaganda in the Spanish zone.[177] It is also interesting to add that after the outbreak of the war, Richter tried to convince the Spanish authorities to adopt anti-Jewish measures in Tetuán. He also tried to entice Muslims against the Jews. But all his efforts failed, as the governor of the city and other Makhzan officials assisted the Jews against any attempt by Muslims and Germans to harm them.[178]

Many years later, Hilali recalled his memories about the German period in many places of his writing. He tried to justify his collaboration with the Nazis by confirming that he was never a "German agent," but a "defending agent" to the Moroccan cause.[179] In a discussion with the vice-consul of the British Consulate in Morocco (who was of Jewish Greek origin, according to Hilali), Hilali did not regret his anticolonial attacks that he had broadcasted on Radio Berlin, as he believed he should defend the rights of his country, just as the Britons tried to defend their country by collaborating with the French. Hilali was convinced that he did the right thing, since the enemy of the enemy was a friend.[180]

Hilali explained that due to his sincere commitment to that cause, he was sometimes obliged to face the danger of war and bombardment in Berlin on his way to the radio building outside Berlin in the metro at night and under the snow. He asserted that he was even obliged to pay the costs of translation and typewriting because the director of the station did not allow the broadcasting of any program before its authorization from four government offices, which he had to pay for himself.[181]

Germany was a fruitful station in Hilali's career, but he was sometimes obliged to justify his collaboration with the "notorious" side after the war. In an unpublished diary document, which he wrote in reaction to the trial of Nazi leaders in Nuremberg (October 22, 1946), Hilali supported the views of some of Nuremberg's critics that it was an invalid trial because it was a form of "victors' justice." Hilali wrote this document as a journal article in Arabic, but failed to publish it in any journal at that time. In his view, the trial was "unprincipled" and "partial," because the claimant was a witness and judge at the same time. It would have been fair if the British and French leaders also had been convicted for their crimes besides their German counterparts, he said.[182]

Hilali did not change his mind after the war regarding the perceived paradoxes of democracy, which the United States, Britain, and France started to propagate after the end of World War II. Freedom of religion and thought, which those nations boasted, was merely an illusion because Muslims under their rule were deprived of them. His intention of documenting his judgment was neither due to his feeling of loyalty nor any commitment to the Nazi *ihsan* (beneficence) to him during his stay in interwar Germany. What he saw from them was merely *isa'ah* (misdeed). Hilali was unfortunately silent about this kind of *isa'ah* that he encountered during his sojourn among the Nazis. As he did not completely trust Hitler's promises to the Arabs, Hilali now said that he wished Germany neither a total victory, nor a complete defeat. Even in his Nazi time, he was always worried that Germany would have tyrannized Muslims, if it had won the war. "[Fearing the German] defeat," he wrote, "was meant to strike a specific balance by which we [Muslims] could hit...[Europeans] with one other; and could therefore resist their injustice."[183]

CONCLUSION

In the above-mentioned analysis, we have tried to reconstruct the academic, intellectual, and propagandist political activities of a unique

Muslim reformist figure functioning during a changing course of actions in Nazi Germany. It is the study of a man in a world of a Pan-Islamic transnational collective action in interwar Europe. It has been clear that Hilali had a uniform anticolonial aim during his stay in the Third Reich.

After the war, Hilali turned to a more conservative *Salafi* trend. However, he did not disconnect himself from the Western academic life in the late 1940s and 1950s. His relationship with his German mentor Kahle remained solid. Hilali used to send Kahle his newly established journal *Lisan al-Din* from Tetuán. From his side, Kahle used to inform his old student about his sick wife, children, and his plan of publishing his book about the Nazification of University of Bonn. In 1948, Kahle had requested Hilali to help him find a publisher for one of his works in Morocco, Egypt, or Syria.[184] In the same year, Hilali published an edition of Ibn Daniyal's plays with an Arabic translation of Kahle's introduction in Baghdad in 1948.[185] In 1953–1954, Hilali was even invited as a guest lecturer at the University of Bonn. In his address to the Pakistan History Conference in Karachi (1956), Kahle still boasted about his Oriental Seminar and praised the contribution of Eastern scholars to it. "They were," he said, "of the greatest value and gave the atmosphere of the Institute a distinctive character, and I have remained on the best terms with them. I may mention here my friend Dr. Takieddin al-Hilali, from Morocco, a great Arabic scholar....We worked together for some years on very difficult Arabic texts with the greatest profit to both of us."[186] After many years, Kahle remained thankful to Curt Prüfer for having made it possible for him to make use of Hilali's knowledge.[187]

It is plausible to argue that due to his training in Germany, Hilali laid his emphasis on philology, and that his positivistic approach to history bolstered his scriptualist and linguistic approach to Islam and made it more persuasive.[188] We have seen, however, that Kahle on his part boasted about the new "excellent" knowledge introduced to him by his Moroccan disciple, which distinguished his work from that of his Orientalist colleague. Hilali's acceptance and defense of Moritz's "revisionist" exegesis of the Quranic Opening Sura in an Egyptian *Salafi* journal in Cairo was remarkable.

Nevertheless, other German Orientalists, such as Brockelmann, were not very enthusiastic about his academic qualities. The disagreement of German Orientalists regarding Hilali's scholarly quality should not be surprising. Kahle and Brockelmann responded differently to his works due to the simple fact that Kahle had for many years worked with non-Europeans (including many Jews) on the Cairo

Genizah project, as well as other projects. Brockelmann on the other hand was trained in a Eurocentric tradition of pure philology.

Reconsidering his role (together with other Arab nationalists) in the Arabic propaganda of Nazi Germany, one could venture to say that their collaboration was a product of its times. It was a continuation of the advent of Pan-Islamic anticolonial movements inside Europe with their self-proclaimed goals of liberating their colonized lands in the wider world politics. His polemical and pragmatic messages were produced in a period of highly charged and acute ideological nationalist divisions. This may be due to his "Occidentalist" point of view that did not inhibit him from talking about his work in the German Arab broadcasting service, and his views of Hitler and National Socialism. On the one hand, Hilali opposed racism, but he was not happy with at least one Jewish colleague.

Hilali's ideological consideration was noticeable. His main contributions to the Arab press and German broadcasts should not be dismissed from the project of the internationalization of the Pan-Islamic struggle against colonialism and the increasing Zionist movements in Palestine. In his pre-German period, Hilali aspired that the Arabs and Muslims should have their own radio waves in their anticolonial struggle. As he did not have any chance to participate in the radio in his early stay in Germany, he opted for the printing press as a medium for spreading the message among his readers regarding radio power. But when he got the chance to take part in it, he regularly articulated heavy opposition to the French colonialism in north Africa, and the "British Jewish" complot to destroy the Arab existence in Palestine.

In many places, Hilali stressed the idea of nationality and its racial resonances as he perceived them in the Nazi context. As a propagandist, he knew the needs of the latent and actual public opinion and the degree of intensity of the subjects he dealt with in his press articles and on radio. His pro-Axis sentiments were therefore reflections of a complex international political situation. However, his contributions to Berlin Arabic Radio expressed his religious beliefs and political ideals; the German propaganda machine had exploited his anti-Jewish sentiments to its maximum because it was in entire harmony with the German international interests.[189]

Notes

1. Peter Wien, "Coming to Terms with the Past," *International Journal of Middle East Studies* 42 (2010): 311–321.
2. Nathalie Clayer and Eric Germain, eds., *Islam in Inter-war Europe* (London: Hurst), 1–2.

3. Götz Nordbruch, "'Cultural Fusion' of Thought and Ambitions? Memory, Politics and the History of Arab–Nazi German Encounters," *Middle Eastern Studies* 47.1 (2011): 183–194.

4. J. Herf, *The Jewish Enemy: Nazi Propaganda during World War II and the Holocaust* (Harvard University Press, 2006); J. Herf, *Nazi Propaganda for the Arab World* (New Haven, CT: Yale University Press, 2009); J. Herf, "Nazi Germany's Propaganda Aimed at Arabs and Muslims During World War II and the Holocaust: Old Themes, New Archival Findings," *Central European History* 42 (2009): 709–736; Matthias Kuentzel, *Jihad and Jew-hatred: Islamism, Nazism and the Roots of 9/11* (New York: Telos Press Publishing, 2007); David G. Dalin et al., *Icon of Evil: Hitler's Mufti and the Rise of Radical Islam* (Transaction Publishers, 2009); K. M. Mallmann and M. Cüppers, *Halbmond und Hakenkreuz: Das Dritte Reich, die Araber und Palästina* (Darmstadt: Wissenschaftliche Buchgesellschaft, 2006).

5. Peter Wien, "The Culpability of Exile: Arabs in Nazi Germany," *Geschichte und Gesellschaft* 37 (2011): 332–358.

6. Wien, "Coming," 311–312. Cf. Israel Gershoni, "Egyptian Liberalism in an Age of 'Crisis of Orientation': Al Risala's Reaction to Fascism and Nazism, 1933–39," *International Journal of Middle East Studies* 31 (1999): 551–576; Israel Gershoni, "'Der verfolgte Jude.' Al-Hilals Reaktionen auf den Antisemitismus in Europa und Hitlers Machtergreifung," in *Blind für die Geschichte? Arabische Begegnungen mit dem Nationalsozialismus*, ed. Gerhard Höpp et al. (Berlin: Klaus Schwarz Verlag, 2004), 39–72.

7. See, for example, Israel Gershoni and James P. Jankowski, *Confronting Fascism in Egypt: Dictatorship versus Democracy in the 1930s* (Stanford: Stanford University Press, 2009).

8. Martin Kramer, *Islam Assembled* (New York: Colombia University Press, 1986), 159; Gerhard Höpp, and Gerdien Jonker, eds., *In fremder Erde: Zur Geschichte und Gegenwart der islamischen Bestattung in Deutschland* (Berlin: Verlag Das Arabische Buch, 1996); Gerhard Höpp, *Arabische und islamische Periodika in Berlin und Brandenburg 1915–1945: Geschichtlicher Abriß und Bibliographie* (Verlag Das Arabische Buch: Berlin, 1994); Gerhard Höpp, *Texte aus der Fremde. Arabische politische Publizistik in Deutschland, 1896–1945: Eine Bibliographie* (Berlin: Verlag Das Arabische Buch, 2000).

9. Wien, "The Culpability," 332.

10. Henri Lauzière, "The Evolution of the Salafiyya in the Twentieth Century through the Life and Thought of Taqi Al-Din Al-Hilali" (PhD dissertation, Georgetown University, 2008), 241.

11. The label is quoted from Lauzière, "The Evolution."

12. Nordbruch, "Cultural Fusion," 187.

13. Lauzière, "The Evolution," 88–89.

14. Taqi al-Din al-Hilali, *Al-Da'wa Ila Allah fi Aqtar Mukhtalifa* (Cairo: Maktabat al-Sahaba and Shariqa: Maktabat al-Tabi'in, 2003), 36, 40–41, 50–51, 131–132.

15. Stefan Wild, "National Socialism in the Arab Near East between 1933 and 1939," *Die Welt des Islams* 25 (1985): 126–173. Wild did not depend on *Al-Fath*, but on an Italian translation of the article in *Oriente Moderno* (1937). On its tenth anniversary, *Al-Fath* published a photo of Hilali, among other contributors, in his European dress with a comment that he, as a writer in the magazine, was like the "sun" that remains "sun" in the east or in the west with his "ripe, useful and enjoyable" contributions (*Al-Fath* 12.551 [July 26, 1937]: 25).

16. Lauzière, "The Evolution," 236–237.

17. Lauzière, "The Evolution," 245–249.

18. Lauzière, "The Evolution," 245–249.

19. Lauzière, "The Evolution," 244.

20. Lauzière, "The Evolution," 250.

21. Shakib Arslan, *Al-Sayyid Rashid Rida aw Ikha' Arba'in Sanah* (Damasacus, 1937), 433, 564–565.

22. E. Said, *Culture and Imperialism* (Vintage, 1994), xxii–xxiii.

23. F. Malti-Douglas, "In the Eyes of Others: The Middle Eastern Response and Reaction to Western Scholarship," *Comparative Civilizations Review* 13.14 (1985): 36–55.

24. Ronen Raz, "The Transparent Mirror: Arab Intellectuals and Orientalism, 1798–1950" (PhD dissertation, Princeton University, 1997), 107–108.

25. Raz, "The Transparent," 136.

26. Lauzière, "The Evolution," 243.

27. Lauzière, "The Evolution," 242.

28. Kramer, *Islam Assembled*, 144–146.

29. Hilali, unpublished dairy, "Min al-Zubayr ila la adri (From Zubayr to I-do-not-know-where)," 1936, Hilali family private papers.

30. Lauzière, "The Evolution," 242.

31. Lauzière, "The Evolution," 252.

32. Ursula Wokoeck, *German Orientalism: The Study of the Middle East and Islam from 1800 to 1945* (Taylor & Francis, 2009), 185–209; cf. Suzanne L. Marchand, *German Orientalism in the Age of Empire: Religion, Race, and Scholarship* (Washington, DC: German Historical Institute, 2009).

33. For more about him, see Donald M. McKale, *Curt Prüfer, German Diplomat from the Kaiser to Hitler* (Kent, OH: Kent State University Press, 1987).

34. Paul Kahle, "Curt Prüfer," *Zeitschrift der Deutschen Morgenländischen Gesellschaft* 111 (1961): 1–3.

35. Paul Kahle, *Three Shadow Plays*, with a critical apparatus by Derek Hopwood (Oxford: Gibb Memorial Trust, 1992), 3.

36. Lauzière, "The Evolution," 254–255.

37. According to Hilali, the quality of this edition was bad and contained many errors, because of the weak print techniques in India (T. al-Hilali, "Kitab al-Jamahir fi al-Jawahir lil-Biruni," *Al-Fath*

14.653 [May 11]: 6–7). For Krenkow, see Otto Spies, "Fritz Krenkow," *Der Islam* 31.2–3 (1956): 228–236.

38. See, for instance, Edward C. Sachau, *Alberuni's India: An Account of the Religion, Philosophy, Literature, Geography, Chronology, Astronomy, Customs, Laws and Astrology of India about A.D. 1030* (London: Kegan Paul, Trench and Trübner), 1910.

39. Hilali, "Kitab al-Jamahir", 7.

40. Hilali, "Kitab," 6.

41. Paul Kahle, *Bonn University in Pre-Nazi and Nazi Times (1929–1939): Experiences of a German Professor* (London: n.p., 1945), 28; H. B. Paksoy, "Basmachi Movement from within: Account of Zeki Velidi Togan," *Nationalities Papers* 23 (1995): 373–399.

42. Raz, "The Transparent," 69.

43. Kahle, *Bonn University*, 27.

44. Kahle, *Bonn University*, 29–30.

45. Kahle, *Bonn University*, 29.

46. Kahle, *Three Shadow*, 3.

47. Shmuel Moreh, "Review of *Three Shadow Plays* by Muhammad Ibn Daniyal; Paul Kahle," *Die Welt des Islams* 34.1 (1994): 126–129.

48. Original text: "Außerdem war es möglich, diesen Text mit Takieddin al-Hilali durchzusprechen, dem alten Freund aus der Bonner Zeit. Ein Futuwwa Text war der erste arabische Texte gewesen, der uns beschäftigt hatte, als Hilali im Herbst 1936 nach Bonn kam, nämlich das Futuwwa-Kapitel aus der Einleitung zu Biruni's Steinbuch." Paul Kahle, *Opera Minora: Festgabe zum 21. Januar 1956*, (Leiden, Netherlands: E. J. Brill, 1956), 216. Kahle was also impressed by Hilali's memorization of the Qur'an and that he was able to find any verse without any help of glossaries.

49. Kahle, *Opera*, 216.

50. Kahle, *Opera*, 217–219.

51. Paul Kahle, "The Arabic Shadow Play in Egypt," *The Journal of the Royal Asiatic Society of Great Britain and Ireland* 1 (1940): 21–34; Kahle, *Opera*, 300.

52. Cyrus Ali Zargar, "The Satiric Method of Ibn Daniyal: Morality and Anti-Morality in 'Tayf al-Khayal,'" *Journal of Arabic Literature* 37.1 (2006), 68–108.

53. Kahle, *Three Shadow*, 3–4.

54. Original text: "Er hat sich bei der Arbeit der wichtigen Mitarbeit eines ausgezeichneten arabischen Gelehrten, prof. Takieddin al-Hilaly, erfreuen können. Er hofft, demnächst den arabischen Text nebst Übersetzung herausgeben zu können." Jean Capart, ed., *Actes du XXe Congrès international des Orientalistes: Bruxelles, 5–10 Septembre 1938* (Louvain: Bureaux du Muséon, 1940), 325.

55. Marchand, *German Orientalism*, 490–492.

56. Marie Kahle, *What Would You Have Done? the Story of the Escape of the Kahle Family from Nazi-Germany* (London: Portsoken Press), 15.

57. Cf. John Mendel, *Legalizing the Holocaust, the Early Phase, 1933–1939* (Garland: Brustein, 1982); William Brustein, *Roots of Hate: Anti-Semitism in Europe before the Holocaust* (Cambridge: Cambridge University Press, 2003).

58. T. Al- Hilali, "Ahl Uruba wa al-Tadayyun," *Al-Fath* 12.559 (July 23, 1937): 9.

59. Lauzière, "The Evolution," 252.

60. Typescript, no date, family archive. According to Hilali, Jakobi died later after a British bombardment that destroyed his house.

61. Lauzière, "The Evolution," 252–353.

62. See his thesis, Taki al-Din al-Hilali, *Die Einleitung zu al-Biruni's Steinbuch* (Leipzig: O. Harrassowitz, 1941).

63. Lauzière, "The Evolution," 252–353; Taqi ed-Din al-Hilali, "Die Kasten in Arabien," *Die Welt des Islams* 22 (1940): 102–110.

64. Lauzière, "The Evolution," 261.

65. As quoted in Lauzière, "The Evolution," 261.

66. P. Kahle, "Al-Biruni," *Journal of the Asiatic Society of Pakistan* 1.1 (1956): 22.

67. Lauzière, "The Evolution," 260–261.

68. T. al-Hilali, "Latifa fi Tafsir al-Basmala," *Al-Fath* 14.654, 28 Rabi' al-Awwal 1358 (May 18, 1939): 14.

69. Wild, "National Socialism," 139.

70. Hilali, "Latifa," 14. In his article in *Al-Fath*, Hilali mentioned that Moritz had shown him a manuscript of a Persian translation of the *Fatiha* in which the word was translated as "loving." This means that the Arabs at this time understood the word in this way. When Hilali showed the German Orientalist his article on the issue, Moritz corrected him by saying that *al-Fatiha* appeared on the papyrus not in Persian, but in Greek translation. Ibid, 10.

71. Abu al-Samh, "Falsafa fi al-Basmala," *Al-Fath* 14.657, 20 Rabi' al-Akhar 1358 (June 9, 1939): 19–21.

72. T. al- Hilali, "Latifa fi ma'na al-Rahim," *Al-Fath* 14.662, 25 Jumada al-Ula 1358 (July 13, 1939): 10.

73. Lauzière, "The Evolution," 238.

74. T. al- Hilali, "Laysa 'indi Harim," *Al-Fath* 12.594, 23 Muharram 1357 (March 26, 1938):, 6–8.

75. Hilali, "Laysa," 7.

76. Hilali, "Laysa," 6.

77. Hilali, "Laysa," 6.

78. Hilali, "Laysa," 7.

79. Hilali, "Laysa," 7.

80. Hilali, "Laysa," 8.

81. Hilali, "Laysa," 8.

82. Hilali, "Laysa," 9. Hilali cited the ideas of the British convert Muhammad Marmaduke Pickthall (1875–1936) about the better status of Muslim women than their Western counterparts; see

P. Clark, *Marmaduke Pickthall: British Muslim* (Quartet Books, 1986).

83. Hilali, "Laysa," 8.
84. T. al-Hilali, "Min 'Aja'ib Ahkam al-Qissisin," *Al-Fath* 13.640, 20 Dhu al-Hijja 1357 (February 10, 1938): 6. Hilali maintained that there were 3,000 out of 100,000 inhabitants of Bonn, who were excommunicated from the church. Those people were always ashamed and faced trouble in the society. His landlady told him that she regretted her visit to a good friend in hospital after having known that she was excommunicated from the church. Because his landlady conveyed to him that she disliked dealing with disbelievers, Hilali described her as a "stubbornly religious and nationalistic person."
85. Hilali, "Min 'Aja'ib," 6.
86. T. al-Hilali, "Al-Rajul al-Abyad wa al-Rajul al-Mulawwan: Muhawarah bayna Imra'ah Amrikiyya wa rajul Jirmani," *Al-Fath* 11.549, 2 Rabi al-Awwal, 1356 (May 13, 1937): 10–11.
87. Hilali," Al-Rajul," 10–11.
88. Hilali," Al-Rajul," 12.
89. T. al-Hilali, "Dawa' al-Shakkin wa Qami' al-Mushakkikin 8," *Da'wat al-Haqq*, 4.1 (October 1960): 10–11.
90. Hilali, "Dawa' 8," 11.
91. Hilali, "Ahl Uruba," 9.
92. Hilali, "Ahl Uruba," 7.
93. Hilali, "Ahl Uruba," 7.
94. Hilali, "Ahl Uruba," 7.
95. Hilali, "Ahl Uruba," 8.
96. The system was embodied in the Weimar Constitution of 1919 and the Basic Law of the Federal Republic of Germany in 1949. See the International Center for the Non-Profit Law, http://www.icnl.org/knowledge/pubs/Percentage_laws_Report.pdf, accessed March 12, 2010.
97. Hilali, "Ahl Uruba," 8.
98. Hilali, "Ahl Uruba," 8–9.
99. Marie Kahle, *What*, 19.
100. Hilali, "Ahl Uruba," 8–9.
101. Hilali, "Ahl Uruba," 9.
102. T. Hilali, "Al-Tara'iq al-Qidad wa 'Awaqibaha al-Wakhima, *Al-Fath* 12.580, 13 Shawwal 1356 (December 16, 1937): 8.
103. T. al-Hilali, "Hajimun Hajam Fa Duhira wa Inhazm," *Al-Fath* 12.592, 8 al-Muharram 1357 (March 11, 1938): 7.
104. Hilali, "Hajimun," 6.
105. Hilali, "Hajimun," 7.
106. T. al-Hilali, "Shurb al-Khamr fi Uruba Mahlakah Kama fi Ghayriha," *Al-Fath* 13.622 13 Sha'ban 1357 (October 7, 1938): 6. It might be interesting to know that "Imran had earlier requested Shakib Arslan, through Rida's magazine *Al-Manar*, to answer the question

of the causes of Muslim decline as compared to the progress of the Western world. Arslan promptly answered the question in the form of a well-known treatise tackling the reasons why Muslim nations stagnated while the others experienced rapid progress." Arslan, 1349/1930–1931. About Imran's life, see, Martin Van Bruinessen, "Basyuni Imran," *Dictionnaire biographique des savants et grandes figures du monde musulman périphérique, du XIXe siècle à nos jours* (Paris: CNRS-EHESS, 1992), 134–141.

107. Hilali, "Shurb," 6.
108. Hilali, "Shurb," 6.
109. Hilali, "Shurb," 7.
110. Hilali, "Shurb", 7–8.
111. Herf, "Nazi Germany's," 709–736.
112. Nordbruch, "'Cultural Fusion,'" 188.
113. Lauzière, "The Evolution," 257.
114. Lauzière, "The Evolution," 258.
115. Lauzière, "The Evolution," 258.
116. Cf. Umar Ryad, "A Printed Muslim 'Lighthouse' in Cairo *al-Manar*'s Early Years, Religious Aspiration and Reception (1898–1903)," *Arabica* 56 (2009): 27–60.
117. T. al-Hilali, "Ta'liqat min Almaniya 'ala al-Idha'a al-Lasilkiyya," *Al-Fath* 12.522, 24 Rabi al-Awwal, 1356 (June 4, 1937): 6–7.
118. T. al-Hilali, "Hadith Tarif fi Ifsad al-Idha'at," *Al-Fath* 13.603, 26 Rabi' al-Awwal 1357 (May 27, 1938): 6.
119. Hilali, "Ta'liqat," 6–7.
120. Julian Hale, *Radio Power: Propaganda and International Broadcasting* (Philadelphia: Temple University Press, 1975), x.
121. T. a-Hilali, "Idha'at al-Qur'an min Misr wa sama'uh fi Uruba," *Al-Fath* 11.541, 5 Muharram 1356 (March 18, 1937): 6–7.
122. Hilali, "Ta'liqat," 6–7. Hilali was aware that some of his Muslim readers disliked listening to music or even prohibited it.
123. Hilali, *Al-Fath*, 12.589: 7. He complained about the weakness of the wave of the Egyptian radio because it was always received on a middle wave beside Radio Brussels, which always disturbed its quality. Hilali ironically stated that he received it at the same time of Brussels' broadcasting for one hour, but this was like a "miracle of a [Sufi] *wali*."
124. Hilali, "Ta'liqat," 6.
125. Hilali, "Hadith," 6. See, Jane M. J. Robbins, *Tokyo Calling: Japanese Overseas Radio Broadcasting 1937–1945* (Fucecchio: European Press Academic, 2001).
126. Hilali, "Hadith," 6. Hilali referred here to the Nazi conferring of the status of Honorary Aryan (Ehrenarier) to the Japanese people due to its great ancient civilization. Cf. Philip Towle (et al.) *Japanese Prisoners of War* (Continuum International Publishing Group, 2000), 128–129.
127. Hilali, "Hadith," 7.

128. Hilali, "Hadith," 6.
129. T. Hilali, "Khutbat Sultan Jimma fi Idha'at Rumiyya al-'Arabiyya: Zalltuh al-Kubra," *Al-Fath* 13.610, 16 Jumada al-Ula 1357 (July 14, 1938): 6–7. About the Kingdom of Jimma, see, for instance, Herbert S. Lewis, *A Galla Monarchy: Jimma Abba Jifar, Ethiopia, 1830–1932* (Madison, WI et al.: The University of Wisconsin Press, 1965); Mockler Anthony, *Haile Selassie's War* (Oxford: Signal Books, 2003).
130. Hilali, "Khutbat," 7.
131. Hilali, "Hadith," 6–7.
132. Hilali, "Hadith," 6.
133. T. al-Hilali, "Chamberlain wa Daladier, Nabiyyan Rasulan aw Qa'iman Maqam Rasul, Riwaya Radio Paris 'an Sahifat al-Zahra al-Tunisiyya," *Al-Fath* 13/626, 11 Ramadan 1357 (November 4, 1938): 6.
134. Hilali, "Chamberlain," 6.
135. T. Hilali, "Waqahat al-Isti'mar al-Faransi la Nihayat laha," *al-'Alam* (May 10, 1939): 4.
136. Hilali, "Chamberlain," 9.
137. Hilali, "Chamberlain," 9.
138. T. al- Hilali, "Al-Radio al-'Arabi al-Hurr," *Al-Fath* 13.646, 2 Safar 1358 (March 23, 1939): 10.
139. T. al- Hilali, "Hadiyya Li Qurra' al-Fath: Fukahat Adabiyya," *Al-Fath* 13.27, 18 Ramadan 1357 (November 11, 1938): 10–11. For more about this, see Tahar Melligi, "Ramadan 1938, naissance de Radio-Tunis." Available at http://www.lapresse.tn/index.php?opt =15&categ=4&news=35186; "Il y a 70 ans, la Radio voyait le jour," at http://www.lapresse.tn/index.php?opt=15&categ=4&news=74068, accessed March 27, 2010.
140. Hilali, "Hadiyya," 11.
141. Hilali, "Hadiyya," 11.
142. T. Hilali, "Makidah Faransiyya Jadida Yuridu al-Faransiyyun Tajribatiha fi Tunis," *Al-Fath* 13.643, 11 Muharram 1357 (March 14, 1938): 11–12.
143. T. Hilali, "Khawatir wa Sawanih fi al-Idha'a," *Al-Fath* 13.629, 2 Shawwal 1357 (November 24, 1938): 6–7.
144. T. Hilali, "Radio Surya al-Kubra," *Al-Fath* 13.644, 18 Muharram 1358 (March 10, 1939): 6–7; "Yasqut al-Intidab, Yasqut al-Isti'mar," *Al-Fath* 13.645, 25 Muharram 1358 (March 17, 1939): 8–9.
145. Hilali, "Yasqut," 8–9.
146. Hilali, "Yasqut," 10.
147. Hilali, "Yasqut," 11.
148. Francis R. Nicosia, *The Third Reich & the Palestine Question* (Transaction Publishers, 2000), 175.
149. T. al-Hilali, "Biritaniya tatharra al-'Adl Bi Za'miha Bayna al-Khusum," *Al-Fath* 12.593, 15 Muharram 1357 (March 18, 1938): 10. See Penny

Sinanoglou, "British Plans for the Partition of Palstine 1929–1938," *The Historical Journal* 52 (2009): 131–152; Lukasz Hirszowicz, "Nazi Germany and the Palestine Partition Plan," *Middle Eastern Studies* 1.1 (October 1964): 40–65.

150. T. al-Hilali, "Ya Lillah Li al-Asra al-Dhina la Nasir Lahum: Filistin, Iskadrūnah Shamal Ifriqiya," *Al-Fath* 13.625, 4 Ramadan 1357 (October 28, 1938): 10.

151. http://www.calvin.edu/academic/cas/gpa/booklet3.htm, accessed April 2, 2010.

152. T. Hilali, "al-Wataniyya al-Sadiqa," *Al-Fath* 13.640, 20 Dhu al-Hijja 1357 (February 10, 1939): 14–15.

153. Lorna L. Waddington, *Hitler's Crusade: Bolshevism and the Myth of the International Jewish Conspiracy* (London: IB Tauris, 2007).

154. Robert H. Whealey, *Hitler and Spain: The Nazi Role in the Spanish Civil War, 1936–1939* (Lexington: University Press of Kentucky, 2005), 95.

155. T. Hilali, "Al-Hadhari al-Hadhari min al-Dasa'is al-Bolshafiyya," *Al-Fath* 11.542, 12 Muharram 1356 (March 25, 1937): 10.

156. Hilali, "Al-Tara'iq," 6; Hilali, "Al-Hadhari," 11–12; "Al-Shuyu'ya A'zam La'nat Hadha al-'Asr," *Al-Fath* 12.581, 20 Shawwal 1356 (December 23, 1937): 6.

157. T. al-Hilali, "Kuhm al-Islam: al-Hukm al-Sha'abi, al-Hukm al-Dimuqrati, al-Hukm al-Shiyu'i, al-Huk al-Istibdadi Ayyuha Aslah," *Al-Fath* 11.545, 4 Safar 1356 (April 16, 1937): 6–7.

158. See, Herwart Vorländer, "NS-Volkswohlfahrt und Winterhilfswerk des Deutschen Volkes," *Vierteljahrshefte für Zeitgeschichte* 34 (1986): 341–380; Florian Tennstedt, "Wohltat und Interesse: Das Winterhilfswerk des Deutschen Volkes: Die Weimarer Vorgeschichte und ihre Instrumentalisierung durch das NS-Regime," *Geschichte und Gesellschaft* 13 (1987): 157–180.

159. Hilali, "Kuhm," 7.

160. Hilali, "Kuhm," 7.

161. Hilali, "Kuhm," 7.

162. Abteilung IVA, Der Drahtlose Dienst, IVA 4078/Pers/318, April 17, 1939, Budesarchiv R. 55/24211—15.3.1896. Other names were Abdin Bey, Riad, and Junis Bahri.

163. May 9, 1939. Budesarchiv R. 55/24211—15.3.1896.

164. August 7, 1939. Budesarchiv R. 55/24211—15.3.1896.

165. May 26, 1939. Budesarchiv R. 55/24211—15.3.1896.

166. T. al-Hilali, "Al-Mahajja al-Bayda: Muhadara La Silkiyya min Berlin," *Al-Fath* 14.653, 21 Rabi al-Awwal, 1358 (May 11, 1939): 20–21.

167. T. al-Hilali, "Al-Hadi al-Nabawi al-Ladhi dayya'uhu al-Mislimūn III," *Al-Fath* 14.667, 2 Rajab 1358 (August 18, 1939): 7–8.

168. Hilali, "Al-Hadi," 8–9.

169. S. Arsenian, "Wartime Propaganda in the Middle East," *Middle East Journal* 2.4 (1948): 420–421.

150 ❖ UMAR RYAD

170. T. al- Hilali, "al-Hadi al-Nabawi al-Ladhi dayya'uhu al-Mislimun I," *Al-Fath* 14.664, Jumada al-Akhira 1358 (August 1939): 8–9.
171. T. al- Hilali, "al-Hadi al-Nabawi al-Ladhi dayya'uhu al-Mislimun II," *Al-Fath* 14.666, 24 Jumada al-Akhira 1358 (August 10, 1939): 8. Hilali's anticolonial radio speeches included a defense of Shakib Arslan against a campaign by the French radio Paris Mondial in 1939. The prince was criticized for his political failure and "opportunism." The French radio recalled early accusations against Arslan because of his former collaboration with Fascist Italy in return for money in 1935. Kramer, *Islam Assembled*, 148. T. al- Hilali, "Al-Amir Shakib Arslan bayna Almaniya wa Faransa," *al-ʾAlam* (July 19, 1939).
172. Lauzière, "The Evolution," 265; Hilali, *al-Daʾwa*, 40–41.
173. Hilali, *al-Daʾwa*, 36.
174. "Weiterleitung der Post für den Grossmufti," Politisches Archiv Auswärtiges Amt, Handakten Ettel Grossmufti, R 27328—vom 1943-bis 1944.
175. "Weiterleitung der Post für den Grossmufti," Politisches Archiv Auswärtiges Amt, Handakten Ettel Grossmufti, R 27324, 1941, 304509.
176. Stanley G. Payne, *Franco and Hitler: Spain, Germany, and World War II* (New Haven: Yale University Press, 2008), 67 and 106–107. See also, Norman J. W. Goda, "Franco's Bid for Empire: Spain, Germany, and the Western Mediterranean in World War II," *Mediterranean Historical Review* 13.1–2 (2008): 168–194.
177. "Weiterleitung der Post für den Grossmufti," Politisches Archiv Auswärtiges Amt, Handakten Ettel Grossmufti, R 27324, 1942, 304507.
178. Michael M. Laskier, *North African Jewry in the Twentieth Century: The Jews of Morocco, Tunisia, and Algeria* (New York and London: NYU Press, 1994), 66.
179. Hilali, *al-Daʾwa*, 51.
180. Hilali, *al-Daʾwa*, 132.
181. Hilali, *al-Daʾwa*, 132–33.
182. Hilali, MS, October 22, 1946, family archive.
183. Hilali, MS, October 22, 1946, family archive.
184. Letters, Paul Kahle, August 6, 1946, Oxford; and March 10, 1948, Hilali's family archive, Morocco.
185. T. al- Hilali, *Thalathat Masrahiyyat ʾArabiyya muththilat fi al-Qurun al-wusta: wadaʾaha Ibn Daniyal al-Mawsili yuqddimuha ilayha al-ʾAlim Professor Kahle* (Baghdad, 1948), as quoted in Kahle, *Three Shadow*, 29.
186. Paul Kahle, "Muslim Contribution to Scholarship: Past, Present and Future," Address given at the Sixth session of the Pakistan History Conference (Karachi, 1956), 8–9.
187. Kahle, "Curt Pruefer."
188. Lauzière, "The Evolution," 241.
189. Arsenian, "Wartime," 417–429.

References

Abdullah, M. S. *Geschichte des Islams in Deutschland.* Graz: Verlag Styria, 1981.

Abteilung IVA, Der Drahtlose Dienst, IVA 4078/Pers/318, April 17, 1939, Budesarchiv R. 55/24211—March 15, 1896.

Abteilung IVA, Der Drahtlose Dienst, IVA 4078/Pers/318, May 9, 1939, Budesarchiv R. 55/24211—March 15, 1896.

Abteilung IVA, Der Drahtlose Dienst, IVA 4078/Pers/318, May 26, 1939, Budesarchiv R. 55/24211—March 15, 1896.

Abteilung IVA, Der Drahtlose Dienst, IVA 4078/Pers/318, August 7, 1939, Budesarchiv R. 55/24211—March 15, 1896.

Al-'Alam (July 19, 1939).

Al-Fath, various articles, 1936–1942.

Al-Shabab (June 23, 1937): 3.

Al-Shabab (December 29, 1937) : 4.

Anthony, Mockler. *Haile Selassie's War.* Oxford: Signal Books, 2003.

Arsenian, S. "Wartime Propaganda in the Middle East." *Middle East Journal* 2.4 (1948): 420–421.

Arslan, Shakib. *Al-Sayyid Rashid Rida aw Ikha Arbain Sanah.* Damascus: Ibn Zaydun, 1937.

———. *Li-madha Ta'akhkhara al-Muslimun wa li-madha Taqaddama Ghayruhum.* Cairo: Matba'at al-Manar, 1930–1931.

———. "Une Soirée au Club Arabe de Berlin." *La Nation Arabe* 18–19 (1938): 1005.

Biruni Muhammad b. Ahmad, al. *The chronology of ancient nations: an English version of the Arabic text of the Athár-ul-bákiya of Albírúní or "Vestiges of the past": coll. and reduced to writing by the author in A.H. 390–1, A.D.1000*, translated and edited, with notes and index, by Eduard Sachau. London: W. H. Allen, 1879.

———. *Kitab al- Jamahir*, edited by S. Krenkow. Deccan: Haydarabad, 1936.

Brustein, William. *Roots of Hate: Anti-Semitism in Europe before the Holocaust.* Cambridge: Cambridge University Press, 2003.

Capart, Jean, ed. *Actes du XXe Congrès international des Orientalistes: Bruxelles, 5–10 Septembre 1938.* Louvain, Belgium: Bureaux du Muséon, 1940.

Choueiri, Youssef. *Arab Nationalism: A History.* London: Wiley-Blackwell, 2000.

Clark, P. *Marmaduke Pickthall: British Muslim.* London: Quartet Books, 1986.

Clayer, Nathalie and Eric Germain, eds. *Islam in Inter-war Europe.* London: Hurst, 2008.

Dalin, David G. et al. *Icon of Evil: Hitlers Mufti and the Rise of Radical Islam.* New Brunswick, NJ: Transaction, 2009.

Davis, Marni. "'No Whisky Amazons in the Tents of Israel': American Jews and the Gilded Age Temperance Movement." *American Jewish History* 94.3 (2008): 143–173.

Dawn, C. Ernest. "An Arab Nationalist View of World Politics and History in the Interwar Period: Darwish al-Miqdadi." In *The Great Powers of the Middle East*, edited by Uriel Dann, 355–369. New York: Holmes & Meier, 1988.

Ende, Werner. "Sollen Frauen schreiben lernen? Eine innerislamische Debatte und ihre Widerspiegelung in *Al-Manär*." In *Gedenkschrift Wolfgang Reuschel: Akten des III. Arabistischen Kolloquiums*, edited by Dieter Bellmann, 49–57. Leipzig: Franz Steiner, 1994.

Gershoni, Israel. "'Der verfolgte Jude.' Al-Hilals Reaktionen auf den Antisemitismus in Europa und Hitlers Machtergreifung." In *Blind für die Geschichte? Arabische Begegnungen mit dem Nationalsozialismus*, edited by G. Höpp et al., 39–72. Berlin: Klaus Schwarz Verlag, 2004.

———. "Egyptian Liberalism in an Age of 'Crisis of Orientation': Al Risala's Reaction to Fascism and Nazism, 1933–39." *International Journal of Middle East Studies* 31 (1999): 551–576.

Gershoni, Israel and James P. Jankowski. *Confronting Fascism in Egypt: Dictatorship versus Democracy in the 1930s*. Stanford: Stanford University Press, 2009.

Goda, Norman J. W. "Franco's Bid for Empire: Spain, Germany, and the Western Mediterranean in World War II." *Mediterranean Historical Review* 13.1–2 (2008): 168–194.

Hale, Julian. *Radio Power: Propaganda and International Broadcasting*. Philadelphia: Temple University Press, 1975.

Hasanain, Fu'ad. *al-Adab al-Yahudi al-Muasir*. Cairo: Ma'had al-Buhuth wa al-Dirasat al-Arabiyya, 1972.

———. *al-Mujtama' al-Israili Hatta Tashriduh*. Cairo: Ma'had al-Dirasat al-'Arabiyya, 1966.

———. *Min al-Adab al-Ibri*. Cairo: The Arab League, 1963.

Heineman, Elizabeth D. *What Difference Does a Husband Make?: Women and Marital Status in Nazi and Postwar Germany*. Berkeley: University of California Press, 2003.

Herf, J. *The Jewish Enemy: Nazi Propaganda during World War II and the Holocaust*. Cambridge, MA: Belknap Press of Harvard University Press, 2006.

———. "Nazi Germany's Propaganda Aimed at Arabs and Muslims during World War II and the Holocaust: Old Themes, New Archival Findings." *Central European History* 42 (2009): 709–736.

———. *Nazi Propaganda for the Arab World*. New Haven, CT: Yale University Press, 2009.

Hilali, Taqi ed-Din al-. "Al-Amir Shakib Arslan bayna Almaniya wa Faransa." *al-'Alam* (July 19, 1939).

———. *al-Da'wa Ila Allah fi Aqtar Mukhtalifah*. Cairo: Maktabat al-Sahaba and Shariqa, 2003.

———. "Dawa' al-Shakkin wa Qami' al-Mushakkikin 7." *Da'wat al-Haqq* 3–10 (July 1960): 11.

———. "Dawa' al-Shakkin wa Qami' al-Mushakkikin 8." *Da'wat al-Haqq* 4–1 (October 1960): 10–11.

———. *Die Einleitung zu al-Biruni's Steinbuch.* Leipzig, Germany: O. Harrassowitz, 1941.

———. "Die Kasten in Arabien." *Die Welt des Islams* 22 (1940): 102–110.

———. "Khutbat Daladier Dhahabat Adraj al-Riyah." *al-'Alam* (May 24, 1939).

———. "Min al-Zubayr ila la adri (From Zubayr to I-Do-Not-Know-Where)." Unpublished dairy, family private papers, 1936.

———. "Min Mahazil al-Ist'mar wa Akadhibih." *al-Shabab* (November 16, 1938).

———. *Thalathat Masrahiyyat 'Arabiyya muththilat fi al-Qurun al-wusta: wada'aha Ibn Daniyal al-Mawsili yuqddimuha ilayha al-'Alim Professor Kahle.* Baghdad: n.p., 1948.

———. "Waqahat al-Isti'mar al-Faransi la Nihayat laha." *al-'Alam* (May 10, 1939).

Hilali, Taqi ed-Din al- et al. *Kitāb al-Futuwwa.* Baghdad: n.p., 1958.

Hirszowicz, Lukasz. "Nazi Germany and the Palestine Partition Plan." *Middle Eastern Studies* 1.1 (October 1964): 40–65.

Höpp, G. *Arabische und islamische Periodika in Berlin und Brandenburg 1915–1945: Geschichtlicher Abriß und Bibliographie.* Berlin: Verlag Das Arabische Buch, 1994.

———. *Texte aus der Fremde. Arabische politische Publizistik in Deutschland, 1896–1945. Eine Bibliographie.* Berlin: Verlag Das Arabische Buch, 2000.

Höpp, G. and G. Jonker. *In fremder Erde. Zur Geschichte und Gegenwart der islamischen Bestattung in Deutschland.* Berlin: Verlag Das Arabische Buch, 1996.

Kahle, Marie. *What Would You Have Done?: The Story of the Escape of the Kahle Family from Nazi-Germany.* London: Portsoken Press, 1945.

Kahle, P. "Al-Biruni," *Journal of the Asiatic Society of Pakistan* 1.1 (1956): 22

Kahle, Paul. "The Arabic Shadow Play in Egypt." *The Journal of the Royal Asiatic Society of Great Britain and Ireland* 1 (1940): 21–34.

———. *Bonn University in Pre-Nazi and Nazi Times (1929–1939). Experiences of a German Professor.* London: n.p., 1945.

———. "Muslim Contribution to Scholarship: Past, Present and Future." *Address given at the Sixth session of the Pakistan History Conference.* Karachi, 1956, 8–9.

———. *Opera Minora: Festgabe zum 21. Januar 1956.* Leiden, Netherlands: E. J. Brill, 1956.

———. *Three Shadow Plays*, with a critical apparatus by Derek Hopwood. Oxford: Gibb Memorial Trust, 1992.

Klieman, Aaron S. "In the Public Domain: The Controversy over Partition for Palestine." *Jewish Social Studies* 42.2 (1980): 147–164.

Kramer, Martin. *Islam Assembled.* New York: Colombia University Press, 1986.

Kuentzel, Matthias. *Jihad and Jew-hatred: Islamism, Nazism and the Roots of 9/11*. New York: Telos Press, 2007.

Laskier, Michael M. *North African Jewry in the Twentieth Century: The Jews of Morocco, Tunisia, and Algeria*. New York and London: NYU Press, 1994.

Lauzière, Henri. "The Evolution of the Salafiyya in the Twentieth Century through the Life and Thought of Taqi Al-Din Al-Hilali." Unpublished PhD dissertation, Georgetown University, 2008.

Lewis, Herbert S. *A Galla Monarchy: Jimma Abba Jifar, Ethiopia, 1830–1932*. Madison: The University of Wisconsin Press, 1965.

Mallmann, K. M. and M. Cüppers. *Halbmond und Hakenkreuz. Das Dritte Reich, die Araber und Palästina*. Darmstadt, Germany: Wissenschaftliche Buchgesellschaft, 2006.

Malti-Douglas, F. "In the Eyes of Others: The Middle Eastern Response and Reaction to Western Scholarship." *Comparative Civilizations Review* 13.14 (1985): 36–55.

Marchand, Suzanne L. *German Orientalism in the Age of Empire: Religion, Race, and Scholarship*. Washington, DC: German Historical Institute, 2009.

Marcus, Harold G. *Haile Sellassie I*. Berkeley: University of California Press, 1987.

McKale, Donald M. *Curt Prüfer, German Diplomat from the Kaiser to Hitler*. Kent, OH: Kent State University Press, 1987.

Mendel, John. *Legalizing the Holocaust, the Early Phase, 1933–1939*. New York: Garland, 1982.

Moreh, Shmuel. "Review of *Three Shadow Plays* by Muhammad Ibn Daniyal; Paul Kahle." *Die Welt des Islams* 34.1 (1994): 126–129.

Mosley, Leonard. *Haile Selassie: The Conquering Lion*. London: Weidenfeld and Nicholson, 1964.

Mouton, Michelle. *From Nurturing the Nation to Purifying the Volk: Weimar and Nazi Family Policy, 1918–1945*. Cambridge and New York: Cambridge University Press, 2007.

Nicosia, Francis R. *The Third Reich & the Palestine Question*. New Brunswick, NJ: Transaction, 2000.

Nordbruch, Götz. "'Cultural Fusion' of Thought and Ambitions? Memory, Politics and the History of Arab–Nazi German Encounters." *Middle Eastern Studies* 47.1 (2011): 183–194

Paksoy, H. B. "Basmachi Movement from Within: Account of Zeki Velidi Togan." *Nationalities Papers* 23 (1995): 373–399.

Payne, Stanley G. *Franco and Hitler: Spain, Germany, and World War II*. New Haven: Yale University Press, 2008.

Pinney, Thomas. *A History of Wine in America: From Prohibition to the Present*, 2 vols. Berkeley: University of California Press, 2005.

Raz, Ronen. "The Transparent Mirror: Arab Intellectuals and Orientalism, 1798–1950." PhD dissertation, Princeton University, 1997.

Rizvi, Sayyid Muhammad. "Muhibb Al-Din Al-Khatib: A Portrait of a Salafi-Arabist (1886–1969)." MA dissertation, Simon Fraser University, 1991.

Robbins, Jane M. J. *Tokyo Calling: Japanese Overseas Radio Broadcasting 1937–1945*. Fucecchio, Italy: European Press Academic Pub, 2001.

Ryad, Umar. "A Printed Muslim 'Lighthouse' in Cairo *al-Manar*'s Early Years, Religious Aspiration and Reception (1898–1903)." *Arabica* 56 (2009): 27–60.

Sachau, Edward C. *Alberunis India: An Account of the Religion, Philosophy, Literature, Geography, Chronology, Astronomy, Customs, Laws and Astrology of India about A.D. 1030*. London: Kegan Paul, Trench and Trübner, 1910.

Said, E. *Culture and Imperialism*. London: Vintage, 1994.

Sinanoglou, Penny. "British Plans for the Partition of Palestine 1929–1938." *The Historical Journal* 52 (2009): 131–152.

Spies, Otto. "Fritz Krenkow." *Der Islam* 31.2–3 (1956): 228–236.

Tennstedt, Florian. "Wohltat und Interesse: Das Winterhilfswerk des Deutschen Volkes: Die Weimarer Vorgeschichte und ihre Instrumentalisierung durch das NS-Regime." *Geschichte und Gesellschaft* 13 (1987): 157–180.

Van Bruinessen, Martin. "Basyuni Imran." *Dictionnaire biographique des savants et grandes figures du monde musulman périphérique, du XIXe siècle à nos jours*. Paris: CNRS-EHESS, 1992.

Vorländer, Herwart "NS-Volkswohlfahrt und Winterhilfswerk des Deutschen Volkes." *Vierteljahrshefte für Zeitgeschichte* 34 (1986): 341–380.

Waddington, Lorna L. "The Anti-Komintern and Nazi Anti-Bolshevik Propaganda in the 1930s." *Journal of Contemporary History* 42.4 (2007): 573–594.

———. *Hitler's Crusade: Bolshevism and the Myth of the International Jewish Conspiracy*. London: IB Tauris, 2007.

Weiterleitung der Post für den Grossmufti, Politisches Archiv Auswärtiges Amt, Hankakten Ettel Grossmufti, R 27328—vom 1943-bis 1944.

Weiterleitung der Post für den Grossmufti, Politisches Archiv Auswärtiges Amt, Hankakten Ettel Grossmufti, R. 27324, 1941, 304509.

Weiterleitung der Post für den Grossmufti, Politisches Archiv Auswärtiges Amt, Hankakten Ettel Grossmufti, R. 27324, 1942, 304507.

Whealey, Robert H. *Hitler and Spain: The Nazi Role in the Spanish Civil War, 1936–1939*. Lexington: University Press of Kentucky, 2005.

Wien, Peter. "Coming to Terms with the Past." *International Journal of Middle East Studies* 42 (2010): 311–321.

———. "The Culpability of Exile: Arabs in Nazi Germany." *Geschichte und Gesellschaft* 37 (2011): 332–358.

———. *Iraqi Arab Nationalism. Authoritarian, Totalitarian, and Pro-fascist Inclinations, 1932–1941*. London and New York: Routledge, 2006.

Wild, Stefan. "National Socialism in the Arab Near East between 1933 and 1939." *Die Welt des Islams* 25 (1985): 126–173.

Wokoeck, Ursula. *German Orientalism: The Study of the Middle East and Islam from 1800 to 1945*. Taylor & Francis, 2009.

Zargar, Cyrus Ali. "The Satiric Method of Ibn Daniyal: Morality and Anti-Morality in 'Tayf al-Khayal.'" *Journal of Arabic Literature* 37.1 (2006), 68–108.

CHAPTER 6

Iranian Journals in Berlin during the Interwar Period

Mohammed Alsulami

I. INTRODUCTION

In many countries across the globe, people have been recurrently forced to leave their homes for religious, ethnic, and sociopolitical reasons. Some others have chosen to leave their homeland and native society without being forced to do so, their voluntary exile being facilitated by a general feeling of estrangement, foreignness, or dissatisfaction with the home culture and ruling system. Yet, such exiles sometimes find it impossible or hard to go back to their homeland because no political and/or cultural change occurs in the country. Furthermore, exile has become a social experience due to the increasing number of emigrants, and exiles have a tendency to develop the formation of national associations in the host country, and they, accordingly, establish a readership that makes it possible for them to publish newspapers, journals, and books.[1]

Exiles played an important role in enriching the varied disciplines of literature in different languages. Yet, most of the available critical writings dealing with the subject of exile literature mostly focus on the works of exiles produced in the language of the host country, rather than studying the works written in the exile's mother tongue. The writings of Iranian activists and intellectuals in interwar Berlin are an example of this genre. As they were mostly produced in the Persian language, their readership was not restricted to a small exile group in Germany or Europe; their works reached the native readers they left behind in the homeland as well.

The Iranians in Berlin during World War I and in the interwar period did not try to make a new "home" in the adopted country, but rather focused mostly on reconstructing their sense of Iranianness and the social and political course their homeland should take on the basis of their long and rich history and traditions. Their experiences in Berlin and their encounters with local intellectual debates profoundly impacted on their own intellectual outlook and related political visions.

Germany was not the first choice of exile for most of Iranian writers in Berlin during this period. On the contrary, it was the German government, as will be shown below, which made a lot of efforts to attract them to Berlin during the Great War. Furthermore, it would not be wrong to emphasize that it was not the intention of those writers to establish journals and newspapers or even to write about political and cultural issues of the homeland before World War I. During World War I, they were serving the interest of the German government. After that, the Iranian exiles were able to disseminate their ideas on issues dealing with their homeland and Persian language and literature in Berlin because they found such activities as their best option before most of them went back to Iran when the political system changed and the Pahlavi dynasty was established.

II. Historical Background

Despite its formal neutrality in World War I, Iran became a battle-field for the competing powers and enjoyed no more than nominal independence. As the Russians in the northwest, the British in the southwest and the Turks and Germans in the west were competing to expand their control, parts of western Iran changed hands a number of times. On the other hand, Germany and its allies aimed to take the war to other parts of the world where the British had colonies. The German political aim in the region was twofold: first, to support Indian nationalists and to benefit from Iran's longstanding conflict with Russia and Great Britain by encouraging Iranians to join the Ottoman Empire in its war against the "enemy"; and second, to redirect British and Russian forces from the main battlefield in Europe by increasing anti-entente feelings and activities in Egypt, Iran, Afghanistan, and India.[2] For these strategic reasons, the German government first founded a department in the Ministry of Foreign Affairs called "The Intelligence Bureau for the East," with the prime task of promoting and sustaining subversive and nationalist agitations in British India as well as in Egypt and Iran.[3] In August 1914, a junior German official, Otto Günter von Wesendonck (1885–1933), established the Indian Independence Committee in Berlin, embracing several Indian revolutionary politicians and students in Europe. This committee was directed by Virendranath Chattopadhyaya (1880–1937), who had previously been engaged in activities aimed at weakening Indian revolutionary groups in England and France.[4]

As for Iran, the central government was too weak to defend its subjects. Most Iranians, therefore, were sympathetic toward the Germans and Ottomans, who were fighting Iran's enemies, Great Britain and Russia. The general attitude of the Iranian public toward the war was different from that of the authorities. Many Iranians were sympathetic toward Germany, and several deputies from the Democratic Party in the Third National Consultative Assembly believed that Iran should go to war against Russia and Britain at the side of the Ottoman Empire. Many Iranians placed much hope on German support to counter these countries' interests in their country.

While Iran was not a top priority for Germany, she had another crucial strategic reason for cultivating Iranian support in the war. Germany sought to encourage the people of India to rise against the British colonial government, but had only limited access to its territories, which was needed to agitate the local population. As the Ottoman Empire had sided with Germany and its allies in this war, there was no problem in using the Ottoman territories as a stepping stone toward India, but the Germans would need to cross the Iranian territory too. Therefore, the suggestion of cooperation with Iranian exiles was made by Indian nationalists in Berlin, some of whom were familiar with Iranian political and geographical conditions, as they had lived in Iran earlier. These Indian nationalists considered cooperation with the Iranian side as necessary, without which they would not be able to achieve their goals.[5] In this context, the Indian nationalists asked the German government to arrange contacts with Iranians—particularly the Democratic Party, which was known for its anti-Russian and anti-British tendencies.[6]

Seyed Hasan Taqizadeh, a reformist politician, played a key role in building these relations. Taqizadeh was born in Tabriz in about 1880 as the son of a local preacher. He was educated in his native town and graduated from Tabriz Government College. During the early days of the Constitutional Revolution (1906–1911), Taqizadeh was elected to the first Iranian parliament (Majlis) as representative of the region of Tabriz, but was soon asked to leave the country because of his political activities in the Democratic Party in his hometown. Taqizadeh sought refuge in the British legation when Mohammad Ali

Shah bombarded the Majlis in 1908. He then left for London, where
he became involved in the formation of a nationalist organization,
the Persia Committee.[7] In June 1909, following the deposition of the
Shah, Taqizadeh returned to Tehran where he was received by his followers with great enthusiasm and became a member of "Temporary
Board of Directors" and was elected as a member of the second
Majlis.[8] In 1910, Taqizadeh was one of the radical democratic leaders
implicated in the assassination of Seyed Abdullah Bihbahani (1840–
1910), a highly influential cleric and veteran of the Constitutional
Revolution.[9] For that reason, he left to Istanbul, where he stayed for
two years, working as coeditor of the *Iran-i now* newspaper with the
Azerbaijani Mohammad Amen Rasulzadeh (1885–1955),[10] and began
to associate himself with the reformers of the Unity Committee. From
there he traveled to Great Britain and France and met the British
Orientalist Edward G. Browne (1862–1926). On another occasion,
he spent six months in Britain, doing research in the British Museum
library in London. During this time, despite being abroad, he was
elected to the Majlis, but preferred not to take his seat. On May 31,
1913, Taqizadeh traveled to the United States of America, where he
stayed for two years, working at the New York Public Library, catego-
rizing Arabic, Turkish, and Persian books.[11]

During this period, the German Consul in New York contacted
Taqizadeh, informing him of the German interest to establish contacts to Iranian nationalist circles. Taqizadeh accepted an invitation
to Berlin and arrived in Germany on January 15, 1915, and soon
started to explore ways of cooperation.[12] On March 7, he handed
to von Wesendonck an untitled document in French, consisting of
eighteen pages and an eight-page index, suggesting the formation of
an Iranian revolutionary movement. In this document, he argued for
financial support to implement the program and raised the option
of harming the interests of the enemy. According to this plan, Iran
would receive the supplies necessary to defend itself against the British
and Russian colonial powers.[13]

III. The Establishment of Iranian Activities in Interwar Berlin

The community of Iranian intellectuals and authors in Berlin during
the interwar years consisted of three groups: first, political activists,
particularly those who were involved in the Constitutional Revolution
of Iran (1906), and who had been invited to come to Germany
from different European countries during the War; second, Iranian

students in Germany; and third, a limited number of Iranians who had settled in Germany before the war, but who had not previously been engaged in relevant political or cultural activities.

The political and cultural activities of the Iranian nationalist group in Berlin started in 1915 with the founding of the Committee of Iranian Nationalists (cumiti-yi miliyun-i iran). As its leader in Berlin, Taqizadeh gathered around him some of his old friends and colleagues from the Democratic Party during the Constitutional Revolution period as well as other Iranian nationalists and students who had settled in Europe. In addition to German activities in Iran, particularly in the south of the country,[14] the committee sent a number of Iranians from Berlin to Iran with certain political objects.[15] In addition to their cooperation with Indian nationalists, the members of the Committee of Iranian Nationalists in Berlin also forged strong contacts with their counterparts in places such as Istanbul and Baghdad. They established links with *Rastakhiz* (Resurrection), a Persian newspaper published in Baghdad and Kirmanshah in 1915–1916, as well as with the Istanbul-based Persian newspaper *Khavar* (the East), edited by Seyed Mohammad Tawfiq, one of Taqizadeh's main foes in Istanbul. The dispute between the two men, however, was soon conciliated.[16] Some committee members, such as Mohammad Ali Jamalzadeh, Isma'il Amir Khan, and Ibrahim Purdavoud, traveled to the region to promote German foreign policy across Iran, but more intensively in Tehran and western regions of the country. Iranian nationalists did not limit themselves to the Committee's activities or their contacts with their colleagues in the region. Rather, they aimed at enlarging their audience, particularly at home, by publishing *Kaveh*, one of the most influential journals in the history of the Iranian press by the diaspora.[17]

In addition to the Committee of Iranian Nationalists, one should mention another association established in Berlin during the war period: the German Persian Society (Deutsch-Persische Gesellschaft), which was sponsored by the German government. According to the *Kaveh* journal (January 30, 1918), about 50 Iranian and German persons came together with the aim of strengthening the relationship between the two countries on both political and social levels. In the meantime, the German minister of state (formerly a German attaché to Tehran), Werner Otto von Hentig (1886–1984) was elected as the first secretary general and Taqizadeh as the second secretary general of the society. In addition, the German Baron Von Richthofen, the former German chargé d'affaires in Tehran, served as the deputy of Hentig, while the Iranian Vahid al-Mulk Shaybani was named deputy of Taqizadeh on the Iranian side. The society organized occasional conferences and lectures, promoting knowledge about Germany and Iran among the respective audiences. The society counted some 350 members; and every month a paper was published under the title "Information of the German-Iranian Society," which was posted to all its members. The society continued its work until late 1933.[18]

Iranian writers and activists in Berlin had a only limited contact with other Muslim counterparts in Berlin. While few contacts existed, the activities of Iranians in Berlin remained largely confined to issues related to Iran and to German-Iranian relations. This also holds true for the Persian journals that were published in the German capital.

IV. *KAVEH* AND THE WAR

The journal *Kaveh*, named after a legendary blacksmith who had launched a national uprising to liberate Iran from the evil foreigner Zahhak, was founded and directed by Taqizadeh.[19] Its first issue appeared on January 24, 1916, and the journal ran for about six years. In total, *Kaveh* published 114 numbers: 35 during the war and 79 after it. The journal was distributed among Iranians in Iran, the Ottoman Empire, India, and the Caucasus, as well as in cities such as Stockholm, Zurich, Geneva, Budapest, and other places. During the war, the journal also focused on distributing its issues in certain cities in Iran such as Tabriz, Isfahan, and Kirmanshah, and had good sales agents in those places as well. In addition to Taqizadeh, who at times wrote under the pen name Mohasil, many Iranian authors and scholars as well as European Orientialists contributed to the journal.

The Iranian émigrés who wrote in this journal came from different social and political backgrounds, some belonging to the courtly and trading (*bazari*) families, others to religious families; among them were a poet, an intellectual, a politician, a student, and a trader. *Kaveh* attracted several Iranians, some of whom came to Berlin soon after the Committee of Iranian Nationalists was established, while others joined the group at a later stage. Among them were Nasir al-Mulk's grandson Ghulam Reza Khan who arrived from Brussels, Nasrullah Khan, Mirza Mahmud Ashrafzadeh and Seyed Mohammad Ali Jamalzadeh (1892–1997) from Switzerland, Bozorg Alavi (1904–1997) who came from Iran to study, Mohammad Qazvini (1874–1949) and Ibrahim Purdavoud (1885–1968) from France, and Hussein Kazimzadeh from England. This small community included several intellectuals who—although full of enthusiasm—promoted reforms based on European experiences, to advance Iranian society. Among the non-Iranian con-tributors to the journal were well-known scholars in the field of Iranian studies, such as the above-mentioned E. G. Browne, Henri Massé, and Arthur Christiansen.

The message of the journal was enforced by the interaction of its authors. The Kaviyani Printing House, which published the journal for a few months during 1921, served as a meeting place of the com-munity. During the weekends, Iranian intellectuals in Berlin used to come together here to discuss cultural, historical, social, and political issues on Iran and read and discuss the essays and articles that were written during that week.[20]

The first issue of the journal consisted of eight large pages. *Kaveh* was intended to be published fortnightly, but in reality it appeared at irregular intervals. In terms of circulation, the first issues of *Kaveh* reached a nominal 3,000 copies, 1,500 of which were distributed by the editorial staff, 1,000 copies were available to the German for-eign office, and 500 copies would be sent to the News Agency of the Orient. The number of copies that were distributed abroad is not clear, however.[21]

During World War I, Taqizadeh saw the world as consisting of nation states participating in a global rivalry of national self-affirmation and political autonomy. In the first issue, Taqizadeh wrote:

> In the midst of this day of resurrection for the nation, several individu-als from a poor and unfortunate nation—that is Iran—have gathered in Berlin, the seat of war, to consider the fate of their nation....Our intention is not to sit idle but to awaken our compatriots...This is the intention of this little journal, to project its weak voice from Berlin to reach the ears of Iranians...Our destiny is tied to the outcome of this war; and our duty is to fight our enemies with all our strength to secure our independence...Our hope is that Iranians will show that the spirit of the nation has not died; and that a wise movement will emerge which will again raise the flag of Kaveh.[22]

Such statements explain the motivation for establishing the journal. During the war it strongly urged the Iranian government to abandon its neutral position by joining the Germans, Austrians, and Ottomans in order to save Iran from what was seen as a shameful and humiliating position that tarnished its illustrious history. In addition, the journal called on the Iranian government to openly challenge Russian and British interests in the country.[23]

During the first period of the journal, *Kaveh* took advantage of the Ottoman Empire's standing as a Muslim state, urging the Iranian government to help their coreligionists against the enemies. *Kaveh* wrote:

> We Muslims see the victory of Germany and its allies as a great benefit for the present and the future, and we pray for his Majesty, William II, the emperor of Germany, and for German troops to obtain victory, since this is considered a victory for the first independent Islamic state, by which we mean the great Ottoman state, for its alliance with Germany is a glory for Islam and a dignity for Muslims.[24]

The journal stressed the importance of unity between Iran and the Ottoman Empire, highlighting what was shared by these neighboring states. In this regard, the journal also emphasized the role of Pan-Islamic activists, such as Sayyid Jamal al-Din Afghani (1838–1897), the main Pan-Islamic agitator in the nineteenth century.[25] The journal saw in Islamic unity a step toward protecting the Islamic world from imperialist domination and gaining its political and economic independence.[26] In early August 1916, Ottoman troops advanced into Iran and occupied Hamadan and Kirmanshah, although the aim was to reach Tehran.[27] Despite the dispute between Iran and the Ottoman Empire, the negative attitude toward the Ottoman Empire changed dramatically during the war, at least in the eyes of Iranian nationalists in Berlin. Commenting on the advance of the Ottoman army, the journal asserted that Iranians should know that advancing Ottoman troops represented a divine intervention on behalf of the oppressed Iranian nation. Under the title "Ittihad-i manafa'-i iran va Osmani" (The Union of Iranian-Ottoman Interests), the journal imagined that an army dispatched by heaven had come to help its eastern coreligionists. Furthermore, Ottoman blood that had been shed on Iranian soil was seen as "pure blood, shed in the sacred duty of liberating its brother from the devil and from impure chains." Ottoman troops, the journal asserted, were the true saviors of Iran.[28]

The representative of the Iranian interim government to Berlin, Vahid al-Mulk Shaybani, nevertheless, revealed his concerns regarding Ottoman objectives in Iran, asking whether a definitive German victory over the Allies would be beneficial for Iran. The victory of the central powers would not be good for the country, he argued, because there remained the possibility of a hidden agreement about Iran between Germany and the Ottoman Empire, whereby the Ottomans might seize at least a part of Azerbaijan.[29] In response to such fears, *Kaveh* explicitly emphasized the concept of Islamic brotherhood and the good intentions of the Ottomans toward Iran. According to the journal, liberating Iran from its Russian warden and granting it full independence through its Ottoman "elder brother" for the sake of sincere brotherhood and without any self-interest, would remain forever in the Iranian national memory.[30] *Kaveh* saw the Ottoman government as the best and the heir of great Muslim caliphs and sultans that was fighting not only to rescue the people under its rule, but also to liberate and rescue Islam and the East as a whole. The victory of the Ottomans would grant new life to the East and resurrect Islam. Their defeat, on the other hand, would be a defeat for the entire Orient and a serious danger for Islam as such. The journal even went further to compare Enver Pasha (1881–1922), the former Turkish war minister and Ottoman commander-in-chief during World War I and nationalist exile in Berlin, to Khalid Ibn al-Walid (592–642), a hero from the early history of Islam who is reputed as a defender of the rights of Muslims.[31]

In that sense, the journal fulfilled the aim of the German propaganda. Its tone in fighting for Islamic unity, particularly between Iran and the Ottoman Empire, implied a call to their Muslim co-emigrants to support Germany and to fight British and Russian imperialism. As soon as the war was over, however, this strategy was abandoned.

V. *KAVEH* IN THE POSTWAR PERIOD

After the war, *Kaveh* had to change its direction completely. It was more organized, since it used to be published monthly and now discussed critical social and political issues that concerned intellectuals of the time. At the same time, *Kaveh* could establish an ideological basis for nationalism and modernization of Iran in the twentieth century. In its first issue after the war (January 22, 1920), the editor wrote:

> Kaveh was born as a result of the prevailing conditions—the war—and therefore it was delivered in a way that suited the period. Now [since] the war is ended and an international peace agreement is signed, Kaveh ends this period and adopts a completely new approach and line of conduct from the beginning of 1920, corresponding with the 9th of Rabi' II 1338 A.H. The main focus has become scientific, historical and literary articles. Its ultimate goal is propagating the European culture in Iran, a *Jihad* against fanaticism, preserving Iranian nationality and unity as well as the purification of the Persian language and literature from the dangers and disorders that threaten them.[32]

Kaveh summarized its new strategy in three main points: The first was the acceptance and propagation of Western culture, with the exception of language, by adopting a Western customs and culture, education, science, and lifestyles, while abandoning any kind of self-admiration and the meaningless objections that were the result of a mistaken patriotism. Second, it should make a serious effort to preserve, develop, and spread the Persian language and literature. Third, *Kaveh* sought to propagate Western learning and to promote the public interest in establishing schools.

The journal emphasized that Iran had never been in such a condition before. Ancient Iran was strong and powerful, but had declined because its people had abandoned almost all of the good features of their predecessors, including "knowing the language and the script of Avesta or old Persian."[33] Furthermore, throughout the pages of *Kaveh*, Taqizadeh and his friends in Berlin employed the device of engaging the deep reservoirs of Persian myths, legends, and symbols, in their perceptions of a modern national guise. In this regard, one of *Kaveh*'s goals was to teach Iranians their forgotten glorious ancient history, an idea that was seen as an important intellectual support for the people of Iran and a vital step toward the reform of their country. Thus, *Kaveh* raised the question of why the national spirit of Iranians had been filled with insecurity and doubt. It proposed two essential reasons: (1) the contemporary political situation of Iran, and (2) the people's ignorance of the glorious and illustrious civilization of the country. For the writers of the journal, both factors played a role in what they called Iran's "identity crisis." According to this argument, "the Iranian, who knows his past well, would never be weak or pessimistic, because the best way to educate the nation politically, spiritually and morally is through teaching it the history of its ancient civilization, particularly a nation like Iran."[34] The aim of *Kaveh* was to strengthen the nationalist foundations of Iran during the era of state-building, thus contributing to the foundation of a new Iran. *Kaveh* strove to revive ancient Iranian culture and customs, introducing a new way of thinking for society in order to build a new Iran upon the old foundations. In addition, the editor of the journal was familiar with contemporary European historical and philological scholarship, which greatly helped him to learn more about the past of his country as represented in Western scholarship. Taqizadeh began a series of articles in his journal under the title: "The Best Western Scholarship about Iran," in which he introduced to his readers some German, French, and English scholarly works dealing with the pre-Islamic religious, geographical, literary, linguistic, and historical affairs of Persia.[35] Furthermore, of central importance to this undertaking was *Kaveh*'s encounter with European Oriental scholarship.

In this context, a long article was devoted to the contents of the two-volume *Grundriss der Iranischen Philologie* (1896–1904), edited by Wilhelm Geiger and Ernst Kuhn. This book can be considered as one of the best works dealing with Western discoveries concerning Persia.[36]

Taqizadeh published the journal at his own expense for one and a half years, but he could not afford it anymore. He complained of people in Persia who never sent him the money collected as subscriptions. Hence, lacking financial support, Taqizadeh sought help from "wise people or those who prefer knowledge and literature," and not from the "political elite." However, he was obliged to stop publishing the journal on March 30, 1922 because he did not succeed in obtaining any financial help.[37]

Kaveh, during the second period in particular, provided Iranian nationalists and reformists in Berlin and other European cities with a suitable vehicle through which they could express their ideas and thoughts. At the same time, it paved the way for the political and mostly cultural and social activists who would later try to elaborate their ideas more explicitly in *Iranshahr*, another journal which was published in Berlin following the closure of *Kaveh*.

VI. *IRANSHAHR*

The second Iranian journal published in Berlin was *Iranshahr*, founded by the Iranian nationalist Hussein Kazimzadeh, who later became known as Iranshahr, after the journal's name. He was born to a religious family in Tabriz in 1884. In 1904, he had traveled to Istanbul to study medicine, but as a result of the Constitutional Revolution, the formation of the parliament, law became an attractive subject, therefore he decided to study law instead, while working at the Iranian Consulate in Istanbul. In 1911, Iranshahr went to Belgium, receiving his bachelor degree in political and social sciences from a college in Louvain in 1912. He then spent a year in Paris, following classes at the Sorbonne and the École des hautes études sociales, before traveling to Cambridge, England, where he taught Persian and worked as an assistant to Edward G. Browne. In 1915, on Taqizadeh's invitation, Kazimzadeh joined Taqizadeh and his Iranian nationalist colleagues in Berlin. Kazimzadeh was one of *Kaveh*'s writers and played a vital role in spreading German propaganda during World War I. in 1915, Kazimzadeh took on the task of traveling to Iran to meet the leaders of democratic parties and to encourage them to join the gendarmerie forces and to defend the country against the colonial powers.[38] He carried out this mission and met some of these leaders in Tehran and other cities before being arrested in Kirmanshah and imprisoned for a few months. After his release, Kazimzadeh returned to Berlin and started to write articles for *Kaveh*, before he decided to publish his own journal, *Iranshahr*, from 1922 to 1927.

The first edition of *Iranshahr* was published on June 26, 1922; the journal had an explicit secular nationalist program, favoring universal secular education, women's rights, and centralization as against local languages and customs. Issues such as public education, sport, translation, equality between men and women, a strong central government, and the need to control tribes, as well as historical investigations, were among the topics that were discussed.[39]

Iranshahr journal was printed in Iranshahr Printing House in Berlin. In addition to the journal, Iranshahr Printing House published some 21 books on Persian literature, Islamic philosophy, the history of Iran, and many other topics.[40] The journal itself was distributed in Europe as well as in Iran, Afghanistan, India, the Ottoman Empire, Egypt, and the Far East (Philippine). From 1922 until 1927 when the journal ceased publication, about 140 writers from different countries had contributed to the journal. Many of the Iranian students and activists in Berlin were among them.[41] Due to the journal's criticism of political and social issues in Iran at the time, the Iranian government banned its distribution in the country soon after its first appearance. However, copies of the journal were sent illegally to Iran and secretly circulated.[42]

A key argument of the journal held the Islamic Arab invasion in the seventh century responsible for the backward state of the country; only a liberation from Islam would allow the country to progress and prosper.[43] In addition, the journal paid close attention to social problems. It criticized Iranian society for sinking in "corruption" and "bad habits," such as lying, cheating, hypocrisy, violence, self-interest, drug taking, and bribery, as well as betraying its homeland, religion, and children. The editor called for a revolt against such bad and dangerous habits, otherwise all the efforts at rescuing Iran from its backwardness would be useless and ineffective.[44]

In the second issue of the journal, the editor set out its aims and the topics that would be at the heart of its philosophy and spirit. He declared that it would publish writing with a focus on three important aims: The first would be to present a conscious and fair description of the current Iranian social status in order to inform the nation of the unfortunate situation of its life and stimulating thoughts for the sake of its remediation. The second would be to impart historical information about ancient Iranian civilization and its people's achievements, comparing the glorious Iranian past with the contemporary situation. According to *Iranshahr*, the Iranian people should be informed about what their ancestors had done and what kind of tasks now faced them, since a nation that does not know its past cannot build up its future. The third aim was to publish useful information on the different technological and scientific developments of European and Eastern states in the last few centuries to provide encouragement and edification as a basis for progress and development.[45] It can be added that the journal voiced anti-clericalism, a hostility toward the Muslim Arab conquest of Iran, and a glorification of pre-Islamic Iran, which became common among Iranian intellectuals.[46]

Taking into consideration the above framework that the journal had drawn for itself, it is not surprising that *Iranshahr* devoted much space to exploring the language and culture of ancient Iran and conveyed a strong belief in strengthening the nationalistic spirit. Nevertheless, at the same time it tried to unify ideas of declaring a national culture and joint identity by using a democratic language in order to reach a broader audience. It aimed at educating the Iranian population, to familiarize Iranians with their history, and to make them proud of their forefathers who were at one time the rulers of the world, as the journal claimed.[47] Echoing the racial terminology of the time, Kazimzadeh emphasized what he and many other Iranian nationalists of the nineteenth and twentieth centuries saw as a connection between Iran and the West,[48] affirming that "the Iranian spirit is the best example of Aryan spirit.... It is true that contemporary Iran has fallen behind its Aryan sisters and that it cannot demonstrate today the genius, breadth of talent and capability which it displayed during previous periods. But this does not mean that its eternal spirit has died."[49]

Thus, the people of Iran, in his opinion, were obliged to remember not only their ancient greatness and strength, but also "the noble race to which they belong."[50] Furthermore, Kazimzadeh praised the Iranian Aryan race by describing it as having an intelligent, extraordinary way of thinking, the capability for progress, and self-confidence; yet he warned that Iranians had not yet used these features properly. He ironically noted that they had instead used "their superior talents in cheating, lying, sedition and corruption."[51]

The point to be taken from all of this is that the journal was strongly devoted to reconstructing the Iranian national identity and national awareness as the only tool for awakening the nation. Articles published in *Iranshahr* included "Stone Cuttings of the Sassanid Period,"

"Education in Ancient Iran," "Khaqani and the Ruins of Madaen," "Cuneiform in Iranian Tablets," "The War Committee of Darius II," "Ancient Industries of Iran," and "A Look at the Ancient Era of Iran," giving a clear sense of the authors' fascination with Iran's pre-Islamic glories and their endeavors to construct an Iranian identity founded on ancient history and the pre-Islamic model.[52] Emphasizing the notion of "Iranianness" and its importance for Iranians and their nationhood, the editor of the journal wrote in 1923:

> Our nationality is Iranian and it is all that we have: our pride, honor, greatness, sacredness, principle and life. If we put nationality in the position of the heart (centre) of our wishes and deeds, we will get rid of the status of "having nothing" and will have everything. Before everything, we must be Iranians, be called Iranians and remain Iranians. Iranian is a holy and collective word which embodies all the members of the Iranian nation under the wings of magnanimity, without any differentiation in terms of religion or language. Every member has Aryan blood running in his/her veins and considers the Iranian soil his homeland, and s/he should be called and considered an Iranian whether s/he is Kurdish or Baluchi, Zoroastrian or Armenian.... Every Iranian ought to be a good example of the nation and face other people with a forehead shining with Iranian honor and nobility. Iranian mothers should raise their children with zealotry's milk of Iranian and occupy their sensitive minds with national pride and pure nationalist emotions.[53]

In this context, one can understand *Iranshahr*'s interest in the Parsi (Zoroastrian) community in India, praising their relative well-being and their supremacy over Iranians in the fields of economy, education, and politics. Furthermore, it encouraged Iranians to ask them for help in order to put Iran on the path of progress and modernity. Such a focus on Indian Parsis forced *Habl al-Matin*, a weekly Persian newspaper based in Calcutta, to accuse *Iranshahr* of obtaining a sum of money annually from the Parsi community in India in order to propagate its faith, a charge that was strongly rejected by the journal's editorship.[54]

This attitude matched with *Iranshahr*'s fascination with German romantic nationalism. In its definition of the "nation," German nationalism of the late eighteenth and early nineteenth century had emphasized shared ethnic and cultural features. It is in this context that *Iranshahr* favorably referred to German philosopher and writer Johann Gottfried Herder (1744–1803), as he considered the nation to be "a group of related people who share one culture, race, religion and language; these elements shape the spirit of the nation."[55] Similar to *Kaveh*, *Iranshahr* was short-lived. After about four years of its publication, Iranshahr decided to stop his journal for two reasons: financial problems making it difficult to bear the costs of publication, and what he called "the lack of ambition or spirit in Iranians." Therefore, he sold the printing machines and left for Swaziland in 1936, where he spent the rest of his life, writing several books and essays in Persian and German. During these final years of his life, he detached himself from thinking about the political and social affairs of the homeland, devoting his life to spiritual and mystical matters.[56]

CONCLUSION

The end of World War I had left a strong impact on the journalistic and cultural activities of the Iranian nationalists in Berlin. While the war years were marked by great expectations of German support for Iranian independence, the interwar period saw a much stronger focus on local conditions and the requirements of social and political reform in Iran itself. While Germany remained a point of reference with regard to culture and thought, it had lost its reputation as a possible political ally. Even more importantly, while the political context of the war years fostered hope in Islamic unity, the defeat of the Ottoman Empire and the end of the caliphate frustrated the belief in an Islamic vision. For the editors and writers of *Kaveh* and *Iranshahr*, Iran's pre-Islamic history was increasingly identified as the golden age of the country that contemporary society had to revive. The decline of contemporary Iranian society was due to its ignorance of its own past. As long as Iranians were ignorant of their pre-Islamic national identity, political reforms were bound to fail. For *Iranshahr*, belief in Islamic unity was replaced by a notion of Iranianness, with a fully romantic assessment of ancient Iran. Hence, it is not surprising that Kazimzadeh saw the land (the Empire of Iran) and the blood (the Aryan race) as the two elements from which one could construct the nation; and, therefore, Iranianness was more important than Islam. For him, such identity was not bound by time, but was "the manifestation of the Iranian soul through history (tajaliyat-i ruh-i irani dar advar tarikh)," an expression of the "Aryan race" and "Aryan intelligence."[57] This attitude, which ignored the diverse factors that had shaped Iranian identity over time, stood for an ethnic chauvinism that had gained currency in other regions of the world—not least in Germany. The names of the two journals and the symbols that were chosen (the blacksmith in the case of *Kaveh* and a picture of ancient Iranian ruins) reveal much about nationalistic and romantic attitudes toward ancient Iran. This was in fact accompanied, particularly during the postwar period, by calls for westernization and the adoption of Western models. Both journals adopted Western academic and research methodologies, which had already been rigorously applied by Western scholars to ancient Iranian history and to Persian language and literature. The two journals exerted a dominant influence on the construction and propagation of nationalist themes during the Pahlavi dynasty. In fact, the policies of Reza Shah during his reign, such as westernization, secularization, the reform of Iran on the ancient Iranian model, and the purification of the Persian language from foreign elements, were in effect an adaptation of what these two journals had called for. The return of many of the Iranian exiles in Berlin to Iran further added to the dissemination of these thoughts. While Kazimzadeh, Iranshahr, and Jamalzadeh stayed in Europe for the rest of their lives, most other Iranian intellectuals over the next few years traveled back to Iran where some of them occupied influential positions close to the ruling elite.

NOTES

1. For more information see, for example, Andrew Gurr, *Writing in Exile: The Home in Modern Literature* (Sussex: The Harvester Press, 1981), 13–32; Lloyd S. Kramer, *Threshold of a New World: Intellectuals and the Exile Experience in Paris, 1830–1848* (Ithaca, NY and Paris: Gronell University Press, 1988); John Neubauer, "Exile: Home of the Twentieth Century," in *The Exile and Return of Writers from East-Central Europe: A Compendium,* ed. John Neubauer and Borbála Zsuzsanna Török (Berlin and New York: Walter de Gruyter, 2009), 4–19; Patrick Ward, *Exile, Emigration and Irish Writing* (Dublin: Irish Academic Press, 2002), 1–26.

2. Thomas G. Fraser, "Germany and Indian Revolution, 1914–18." *Journal of Contemporary History* 12.2 (1977): 259; and Rouhollah K. Ramazani, *The Foreign Policy of Iran 1500–1941: A Developing Nation in World Affairs.* (Charlottesville: University Press of Virginia, 1966), 117–120.

3. The German Chancellor in India, Bethmann Hollweg, stressed the aim of Germany in weakening Britain in India: "England appears determined to wage war to the bitter end…Thus one of our main tasks is gradually to wear England down through unrest in India and Egypt, which will only be possible from there," Bethmann Hollweg to Auswärtiges Amt, September 4, 1914, GFM 397/00326, quoted in Richard J. Popplewell, *Intelligence and Imperial Defence: The British Intelligence and the Defence of the Indian Empire 1904–1924* (London: Frank Cass, 1995), 176–177.

4. Nigel Collett, *The Butcher of Amritsar: General Reginald Dyer* (London: Hambledon, 2007), 143; and Uma Mukherjee, *Two Great Indian Revolutionaries: Rash Behari Bose and Jyotindra Nath Mukherjee* (Calcutta: Firma K. L. Mukhopadhyay, 1966), 77–79.

5. Thomas G. Fraser, "Germany and Indian Revolution, 1914–18," *Journal of Contemporary History* 12.2 (1977): 259–260.

6. Fraser, "Germany," 259; and Uma Mukherjee, *Two Great Indian Revolutionaries*, 85–96.

7. This committee was established on October 30, 1908 as a part of other activities aimed first at "stimulating public interest in the Persian people and in their efforts to regenerate Persia; and to enlist it on the side of the declared policy of Great Britain and Russia—namely, non-intervention in Persia" and second at "rendering articulate public opinion in favour of the restoration of the Persian constitution with the three essential conditions of (i) amnesty for political offences, (ii) freedom of election to the Majlis, and (iii) effective control by the Majlis over the national finances." George Lloyd Papers: GLLD 16/46 (Churchill College, Cambridge) cited in Mansour Bonakdarian, "The Persia Committee and the Constitutional Revolution in Iran," *British Journal of Middle Eastern Studies* 18.2 (1991): 191; see also Mansour Bonakdarian, *Britain and the Iranian Constitutional Revolution of 1906–1911: Foreign Policy, Imperialism, and Dissent* (Syracuse, NY: Syracuse University Press, 2006), 133 and Hasan Javadi and Edward G. Browne, *Letters from Tabriz: The Russian Suppression of the Iranian Constitutional Movement* (Washington, DC: Mage, 2008).

8. Iraj Afshar, ed., *S.H. Taqizadeh's Articles and Essays*, vol. VII (Tehran: Shekufan, 1977), 777–781.

9. Farzin Vahdat, *God and Juggernaut: Iran's Intellectual Encounter with Modernity* (New York: Syracuse University Press, 2002), 76; and Nikki R. Keddie, "Iran under later Qajar, 1848–1922." in *Cambridge History of Iran: From Nadir Shah to the Islamic Republic*, ed. P. Avery et al. (Cambridge: Cambridge University Press, 1991), vol. 7, 205.

10. Rasulzadeh was a pre-Soviet leading ideologue of Azeri nationalism and known later as the founder of the first Republic of Azerbaijan. For more information on Rasulzadeh see, for instance, Touraj Atabaki, *Azerbaijan: Ethnicity and the Struggle for Power in Iran* (London: IB Tauris, 2000); and Nassereddin Parvin, "Iran-e now," in *Encyclopedia Iranica*, vol. XIII, ed. Ehsan Yarshater (New York: The Encyclopedia Iranica Foundation, 2006), 498–500.

11. Hasan Taqizadeh, *zandiqi tufani*, ed. Iraj Afshar (Tehran: Intisharat Mohammad Ali Alami, 1990), 177–178.

12. The German Consul also told him that Germany had many war prisoners from different countries, some of whom were Muslims and that those Muslims were separated from other prisoners in order to convince them (who?) that the benefit is in supporting Germany. Therefore, the German authorities needed some people who could

propagate such ideas among the prisoners. For more information about how the German convinced him to travel to Berlin see Hasan Taqizadeh, *zandiqi tufani*, 174–188.

13. Iliza Itschernska, "Taqizadeh dar Alman-i Qaisari," *Iran nameh* XXI.1–2 (2003): 53.

14. The most famous German activist in Iran during the war was Wilhelm Wassmuss, a former consul in Bushire, who became known as "the German Lawrence." Wassmuss was active in the southern part of Iran, promoting German interests among Iranian tribes, arming them, and causing instability in the country. During this period, the British area of influence came under German control, disconnecting the British from the Iranian capital and force forcing it to redirect its troops from Mesopotamia to defend the oilfields in Khuzistan (Elina Andreeva, "Iran During World War I," in *Conflict and Conquest in the Islamic World: A Historical Encyclopedia,* ed. Alexander Mikaberidze (Santa Barbara: ABC-CLIO, 2011) vol. I, 411. Popplewell, *Intelligence and Imperial Defence*, 177–179.

15. Jamshid Bihnam, *Barlini-ha: Andishmandan-i irani dar birlin 1915–1930* (Tehran: Farzan, 1379/2000), 28–32.

16. J. P. Luft, "The Iranian Nationalists in Istanbul During World War I," in *Studies in Honour of Clifford Edmund Bosworth*, ed. Carole Hillenbrand (Leiden, Netherlands; London; and Boston: E. J. Brill, 2000), vol. II, 260–262.

17. Abbas Milani, *Eminent Persians: The Men and Women Who Made Modern Iran, 1941–1979* vol. 1 (Syracuse, NY and London: Syracuse University Press, 2008), 324. In addition to *Kaveh* and *Iranshahr*, there was another Iranian journal called *Farngistan* (The Western world) published by Iranian students in Berlin in May 1924, under the editorship of Murtaza Mushfiq Kazimi. The journal had dealt with social, political, scientific, and literary subjects. In its ideas and attitude toward the conditions of Iran at the time, the journal resembled *Kaveh* and *Iranshah*r, yet with a stronger and harsher language. Therefore, it was forbidden in Iran after its third issue, yet it continued its publication until April 1925. Bihnam, *Birlini-ha*, 96–100.

18. *Kaveh* 3.25 (February 15, 1918): 10–11; and Ahmad Mahrad, *Die Deutsch-persischen Beziehungen von 1918–1933* (Frankfurt and Las Vegas: Peter Lang, 1979).

19. P. O. Sklervo. "Azdaha," in *Encyclopedia Iranica*, ed. Ehsan Yarshater (London and New York: Roultedge and Kegan Paul, 1989), vol. III, 191–199; Theodor Nöldeke, *The Iranian National Epic, or Shahnameh*, trans. Leonid Bogdanov (Bombay: Fort Printing Press, 1930), 31.

20. Bihnam, *Barlini-ha*, 54–55; Raziya Mohib, "Chapkhaneh-yi Kaviyani," *kitab mah-i tarikh va jughrafia*, Murdad 147 (1389/2010): 22

21. Tim Epkenhans, *Die Iranische Moderne im Exil: Bibliographie der Zeitschrift Kave, Berlin 1916–1922* (Berlin: Klaus Schwarz Verlag, 2000), 59–60.

22. *Kaveh* 1.1 (January 24, 1916): 1–3.
23. Ibid., 4.
24. Ibid., 8.
25. On this subject, see for example, Anvar Moazzam, *Jamal al-Din al-Afghani: A Muslim Intellectual* (New Delhi: Naurang Rai, 1984); Mansoor Moaddel, *Islamic Modernism, Nationalism, and Fundamentalism: Episode and Discourse* (London: University of Chicago Press, 2005); and Nikki R. Keddie, *An Islamic Response to Imperialism: Political and Religious Writings of Sayyid Jamāl Ad-Dīn "al-Afghānī"* (Berkeley: University of California Press, 1968).
26. *Kaveh* 1.12 (September 15, 1916): 8.
27. On the events of this period and the position of Iran during the World War I, see for example, Touraj Atabaki, *Iran and the First World War: Battleground of the Great powers* (New York: IB Tauris, 2006); Frederick Moberly, *Operations in Persia, 1914–1919* (London: HMSO, 1987); Ervand Abrahamian, *Iran between Two Revolutions* (Princeton: Princeton University Press, 1982) and Houshang Sabahi, *British Policy in Persia, 1918–1925* (London: Frank Cass, 1990).
28. *Kaveh* 1.12 (September 15, 1916): 3.
29. AbdulHussein Shaybani, *Khatirat mohajart az dawlat-i movaqat ta kometeh-i birlin*, eds. Iraj Afshar and Kaveh Bayat (Tehran: Shirazeh, 1378/1999), 171 and 198.
30. *Kaveh* 1.12 (September 15, 1916): 4.
31. *Kaveh* 1.15 (December 15, 1916): 1–2.
32. *Kaveh* 5.1 (January 22, 1920): 1–2.
33. *Kaveh* 2.22 (August 15, 1917): 2–5.
34. *Kaveh* 3.25 (February 15, 1918): 13.
35. *Kaveh* included a number of articles about Western scholarship on Iran. For more information see *Kaveh*, issues 25–33 under the title "Bihtarin-i ta'lifat-i farngiha dar barah-yi Iran." The journal also included several long articles about the celebrated Iranian poet Abu al-Qasim Firdowsi (940–1020) and his epic, the Shahnameh, and the pre-Islamic Iranian prophet, Mazdak (d. 524). See *Kaveh* 5.3 (March 21, 1920): 3–11.
36. Wilhelm Geiger and Ernst Kuhn, eds., *Grundriss Der Iranischen Philologie* (Strassburg: 1895–1904); see Afshin Marashi, *Nationalizing Iran: Culture, Power and the State, 1870–1940* (Washington, DC: University of Washington Press, 2008), 81.
37. Bihnam, *Barlini-ha*; and Iraj Afšar, in *Encyclopedia Iranica*, under "Kava Newspaper," accessed September 29, 2013, http://www.iranicaonline.org/articles/kava.
38. Hussein Kazimzadeh, *Sharh-i hal-i nigarandeh-i kitab usul-i isasi fann-i tarbiat* (Tehran: Iqbal, 1329/1950), 28–37.
39. The journal had a strong influence on political and intellectual circles in Iran. During its four years, *Iranshahr* published 48 issues containing 236 articles, of which 73 dealt with the importance of civil and public education, 45 tackled the situation of women, 30 were about

Iran's pre-Islamic period and 40 addressed various philosophical subjects. Jamshid Behnam, "Iranšahr," in *Encyclopedia Iranica*, ed. Ehsan Yarshater (New York: The Encyclopedia Iranica Foundation, 2006), vol. XIII, 535–536.

40. Yahiya Aryanpur, *as Saba ta nima: tarikh sad va panjah sal adab-i farisi* (Tehran: Nawid, 1367/1989), vol. II, 233.

41. Bihnam, *Barlini-ha*, 92.

42. Bihnam, *Barlini-ha*, 99.

43. Abrahamian, *Iran between Two Revolutions*, 124.

44. *Iranshahr* 1.4 (September 23, 1922): 63–66.

45. *Iranshahr* 2.2 (October 18, 1923): 84–85. The journal also asserted that the east was in need of Western knowledge and science, and in order to do that easterners need to establish an organization to be called "Occidentalists," consisting of people familiar with the situation in the west (whether they studied, traveled, or worked in this part of the world). Their task was to transfer what they knew into their own countries and societies. *Iranshahr* 1.1, 13–14 (June 26, 1922).

46. Nikki R. Keddie, *Qajar Iran and the Rise of Reza Khan, 1796–1925*, (Costa Mesa, CA: Mazda Press, 1999), 83.

47. *Iranshahr* 1.3 (August 24, 1922): 36–37.

48. For more information see, for example, Mohammad Tavakoli-Targhi, *Refashioning Iran, Orientalism, Occidentalism and Historiography* (New York: Palgrave, 2001); and Mangol Bayat-Philipp, *Mysticism and Dissent: Socioreligious thought in Qajar Iran* (Syracuse, NY: Syracuse University Press, 1982). In addition, I am currently researching this notion and the way in which some Iranian nationalists looked at two other groups—Arabs and westerners—by using some nineteenth-century racial theories such as Aryan race theory and Darwinism.

49. *Iranshahr* 2.9 (May 21, 1924): 499.

50. *Iranshahr* 1.4 (September 23, 1922): 60.

51. *Iranshahr* 1.4, 60–61. On Aryanism in Iran see, for example, Reza Zia Ebrahimi, "Self-Orientalization and Dislocation: The Uses and Abuses of 'Aryan' Discourse in Iran," *Iranian Studies* 44.4, (2011): 445–472.

52. Nader Entikhabi, "Nasionalism va tajadud dar farhang-i siasi-i iran," *Iran Nameh* 11.2 (1372/ 1993): 195–196. In addition, *Iranshahr* frequently published articles and poems supporting the establishment of a republican form of government in Iran under titles such as "Republic of Iran and Iranians in Berlin," "Republic and the Social Revolution," "Republic and Our Sciences," and "Congratulation for the Republic and Spring." The journal also reported that on March 31, 1924, Iranian residents of Berlin held a meeting in which they conveyed their hatred of the Qajar government and insisted on the need to change the constitution and establish a republican system in Iran. *Iranshahr* 2.1 (September 18, 1923): iv; Ibid., 5–6 (February 15, 1924): 257; Ibid., 7 (March 22, 1924): 369–374. The republican

movement, however, faced serious resistance from the followers of Bazar religious leaders and some members of the Majlis. Firoozeh Kashani-Sabet, *Frontier Fictions: Shaping the Iranian Nation 1804–1946* (London: IB Tauris, 2000), 168–174; and 'Abd al-Hadi Hairi, *Shi'ism and Constitutionalism in Iran: A Study of the Role Played by the Persian Residents of Iraq in Iranian Politics* (Leiden, Netherlands: E. J. Brill, 1977), 140–141.

53. *Iranshahr* 2.2 (October 18, 1923): 74–76. In addition, the writer stresses what it is to be an Iranian and greatly emphasizes the meaning of being a part of this nation and holding its nationality.

"We say that the Iranian nation has not lost its racial talent (ist'dad-i nizhadi) and Aryan intelligence, and it is still able to build a brilliant civilization from its own. [This civilization] can do great deeds in science, reality and industry, because Iranian natural intelligence and cleverness are still alive, and the sapling of sagacity and knowledge has not yet dried entirely from the country of Iran. It only needs to be irrigated from the profuse spring of civility and the shining sun of encouragement. Spring and sun are nothing other than knowledge and freedom. [When they obtain these two], you will see the jewels of grace and knowledge that will flow from the mine of Aryan intelligence, and at that time will see what symbols of civilization and knowledge come from the hands of the national masses. At that time you will [also] believe that the soul of this nation has not died, but it was dejected. At that time you will understand that reviving ancient Iran and restoring its civilization is not impossible, bringing forth a 'young and free Iran' in which our utmost desire must be in our own hands." *Iranshahr* 2.4 (December 17, 1923): 194–198.

54. *Iranshahr* 4.5, July 23, 1926, 319; and Nassereddin Parvin, "habl al-matin." in *Encyclopedia Iranica,* ed. Ehsan Yarshater (New York: The Encyclopedia Iranica Foundation, 2003), vol. XI, 431–434.

55. Bihnam, *Barlini-ha*, 178.

56. Vahdat, *God and Juggernaut*, 84–85.

57. *Iranshahr* 1.4 (September 23, 1922): 58–60; *Iranshahr* 2.2 (October 18, 1923): 74; and *Iranshahr* 2.9 (May 21, 1924): 495–507.

REFERENCES

Abrahamian, Ervand. *Iran between Two Revolutions.* Princeton: Princeton University Press, 1982.

Afshar, Iraj. In *Encyclopedia Iranica,* under "Kava Newspaper." Accessed September 12, 2013. http://www.iranicaonline.org/articles/kava.

———, ed. *S. H. Taqizadeh's Articles and Essays,* vol. VII. Tehran: Shekufan, 1977.

Andreeva, Elina. "Iran During World War I." In *Conflict and Conquest in the Islamic World: A Historical Encyclopedia,* edited by Alexander Mikaberidze, vol. I, 410–412. Santa Barbara: ABC-CLIO, 2011.

Aryanpur, Yahiya. *as Saba ta nima: tarikh sad va panjah sal adab-i farisi*, vol. II. Tehran: Nawid, 1367/ 1989.

Atabaki, Touraj. *Azerbaijan: Ethnicity and the Struggle for Power in Iran*. London: IB Tauris, 2000.

———. *Iran and the First World War: Battleground of the Great Powers*. New York: IB Tauris, 2006.

Bayat-Philipp, Mangol. *Mysticism and Dissent: Socioreligious Thought in Qajar Iran*. Syracuse, NY: Syracuse University Press, 1982.

Bihnam, Jamshid. *Barlini-ha: Andishmandan-i irani dar birlin 1915–1930*. Tehran: Farzan, 1379/2000.

———. "Iranšahr." In *Encyclopedia Iranica*, edited by Ehsan Yarshater, vol. XIII, 535–536. New York: The Encyclopedia Iranica Foundation, 2006.

Bonakdarian, Mansour. *Britain and the Iranian Constitutional Revolution of 1906–1911: Foreign Policy, Imperialism, and Dissent*. Syracuse, NY: Syracuse University Press, 2006.

———. "The Persia Committee and the Constitutional Revolution in Iran." *British Journal of Middle Eastern Studies* 18.2 (1991):186–207.

Browne, Edward. G. *A Literary History of Persia*. Cambridge: Cambridge University Press, 1959.

Collett, Nigel. *The Butcher of Amritsar: General Reginald Dyer*. London: Hambledon, 2007.

Entikhabi, Nader. "Nasionalism va tajadud dar farhang-i siasi-i iran." *Iran Nameh* 11.2 (1372/ 1993):185–208.

Epkenhans, Tim. *Die Iranische Moderne im Exil: Bibliographie der Zeitschrift Kave, Berlin 1916–1922*. Berlin: Klaus Schwarz Verlag, 2000.

Fraser, Thomas G. "Germany and Indian Revolution, 1914–18." *Journal of Contemporary History* 12.2 (1977): 255–272.

Gurr, Andrew. *Writing in Exile: The Home in Modern Literature*. Sussex: The Harvester Press, 1981.

Hairi, 'Abd al-Hadi. *Shi'ism and Constitutionalism in Iran: A Study of the Role Played by the Persian Residents of Iraq in Iranian Politics*. Leiden, Netherlands: E. J. Brill, 1977.

Itschernska, Iliza. "Taqizadeh dar Alman-i Qaisari." *Iran nameh* XXI.1–2 (2003): 49–75.

Jamalzadeh, Mohammad A. "Taqizadeh be Qalam-i Jamalzadeh." *Rāhnamā-yi kitāb* 13.3–4 (1349/1970):165–188.

Javadi, Hasan and Edward G. Browne. *Letters from Tabriz: The Russian Suppression of the Iranian Constitutional Movement*. Washington, DC: Mage, 2008.

Kashani-Sabet, Firoozeh. *Frontier Fictions: Shaping the Iranian Nation 1804–1946*. London: IB Tauris, 2000.

Kazimzadeh, Hussein, ed. *Iranshahr*. Berlin, 1922–1927.

———. *Sharh-i hal-i nigarandeh-i kitab usul-i isasi fann-i tarbiat*. Tehran: Iqbal, 1329/1950.

Keddie, Nikki R. "Iran under Later Qajar, 1848–1922." In *Cambridge History of Iran: From Nadir Shah to the Islamic Republic*, edited by

P. Avery et al., vol. 7, 147–212. Cambridge: Cambridge University Press, 1991.

———. *An Islamic Response to Imperialism: Political and Religious Writings of Sayyid Jamāl Ad-Dīn "al-Afghānī"* Berkeley: University of California Press, 1968.

———. *Qajar Iran and the Rise of Reza Khan, 1796–1925.* Costa Mesa, CA: Mazda Press, 1999.

Kramer, Lloyd S. *Threshold of a New World: Intellectuals and the Exile Experience in Paris, 1830–1848.* Ithaca, NY and Paris: Gronell University Press, 1988.

Luft, J. P. "The Iranian Nationalists in Istanbul During World War I." In *Studies in Honour of Clifford Edmund Bosworth,* edited by Carole Hillenbrand, vol. II, 246–271. Leiden, Netherlands; London; and Boston: E. J. Brill, 2000.

Mahrad, Ahmad. *Die Deutsch-persischen Beziehungen von 1918–1933.* Frankfurt and Las Vegas: Peter Lang, 1979.

Marashi, Afshin. *Nationalizing Iran: Culture, Power and the State, 1870–1940.* Washington: University of Washington Press, 2008.

Milani, Abbas. *Eminent Persians: The Men and Women Who Made Modern Iran, 1941–1979,* vol. 1. Syracuse, NY and London: Syracuse University Press, 2008.

———. *Tajaddud va tajaddudsitizi dar iran.* Essen: Nima, 1998.

Moaddel, Mansoor. *Islamic Modernism, Nationalism, and Fundamentalism: Episode and Discourse.* London: University of Chicago Press, 2005.

Moazzam, Anvar. *Jamal al-Din al-Afghani: A Muslim Intellectual.* New Delhi: Naurang Rai, 1984.

Moberly, Frederick. *Operations in Persia, 1914–1919.* London: HMSO, 1987.

Mohib, Raziya. "Chapkhaneh-yi Kaviyani." *kitab mah-i tarikh va jughrafia,* Murdad 147 (1389/2010): 22–28.

Mukherjee, Uma. *Two Great Indian Revolutionaries: Rash Behari Bose and Jyotindra Nath Mukherjee.* Calcutta: Firma K. L. Mukhopadhyay, 1966.

Neubauer, John. "Exile: Home of the Twentieth Century." In *The Exile and Return of Writers from East-Central Europe: A Compendium,* edited by John Neubauer and Borbála Zsuzsanna Török, 4–103. Berlin and New York: Walter de Gruyter, 2009.

Nöldeke, Theodor. *The Iranian National Epic, or Shahnameh,* translated by Leonid Bogdanov. Bombay: Fort Printing Press, 1930.

Parvin, Nassereddin. "habl al-matin." In *Encyclopedia Iranica,* edited by Ehsan Yarshater, vol. XI, 431–4. New York: The Encyclopedia Iranica Foundation, 2003.

———. "Iran-e now." In *Encyclopedia Iranica,* edited by Ehsan Yarshater, vol. XIII, 498–500. New York: The Encyclopedia Iranica Foundation, 2006.

Popplewell, Richard J. *Intelligence and Imperial Defence: The British Intelligence and the Defence of the Indian Empire 1904–1924.* London: Frank Cass, 1995.

Ramazani, Rouhollah K. *The Foreign Policy of Iran 1500–1941: A Developing Nation in World Affairs.* Charlottesville: University Press of Virginia, 1966.

Sabahi, Houshang. *British Policy in Persia, 1918–1925.* London: Frank Cass, 1990.

Shaybani, AbdulHussein. *Khatirat mohajart az dawlat-i movaqat ta kometeh-i berlin,* edited by Iraj Afshar and Kaveh Bayat. Tehran: Shirazeh, 1378/1999.

Sklervo, P.O. "Azdaha." In *Encyclopedia Iranica,* edited by Ehsan Yarshater, vol. III, 191–199. London and New York: Routledge and Kegan Paul, (1989).

Taqizadeh, Hasan, ed. *Kaveh Journal,* Berlin: n.p., 1916–1922.

———. *zandiqi tufani,* edited by Iraj Afshar. Tehran: Intisharat Mohammad Ali Alami, 1990.

Tavakoli-Targhi, Mohammad. *Refashioning Iran, Orientalism, Occidentalism and Historiography.* New York: Palgrave, 2001.

Vahdat, Farzin. *God and Juggernaut: Iran's Intellectual Encounter with Modernity.* New York: Syracuse University Press, 2002.

Ward, Patrick. *Exile, Emigration and Irish Writing.* Dublin: Irish Academic Press, 2002.

Zia Ebrahimi, Reza. "Self-Orientalization and Dislocation: The Uses and Abuses of 'Aryan' Discourse in Iran." *Iranian Studies,* 44.4 (2011): 445–472.

CHAPTER 7

Maulana Barkatullah Bhopali's Transnationalism: Pan-Islamism, Colonialism, and Radical Politics

Humayun Ansari

Muslim challenges to Western hegemony over the past two centuries have received much scholarly attention in recent years. This, in turn, has generated growing interest in their role as a marker of resistance to imperialism, stretching from the middle of the nineteenth century to the beginning of decolonization following World War II. In many parts of the so-called Muslim world, this defiance assumed the guise of Pan-Islamism, which burst onto the political scene in the form of mass mobilizations such as that associated with the Khilafat Movement in India (1919–1924) during the early interwar period. Such developments raised the question of the significance of this Pan-Islamic movement. Not surprisingly, contrasting perspectives have emerged, some arguing that the movement posed a serious threat to the West, while others have judged this insistence by contemporary agents of political surveillance on its severity to be largely an attack of the nerves. Indeed, as far as this second response is concerned, it would seem that target populations often took the writings and programs of Pan-Islamic leaders with a proverbial "grain of salt" and were skeptical of their radicalism, while colonial authorities tended to overinflate their impact.

The focus of this chapter is to explore the significance of Pan-Islamism as a political force by unpicking an important, but largely overlooked, aspect of Muslim involvement in anticolonial, sometimes anti-Western, networks that developed in Europe in the 1920s and

1930s—namely the activities and contribution of Maulana Barkatullah Bhopali (1859–1927), a leading Muslim radical of his time who was based in Moscow and Berlin between 1919 and 1927 (when he died). Barkatullah's political journey is worth studying because of its direct historical relevance for unfolding discourses among and about Muslims in the early twenty-first century; but also more specifically because, located in the context of European imperial developments of one hundred years ago, such an exploration can shed valuable insights and understandings into "Muslim" sensibilities, the contours of more contemporary militant Islamic political movements, and the ways in which Muslims opposed colonial rule. Of particular interest is the way Barkatullah tried to synthesize the various religious and secular strands within his thinking and his attempts to translate them into relatively coherent actions.

In order to evaluate the significance of his contribution to Pan-Islamism after World War I, however, it will first be necessary to examine Barkatullah's three decades of earlier interaction with various radical—Pan-Islamist and revolutionary nationalist—groups working across three continents—Asia, Europe, and North America. Only by contextualizing his activities in the pre-1919 period—his role in earlier networks that themselves formed the basis of later complex interwar connections—will it be possible to assess his involvement and role.

In the late nineteenth century, Muslims in India as elsewhere became acutely aware of how the expansion of European power was increasingly subjecting their coreligionists to Christian rule. Among those who articulated their concern was Sayyid Jamal al-Din Afghani (1837–1897) who saw the reasons for the decline of Islamic power in its military, technological, and political weakness. What caused particular anxiety was the intense attack mounted on the Ottoman Empire, the last substantial power in a position to defend the integrity of Islam against European powers such as Britain and Russia. Feelings of Muslim defensive solidarity were aroused.

Maulana Barkatullah was one of those Indian Muslims who met al-Afghani, who, having been expelled from Egypt at the time of the Urabi rebellion, had arrived in the subcontinent in 1881. He was part of a group of Muslims who were dubbed by contemporaries as "professional agitators," "extremists," and "militant Indian Muslim nationalists." The majority of these Muslims came from the lower ranks of the service class and their experience of the collapse of Islamic power became a major factor in radicalizing ideological and political outlook. They suffered a crisis of conscience as Western powers tightened their grip on Muslims. Retrieving lost self-esteem and restoring the past glories of Islam became a burning quest for them. Influenced by al-Afghani's proto-nationalist ideas, many of the younger ones chose to eschew constitutional approaches to achieving political freedom and favored a more openly revolutionary anti-British struggle. They pursued al-Afghani's vision with intense passion. Barkatullah had been immediately persuaded by his brand of radical Pan-Islamism, which advocated mobilizing Muslims to fight against Western control and conquest of the Islamic world. Of particular appeal were al-Afghani's call for Muslim unity, his stress on *jihad* against western expansion, and his insistence that the Qur'an enjoined the acquisition of the most modern military methods with which to wage this fight.[1] However, while al-Afghani considered the solidarity of the Muslim community a prerequisite for its defense, the more immediate task for him was to resist foreign aggression; hence, he also stressed national unity (in India, Hindu-Muslim unity) as part of his anti-imperialist and anti-British strategy. Al-Afghani's greatest merit, in our context, was to have shown that, in his days at least, Pan-Islamism and nationalism could be mutually complementary.

What appealed to Barkatullah (who was himself trained as an *alim* at the *Madrasa-i-Sulaimanya* in Bhopal) in al-Afghani's approach was that, in contrast to the traditionalist *ulama*, his Islam was compatible with reason, freedom of thought, and other modern virtues; indeed al-Afghani recognized that Muslim freedom was possible only if the secrets of European intellectual, military, technological, and political superiority had been mastered. Barkatullah agreed and soon left India in quest of Western verities. As he observed on his arrival in England, "Education of the masses was neglected and superstition prevailed all over the Islamic countries. Democracy was crushed down under the feet of despotism . . . it is time now for the sun of Islam to rise from the West," because "Muslims in the West are Muslims by reason, not by birth, they promise to be the pioneers of future civilisation."[2]

Yet, Barkatullah experience of England at the end of the nineteenth century became increasingly disillusioning. As Islam and the Ottoman Caliph were subjected to unrestrained popular and official ridicule and insults, from pulpits and platforms no less than in the press, he quickly became disenchanted and his interactions with the British at the institutional and popular levels became increasingly toxic. The more he defended Islam and Muslims, the more he came under surveillance from the British state. His discussions with a growing circle of radical Indian revolutionaries convinced him that freedom from British rule could be achieved not by constitutional but only by revolutionary means. From then onward, Barkatullah immersed himself into the task of yoking his Pan-Islamism to nationalist goals, pursuing them through propaganda and organization. His vision and strategies, in particular in a variety of transnational, predominantly secular networks in which he was involved in London, Paris, Berlin, New York, San Francisco, Tokyo, Kabul, and Moscow, were predicated upon the expediency of achieving the freedom of colonized people, Muslim and non-Muslim, from British imperial rule primarily by revolutionary means. Hence his part in the foundation of the "terrorist" *Ghadr* (Revolutionary) Party, his collaboration with the German Foreign Ministry seeking military support against the British in India, his role as prime minister of the provisional Government of India in Kabul, and his efforts to gain political and financial help from the Bolsheviks and, with their blessings, Mussolini after the defeat of Germany and its ally, Turkey, in World War I.

This chapter explores Barkatullah's political journey by locating it in the context of the late nineteenth and early twentieth centuries' European imperial developments. What is particularly fascinating is how he synthesized the religious and secular strands within his thinking and sought to translate them into relatively coherent actions. More importantly, it permits not only valuable insights and understandings into wider Muslim sensibilities, contours of Islamic political movements, and engagement of Muslim opposition to colonial rule in the interwar period, but also their relevance in the new millennium.

I. THE PRE-1919 PERIOD

By the time Barkatullah arrived in England, a number of Pan-Islamic networks had begun to surface. The Liverpool Muslim Institute (LMI)—he became its first *imam* and *muezzin*[3]—represented the pivot of one such network. Founded by Abdullah Quilliam after his conversion to Islam in 1887, it served until 1908 not just as a place of worship, but also as a meeting place "for thousands of Mahommedans, merchants, sailors, travellers, who pass[ed] through the port."[4] Among the objectives of the LMI was the promotion of worldwide Muslim unity. In pursuance of this vision, it vociferously proclaimed its support for the Ottoman caliphate. While its resident membership reached about two hundred, thanks to Quilliam's travels and connections it became a genuinely global Muslim network. For instance, he met the Qajar Shah of Persia when he visited Liverpool in 1889, who later appointed him his consul. In 1894, the Ottoman ruler conferred on him the title of *Sheikh al-Islam* of the British Isles.

Further recognition came when Nasrullah Khan, the brother of the Amir of Afghanistan, visited him in 1895 bestowing upon him a gift of £2,500 and the *Koola-Izzat* (hat of honour).

Pan-Islamist Muslims living in Britain at this time had mixed feelings. While they recognized the technological and military superiority of the European powers, they were also dismayed by the subordination of the Muslim world from which they themselves hailed. When Barkatullah arrived in England in the late 1880s, he must have immediately become aware of the rising hostility toward Islam and more specifically toward the Ottoman Empire. In Liverpool, for instance, Islam was being condemned "as an exotic...un-English religion."[5] Anti-Muslim popular sentiment was fuelled by the depiction of Muslims as tyrannical, brutal, and morally decadent in cartoons, music-hall songs, novels, and religious journals. At a time when Gladstone, four-time British prime minister, fulminated against the sultan as "the unspeakable Turk," denouncing him for his tyranny, his moral decrepitude, and his alleged brutality against its Christian populations in the Balkans, the LMI became the target of the local population as well as the press, attracting insult, ridicule, and violent protest. The personal experience of these violent outbursts accompanied by jeers and abuse as he called the faithful to prayers, would have reminded Barkatullah of the antipathy toward Muslims in wider society, confirming his own negative view of the British.

As attacks on Islam and Muslims became more vitriolic, responses from the institute too became increasingly strident. Barkatullah also made speeches and wrote pieces strongly critical of British imperial campaigns and policy vis-à-vis Turkey, increasingly causing the British authorities concern. He was put under surveillance; while British intelligence regarded him as "a highly educated man...an excellent scholar of Arabic," they also suspected him to be "a man of strong revolutionary tendencies,"[6] and acting as "a secret agent of the Ameer of Afghanistan."[7] This experience of the popular and official targeting of Islam and Muslims in all likelihood further reinforced Barkatullah's acceptance of al-Afghani's ideas, especially those that favored a more openly anti-British Pan-Islamic struggle to secure the freedom of the Muslim world from Western dominance.

By the time Barkatullah shifted to London, there had emerged a significant cluster of Muslim activists in Britain who constituted a network that favored such a struggle. Among them were law students—Mushir Husain Kidwai and the "untrustworthy adventurer" Rafiuddin Ahmad, a friend of Queen Victoria's Indian secretary, Munshi Abdul Karim. The former had also been vice president of Quilliam's Liverpool Moslem Association.[8] The Anjuman-i Islam (a society set up in 1886 ostensibly for "the protection of the political interests of Moslem community at large" and to act as "a powerful lever for the regeneration of the Moslem nations"[9]), had already robustly begun to respond to the rising tide of anti-Muslim feeling. Barkatullah had become involved in the two diasporic Muslims bodies—the Anjuman-i-Islam and the Moslem Patriotic League—as well as congregations organized at the temporary mosque in Albert Street. Representing "Indian Mohamedans in London," he played a leading role in refuting the "monstrous calumnies" printed in British newspapers about the sultan of Turkey, protesting "against the gross misrepresentation of the Moslem law and religion."[10] He remained in contact with Quilliam[11] and continued to contribute to the latter's somewhat confrontational Pan-Islamism especially as propagated through his weekly and monthly periodicals, *The Crescent* and *The Islamic World* respectively.

In London, Barkatullah's ideas began to converge with those of the more radical strands of anticolonial nationalism. He was particularly impressed by the strategies of Irish nationalist agitators for home rule. He also came into contact with non-Muslim Indian nationalists, who had increasingly become impatient with the constitutional progress toward home rule in India. But with little wriggle room to pursue his anti-British politics in London, Barkatullah, at the invitation of Muhammad Alexander Russell Webb, a convert to Islam in a similar mould to Abdullah Quilliam, set sail for New York in 1903; he felt that he would have greater opportunity to mobilize Indian nationalists for revolutionary action in a country that itself had won independence from Britain through armed struggle and where there seemed to be visible sympathy for colonial people's aspirations of freedom. With the United States viewed as an organizational haven for other anticolonial groups, in particular Irish nationalists, he was more optimistic about the chances of pursuing his radical Pan-Islamist activities there. The expression of support in periodicals such as *Gaelic American* for "all the countries held in subjection by the British" further encouraged his move to New York.[12]

For the following six years he immersed himself in anti-imperial networks, establishing contacts with Indians who were supportive of similar political activities in other parts of North America and Canada. He wrote numerous articles on Islam and India in Webb's *The Muslim World* as well as in mainstream newspapers such as the *Forum*, exhorting revolutionary action. Here he "tried to organise various disloyal societies."[13] With the support of "Irish-American extremists," especially George Freeman and John Davey, Barkatullah, together with S. L. Joshi, founded the Pan-Aryan Association in October 1906. Its purpose was to disseminate anti-British propaganda among Indians immigrants and students. By now Barkatullah had developed an incisive socioeconomic critique and views on the damaging political impact of British rule in India and the broader Muslim world. In May 1907, in a letter to the Indian journal *Urdu-i Mualla*, he argued:

> Indian crafts and industry had been destroyed by high tariffs on Indian manufacture and the import of cheap English goods...[consequently] India was transformed into an agrarian country....Unequal terms of trade, primitive methods of cultivation and the burden of imperial expenditure had bankrupted India.[14]

On the other hand, he claimed, it was by India's wealth that the English maintained their military strength, and by India's wealth that they brought into subjection Egypt, the Soudan, Persia, the Persian Gulf, and the Muslim countries lying to the north and east of Africa.

He further contended that "it is the Mohamedans of India who, by their loyalty to the British Government, are laying the axe at the root of the stability of the independent Islamic countries." He concluded that "in order to get rid of this corrupt organisation and absurd form of Government (meaning the British) it is necessary that Hindus and Muslims should unite and claim equal rights and privileges."[15]

While he was in New York, Barkatullah maintained his transatlantic contacts with those Indian exiles in Britain and Europe whose policies were rapidly moving toward revolution. However, conditions for these radicals were becoming increasingly hazardous, especially in England. Hence the reluctant shifting of their operations to Europe: Madame Cama brought out her monthly journal, *Bande Mataram*, from Geneva; *Talwar* (Sword) appeared in Berlin—"The capital of the country which is at present most hostile in spirit to England."[16] Krishnavarma, one of Barkatullah's close friends, who, in 1905, had set up a radical hub "India House" in London, and started publishing his radical nationalist monthly *Indian Sociologist* ("An Organ of Freedom, of Political, Social and Religious Reform") had moved to Paris. The knot was also tightening around Bepin Chandra Pal, Virendranath Chattopadhyaya, and V. D. Savarkar who were seen as the leaders of the movement promoting violent methods to achieve nationalist ends. They likewise moved to Europe.

In New York, Barkatullah remained actively involved in the anti-British circles. At the end of 1908, joint Indian-Irish meetings were held "twice a week at Barkatullah's house to discuss the situation."[17] Though he had moved to the United States, his ideas continued to evolve under the influence of the Indian radicals in Europe. His close association with revolutionary nationalists and his intellectual engagement with their vision, their political strategies, objectives, and programs of activities helped him to develop a reasoned reconciliation between his radical brand of Pan-Islamism and revolutionary nationalism.

In achieving this convergence, Barkatullah was undoubtedly helped by political developments in India and elsewhere. Between 1908 and the outbreak of World War I, Pan-Islamism in India erupted into active opposition to the British. Italy's assault on Ottoman Libya in 1911–1912, and European support for Balkan Christians from 1911 to 1913, came as painful blows to any illusions that Indian Muslims might still have had regarding the goodwill of European powers toward the Ottomans. Having concluded that the British were bent upon destroying the worldwide Muslim community, they formulated strategies to resist the perceived British onslaught, and even advocated organizing a *jihad*, from abroad if necessary.[18] The leaders of this radical strand of Pan-Islamism—Mahmud al-Hasan, the principle of the Islamic seminary at Deoband, and Maulana Ubaidullah Sindhi, a Deobandi-trained Sikh convert—planned to leave India for the Hijas and Kabul respectively, the latter to persuade Amir Habibullah of Afghanistan to withdraw his neutrality and declare war against the British in India with the help of Germany and Turkey, while simultaneously instigating a Muslim insurrection from the tribal belt in India.

In the Pacific region, similar efforts were being initiated, with the help of a growing body of Indian revolutionaries among mainly Sikh and Hindu immigrants in California and British Columbia, to produce propaganda for dissemination among the troops of the British Indian Army as well as for circulation in India. Japan, where because of its strategic location in the Far East sizeable groups of Indians had become established, was seen as holding some promise for anti-British operations. Accordingly, Barkatullah was encouraged by Freeman and Joshi to go there. Through Krishnavarma and Madame Cama's connections, he obtained an appointment as Professor of Hindustani at the School of Foreign Languages in Tokyo, where he arrived in early 1909. From his home he began disseminating revolutionary journals from other parts of the world. In early 1910, he took on the editorship of the weekly periodical *Islamic Fraternity*, whose front cover had the following caption: "An organ devoted to providing fraternal feeling among the followers of Islam and those of other religions,"[19] but which was viewed by British intelligence as one that propagated "a rather militant form of Pan-Islamism."[20] As the situation in the Balkans deteriorated, its anti-British tone grew sharper; in the March 1912 number, quoting a Roman poet's description of the Anglo-Saxons of his time as "the seawolves...who lived on the pillage of the world," Barkatullah bemoaned that "the predatory instinct of the race is not softened. If anything at all has been added to it, it is the refinement of hypocrisy which sharpens the edge of brutality."[21] In October, the paper was banned from India (as was its successor *El Islam*) and, on British representations, "suppressed by the Japanese Government."[22]

Undeterred, Barkatullah turned to writing anti-British pamphlets. In June 1913, *The Sword is the Last Resort* blamed the atrocities in the Balkan war and misfortunes of Islam on England, exhorting Muslims "to form secret societies and endeavour to annihilate the oppressive English who are robbing and plundering India. They should destroy the feeling of fear of the English which is a 'spider's web of deceit.'" It went on:

> Those Indian spies [i.e., the *mullahs* in mosques, *pujaris* in temples, prostitutes, street hawkers, shop-keepers, teachers connected with the Criminal Investigation Department] who are faithful to the English should be picked out and killed.... [In anticipation] of a war between England and Germany, Indians should make preparations for an armed rising.[23]

The British saw Barkatullah as "a sort of connecting link between three different movements, namely, the Pan-Islamic, Asia for Asiatics, and Indian sedition. The common aim of all those movements was, of course, the release of Asia, in which was included Turkey, from European domination."[24] His travel movements in 1911—under British surveillance—which took him to his contacts in Constantinople, Cairo, and St Petersburg, before returning to Tokyo in October, revealed his linking role in these widely dispersed networks. With intelligence reports indicating worldwide circulation of Barkatullah's, in their view, dangerously subversive papers and pamphlets, the British authorities took steps to suppress him. They furnished the Japanese with information that proved sufficiently persuasive for them to act: "He was dismissed from his post, at the instance [sic] of the British Ambassador in Tokio"; on May 6, 1914, accompanied by a rising star in the Indian revolutionary movement Bhagwan Singh, he left for the United States, where he became "an active member of the Ghadr Party."[25] He also took over and ran the publication *Ghadr* (after Har Dayal was compelled to leave by the US authorities) in which he articulated an uncompromising revolutionary strategy. For the success of the "war" he advocated the necessity of starting newspapers, publishing books, learning military exercises; he called for the formation of secret societies and made passionate appeals for collection of funds and to foreign nations for help. The *Ghadr* advocated that Indians should return to India with the express objective of creating a rising in conjunction with the enemies of the Empire, murder all Europeans and loyal Indian subjects, overthrow the existing government, and lay the foundation of a republic.[26] At a meeting reported in *Ghadr* on August 4, 1914, the day Britain declared war, Barkatullah declared that the time for the rebellion had come; the British were to be expelled from India as war in Europe commenced; it was a splendid opportunity to go to India, seduce troops, and start the rebellion there.[27]

As the war began, Germany's strategy converged with Barkatullah's own thoughts: along with many of his compatriots he had concluded some time ago that "England's difficulty would be India's opportunity."[28] Germany, he believed, could help in creating such an opportunity. Already, in 1912, he saw Kaiser Wilhelm of Germany as "really one man who holds the peace of the world in the hollow of his hand." So, "in case of a European war," he declared, "it is the duty of the Muslims to be united to stand by the [Ottoman] Khalif...and to side with Germany." *Ghadr*, on July 21, 1914, likewise reiterated, "Germany being the enemy of England, which is also our enemy, we should regard the former country as our friend."[29]

The German government too was persuaded by Max von Oppenheim, a diplomat with specialist knowledge and experience of the Middle East that its enemies could be weakened from within by "fomenting rebellion in the Islamic territories" by mobilizing the Pan-Islamist potential of discontented Muslims under their imperial control.[30] A key element in this strategy, once he took over responsibility for the Islamic regions at the German Foreign Office, was to cajole the Turkish sultan to declare a *jihad* against the British, the French, and the Russians. The targets were Muslims in India, north Africa, and Asia, who were to be incited to rise up against their imperial masters. On November 9, 1914, the *Sheikh al-Islam* in Istanbul duly proclaimed that it was "the duty of all Mahomedans" to do so.[31]

In Berlin, Oppenheim embarked upon recruiting groups of men outside India and other colonized regions whom he thought to be in search of a powerful ally for their anti-imperialist cause. In the United States, Barkatullah was one such Indian recognized as suitable material.[32] Har Dayal, the founder of the Ghadr Party in the United States, introduced Barkatullah "as a person of confidence...and as the most important leader of the Muslim nationalists of India." His credentials were, "A friend of the leading men in Kabul," including "the brother of the Emir and the editor of the only newspaper of Afghanistan, Serajul Akhbar," speaker and writer in English, Arabic, Persian, and Hindi, and "well known in Constantinople," which clearly impressed the Germans. He arrived in Berlin in early 1915 on a German passport where he was given "lessons in order to learn about the production and use of hand grenades and explosives"[33] in preparation for revolutionary work in Afghanistan among the frontier tribes on the Indo-Afghan border.

Working closely with Oppenheim's unit in the German Foreign Office, he, in conjunction with other anti-imperialist exiles, produced news of the war and their ideas on insurrection in conjunction. He helped to produce pamphlets and journals that called for *jihad*, for systematic assassination and extermination of Christian neighbors within Islamic lands.[34] He was involved in preparing similar literature exhorting Muslim soldiers and prisoners of war either to desert or to join the Central Powers in the conflict against their enemies or to promote the anticolonial struggles after returning to their homelands. An influential member of the Indian Committee, he visited the prisoners of war (POW) camp at Wünsdorf near Berlin,[35] delivering lectures and holding informal discussions along with his colleagues such as Dr. Mansur Ahmed and Mahendra Pratap, with the purpose of persuading them to fight the British and their allies.[36] He repeatedly traveled to Hamburg in 1915 and 1916 in order to recruit new members for the Indian Independence Committee among Indian sailors.[37]

While Pan-Islamism was the preferred propagandistic strategy of von Oppenheim and the Foreign Office, it was conceded with some reluctance that giving nationalism precedence over Pan-Islamism (without fully giving up the latter) was the more promising strategy in the Indian case.[38] Indeed, as the war progressed, doubts regarding the efficacy of the *jihad* propaganda were voiced in the German diplomatic establishment with increasing frequency.[39] While an uneasiness to fight for the British against Muslims or on what they regarded as holy land was quoted repeatedly as a prevalent attitude among the Indian Muslim POWs,[40] and some Muslim soldiers did indeed not only refuse "to take up arms against their brother Muslims" (when they reached Basra in Mesopotamia)[41] but also deserted in order "to take

part in Jehad against the English,"[42] by and large the efforts whether
of the German authorities or the Indian revolutionaries at mobilizing large numbers of POWs or persuading soldiers to abscond were
not particularly successful, even though there was some evidence of
the existence not only of "a vague panislamism [sic]" among Muslim
soldiers but also among "Punjabi soldiers...of resentment against
deployment in Muslim lands."[43] Nevertheless, Barkatullah remained
optimistic about the potential for an anti-British Pan-Islamist rebellion being ignited in Afghanistan.[44] Germans too felt that their *jihad*
strategy was winning them support among a significant number of
Indian Muslims, especially the pro-Turkish tribes in the Afghan–India
border regions. In early 1915, Raja Mahendra Pratap (1886–1979),
a revolutionary nationalist from a Hindu background with "decisive sympathy for the Germans who were fighting this dirty British
Empire"[45] arrived in Berlin. He was able to convince the Germans
to send a mission to Afghanistan and seek Amir Habibullah's assistance in operations against Britain, for "if Afghanistan should enter
the war, this would greatly enhance the chances of an Indian uprising against England."[46] Barkatullah, who knew Mahendra Pratap
well, was asked to join the Indo-German-Turkish Mission because
of his cordial relations and influence with the Afghan amir's brother,
Nasrullah Khan, the prime minister; he shared Barkatullah's Pan-
Islamic vision.[47] While the mission on arrival in Kabul received an
enthusiastic welcome from an increasingly Pan-Islamist public, the
astute amir, sensitive to the British anxieties and reluctant to "break
his alliance with the Government of Great Britain,"[48] kept them waiting for several weeks before meeting them. In early 1916, while members of the German mission signed a treaty of friendship recognizing
Afghan independence, they left Kabul without persuading the amir
to join the war.

Even so, Barkatullah, like Mahendra Pratap, saw considerable revolutionary potential, and both decided to stay on in Kabul, where they
received encouragement from the Pan-Islamist Mahmud Tarzi, editor
of the influential journal *Siraj al-Akhbar*, and other members of the
"war party." In the journal, they were allowed to write anti-British
and pro–central powers articles. In April 1916 when Barkatullah tem-
porarily took over its editorship, he reproduced from a newspaper
in Constantinople a speech by Taraknath Das, one of Barkatullah's
associates in the United States, in which he applauded the Ottoman's
alliance with Germany "to save the unfortunate inhabitants of India,
Egypt, Persia, Morocco and Africa from the English, French and
Russians who had forcibly seized and reduced them to slavery."[49]

Under Barkatullah's "seditionist" editorship, the journal's tone became so "dangerously anti-British" and "objectionable" that the alarmed viceroy in India ordered its interception to avoid giving any publicity to the revolutionary views expressed therein.[50] Coinciding with the German mission, Ubaidullah Sindhi's arrival from India in October 1915 with plans to initiate a *jihad* against the British provided a further fillip. Together they set about establishing "The Provisional Government of India" (PGI) or *Hukumat-i- Moogita-i-Hind*. With Mahendra Pratap as president, Barkatullah was appointed prime minister and Ubaidullah as minister for India. Its aim was to create alliances with countries opposed to the British and, with their help, to liberate India. It issued a "general proclamation to the Indian Army," "inciting" Indian troops to mutiny. It invited, in particular, the tsar of Russia to renounce his alliance with Great Britain, and "assist in the overthrow of British rule in India." Messengers were sent to China to seek support from the Republican regime.[51] The creation of *Al Janud-a-Rabbania* (The Army of God), with the Ottoman sultan, the shah of Persia and the amir of Afghanistan as its patrons, was also announced.

This so-called Pan-Islamist conspiracy did not succeed, for several reasons. It suffered from lack of unity of purpose among Muslims themselves. The Arabs, assisted by the British, revolted against the Ottomans. Afghanistan's ruling group was also divided about the PGI: while Nasrullah supported it, Habibullah disapproved of its subversive activities. Moreover, the promised military and financial help from Germany and Turkey, without which Habibullah was certainly not prepared to enter the war, had not materialized. When Barkatullah requested the German Foreign Office for money "and at least ten thousand troops...to Afghanistan for Indian work,"[52] he was ignored. Nevertheless, even under these unpropitious circumstances, the PGI persisted, through diplomatic channels, in soliciting support from various foreign governments for its activities against the British.

But while the war, with the central powers facing defeat, certainly represented a major setback for Barkatullah and his associates' plans, the exiled Indian revolutionaries were given fresh impetus by the success of the Russian revolution in October 1917. Their fortunes were further boosted by the assassination of Habibullah and the enthronement in April 1919 of his considerably more anti-British son, Amanullah. Amanullah, no less keen than the Bolsheviks to reduce British influence, declared war against the British in May 1919, invading the Frontier districts in India. While he was compelled to agree a truce after just 11 days, in the ensuing negotiations he secured British recognition of Afghanistan's independence. The Indians assembled in Kabul also benefited from the friendly relations that developed between him and Lenin.

From his base in Kabul, Barkatullah increasingly involved himself in developing the relationship with the Bolsheviks. He was undoubtedly attracted by the methods that they had recently deployed to demolish the tsarist regime. Russia's annulment of all secret treaties imposed by the imperialist governments, agreeing "to Tsarist annexation of Constantinople, partition of Persia and the dismemberment of Turkey," and its proclamation of "the right of all peoples, no matter how small they be, to determine their own destiny" had impressed him greatly.[53] He was particularly drawn toward them for their moral and material support to Turkey, Persia, and Afghanistan in their resistance to foreign domination. Indeed, it is arguable that on most political matters and in his socioeconomic analysis there seems to be considerable congruence between them, though he continued to hold fast to his theological position. In a speech published in *Ishtraquiun* (Tashkent) he openly called for the abolition of private property.[54] So the question remained, to what extent did he consider it expedient to view the Bolsheviks as allies in order to secure his Pan-Islamic goals? Did he join them only because, for him, they were "the enemies of their enemies"?[55] After all, Barkatullah categorically stated that he was an "irreconcilable enemy of European capitalism in Asia whose main representative is the English." He believed that "the ideas of the Bolsheviks [had] caught on among the Indian masses" and that "in India have matured the same prerequisites of revolution which existed in Russia in October 1917."[56] In a proclamation addressed to "All the Moslems of Asia," he declared that "all democracies of the world are enthusiastically embracing the idea of Bolshevism." He called on them to "unite around Soviet Power and to take up arms against the British, the universal oppressors of the rights of humanity and autonomy of peoples and especially the perpetual and avowed enemies of Islam."[57] However, in an interview with *Petrograd Pravda* in 1919 he elaborated his position: "I am neither a Communist nor a Socialist, but my political programme is the expulsion of the English from Asia...In this I concur with the communists and in this respect we are genuine allies."

So, while he did not consider himself a Bolshevik, Barkatullah did believe that the Bolshevik movement was in essence consistent with the principles of Islam. In *Bolshevism and the Islamic Body Politick*, which was printed in several languages and circulated among his networks in central Asia and India, he appealed to Muslims of the world "to understand the noble principles of Russian socialism and to embrace it seriously and enthusiastically." "Oh, Muhammedans," he wrote, "listen to this divine cry. Respond to this call of liberty, equality and brotherhood which Comrade Lenin and the Soviet Government of Russia are offering to you."[58]

II. Barkatullah in Russia and Germany from 1919 Onward

Thus, after Germany's and Turkey's defeat in the war, the centre of gravity of the Indian revolutionaries' activities shifted to the Soviet Union for quite obvious reasons. Some of the key members of the now-dissolved Berlin Committee likewise saw Britain and France, the victors, dismembering the Ottoman Empire, and carving out mandates for themselves and sought allies in resistance to them. Soviet Union, which had "annulled and torn up...the secret treaties made between the deposed Emperor [the Tsar] and other states as regards the occupation of Constantinople as well as treaties ratified by the dismissed Kerensky" seemed a promising prospect in this regard.[59] Groups of Indian revolutionaries began to gravitate around Moscow. In March 1919, Barkatullah, together with Abdul Rab, whom he knew from Kabul, went to Moscow via Tashkent on a German passport as Amanullah's "ambassador extraordinary," tasked with establishing "permanent relations with Soviet Russia." His interview with Lenin, Chicherin, Karakhan, and other Bolsheviks suggested that the Soviet Government, which was keen to establish cordial relations with neighboring Muslim peoples and, moreover, for strategic and ideological reasons, committed to give moral and material support to those who were fighting to free themselves, saw Barkatullah as a significant political figure. He too was enthusiastic about playing a major role in helping the Soviet Union in its attempts to mobilize Muslims against their imperial masters. To this end, in June 1919, a leaflet signed by him and addressed "To all Muslims of Asia" stated that the British and their allies by stratagem and treachery had taken possession of Mecca, Medina, Baghdad, Syria, Jerusalem, Najaf, Kerbala, and Meshad, the holy places of Islam. The English and the Americans, contrary to all promises, had advanced on Constantinople and Anatolia and had reduced to shreds the Turkish dominions, because, as Barkatullah saw it, they wished to drive Turkey out of Europe.

The defeat of the Ottoman Empire threatened its dismemberment by the victorious entente powers.[60] For Indian Muslims, whether at home or abroad, the outcome of the war was little short of a catastrophe. The British authorities in India were well aware of the intensity of Muslim sentiment.[61] The caliphate was the symbol of Islam's world power and of the unity of Islamic people. With the caliphate on the verge of being destroyed, their minority situation meant that they were left feeling extremely vulnerable. Few concessions were made at the Versailles Peace Conference in 1919. The Treaty of Sevres in August 1920 confirmed their worst fears. What was left of Turkey after the imperial carve up through this treaty was an independent state only in name.

Muslims in India were up in arms. Powerfully supported by the Indian nationalist movement, within a few months of its initiation, the Khilafat agitation, with its objective "to secure a just and honourable peace for Turkey," reached mass proportions.[62] In the spring of 1920, the Khilafat leaders escalated the protests further by proclaiming British India *Dar al-Harb* (House of War) and enjoined Muslim emigration, in the first instance to Afghanistan, a Muslim state from where, with Amir Amanullah's help, an armed challenge against the British could be mounted. Of the 30,000 or so who left India as a result, some arrived in Moscow, where, together with Barkatullah and other Indian revolutionaries, they became energetically involved in attacking the British rule.

In London too there were some Indian Muslims who became active in defense of the caliphate. These were all men who were convinced that the true interests of Muslims, in India as elsewhere, could only be secured through total political independence from Britain, forging of greater unity among Muslim nations, and not entirely or necessarily by constitutional means. Moreover, Mushir Husain Kidwai, a barrister based in London, together with a small group of Indian radicals, was particularly influenced by Bolshevik ideas. Like Barkatullah, he believed that revolutionary socialism was wholly compatible with the achievement of Muslim aims and even before the outbreak of the war, in 1913, published *Islam and Socialism* setting out his argument. Consequently, similar to Barkatullah, he worked hard to bring about a closer relationship between the Bolsheviks and the Ottoman Caliphate, Afghanistan, and Persia, the only independent Muslim states left with some hope of withstanding the power of the West. These Pan-Islamists had been especially encouraged by Bolsheviks' signing of the Peace Treaty at Brest-Litovsk with the central powers in March 1918, their annulment of the secret treaties with the entente powers, and their promises to provide financial and military support to anticolonial and national liberation struggles.

This network of Pan-Islamist activists established a range of political pressure groups centered on London, which shared the broad aim of stemming the decline of the *umma*. They became active in high-profile initiatives such as the visit of the Indian Mohamed Ali–led Khilafat deputation to Europe from India in March 1920, making the necessary financial and logistical arrangements in Britain and Paris, organizing public meetings chaired by some of the leading lights of Britain's political elite, handling its correspondence and interviews and articulating and disseminating its views and demands through various media channels. The stream of telegrams from India regarding the caliphate, disseminated through Kidwai's London newssheet *Muslim Outlook*, as well as news from different parts of the Muslim world, highlighted the transnational reach of this Pan-Islamic network, as well as the breadth of its connections and its capacity to mobilize international opinion and action around Islamic issues. All were underpinned by a coherent principle that opposition to imperialism and domination of the African and Asian people, the struggle for freedom, required solidarity with the remaining few non-European independent powers. Among these, the Ottoman Empire remained the most prominent, but its defense, they felt, could only be mounted under the guise of Pan-Islamism, and so their efforts were geared toward sharpening this solidarity.

Barkatullah, during this postwar period, continued to work with Muslim and non-Muslim Indian revolutionaries in Europe and the Soviet Union. With the defeat of Germany, the Berlin Committee was dissolved in December 1918.[63] While some Indian nationalists residing in Germany continued to be supported by the Government,[64] a number moved to Petrograd and joined the activists at the Russian Propaganda Centre.[65] Barkatullah had maintained contacts with them and others who had dispersed to various parts of Europe, promising to help them financially and otherwise from Moscow. Between 1920 and 1922, he was in touch with the groups of anticolonial radicals still based in Berlin. A large number among them thought that the Soviet strategy of rendering assistance to the Pan-Islamic movement, which Barkatullah was presumed to have supported, was "highly detrimental to the interest of Indian Independence."[66] Indeed, British intelligence at the time reported that "considerable friction exists between the Hindu and Muhammadan members."[67] These discussions were beset by wrangling over the nature of political program—Barkatullah and the PGI were in favor of a political revolution, while M. N. Roy (who had announced the foundation of the Communist Party of India, albeit in Tashkent in 1920) and his associates wanted to do purely Communistic work.[68] While M. N. Roy, whose views on Indian affairs were perhaps regarded more highly by the Soviet high command than those of any other Indian revolutionary, disagreed with Barkatullah ideologically and had conveyed a poor opinion of his political capabilities,[69] as late as March 1923, prominent Russian Bolshevik leaders, regarded him, as "one of their most trusted agents."[70] This was reflected in the Soviet leader's support for Barkatullah and his group through the supply of funds and publication and dissemination of its organ, *Indian Independence*.

After the Genoa Pan-European Conference in April 1922, Georgy Chicherin, the Soviet Commissar for Foreign Affairs, encouraged Barkatullah to go to Berlin and bring the Indian revolutionaries there together. Accordingly, upon arrival in Berlin, Barkatullah set about forming a new party called the Indian Independence Party; he was appointed president and B. N. Dutt, general secretary. Other "prominent seditionists"—Acharya, Dr. Mansur and Muhammad Ali—joined it.[71] Dr. Abdul Hafiz agreed to become a member of the Central Executive Committee. In June 1923, Ubaidullah, stationed in Petrograd, also accepted its membership, agreeing to work in its interest in the Soviet Union.

Barkatullah wrote to Chicherin in Moscow in October 1922, outlining clearly the scope of the work—organizing the *Mujahiddin* in India's North West Frontier, disseminating revolutionary propaganda—which the Indian Independence Party intended to follow[72] with modest financial assistance from Soviet Russia.[73] This work was actually started—a number of schools were set up, and a newspaper *Al-Mujahid* was printed with more or less regularity—but the revolt against the British never really got off the ground.[74]

With the abolition of the Ottoman Sultanate on November 1, 1922, while still concerned about the threat to Turkish sovereignty and independence, Barkatullah's gaze shifted to anti-imperialist and national liberation struggles. At the Lausanne Conference, held to revise the Treaty of Sevres (against its imposition by the victorious imperial powers, Mustafa Kemal Pasha [1881–1938] had waged a successful Turkish nationalist armed struggle, and which his government in Ankara no longer recognized), Barkatullah in his capacity as its representative circulated a manifesto of the Indian Independence Party, headed "The Perfidious Albion," among the peace delegates. This pamphlet denounced the British ambition "to monopolise the whole planet":

> There was no strategic position on the face of the earth [he said] where they had not established their effective control and reduced thereby all the nations, great and small, to be at their mercy and sweet will.

In the chain of their selfish designs there remained only one link, the straits of Dardanelles and the Bosphorus, to complete their domination over all nations of Europe. Hence they came to the Lausanne Conference with their mouths professing peace and good will to all men, while their heads are full of designs of world subjugation. The Indian Independence Party has a message to all oppressed nations of Europe, Asia and Africa...that all should adopt an economic policy based on common interests against Great Britain.[75]

Undeterred by the German Government's "suppression" of *Indian Independence*, on representation from Britain[76] at the beginning of December 1922, Barkatullah published another anti-British circular for distribution to the delegates at the Lausanne Conference. This presented the program of the Indian Independence Party that included the attainment of "complete and absolute independence by all possible means" and the establishment of "the Federated Democratic Republic [of India] in which the sovereignty must rest with the people"; it included the formation of "friendly alliances with the peoples and nations of the world" and the extension of "co-operation and affiliation with all organisations in or outside India having similar objects and those having socio-economic revolutionary programmes."[77] In respect of its constitution and general aims, this new party embraced members of the old "Indian Revolutionary Council." Chicherin had, at Lausanne, already informed Barkatullah that he accepted this program and had asked Moscow to provide funds.[78] So Barkatullah and his network in Europe were able to continue their operations, advising Indians to follow the epoch-making revolution in Russia.

In 1923 and 1924, however, Barkatullah's Pan-Islamist aspirations suffered further setbacks. The Soviet Union had become increasingly supportive of the Turkish national movement. Then Mustapha Kemal established the secular Grand National Assembly in Ankara, stripping the caliphate of all sovereign authority. Tired of the caliph's political meddling, Mustapha Kemal abolished the office of the caliphate in March 1924, and banished him to Switzerland. The broad reaction among Indian Muslims was a mixture of disbelief, shock, and grief. The anger against Mustapha Kemal was intense. His actions were seen as threatening the worldwide Muslim polity. But Pan-Islamism as a viable political philosophy had suffered a major defeat. Indian Muslims abroad too protested. From Berlin, Abdul Jabbar Kheri, the president of the pro-caliphate "Islamische Gemeinde," "condemned what he called the utterly 'anti-Islamic' and 'mischievous' action of the Kemalists."[79]

Barkatullah, however, was more measured in his assessment. Having left Rome, where he had been busy seeking, albeit unsuccessfully,

Mussolini's help, he settled in St. Gallen, Switzerland, where, in the autumn of 1924, he wrote an Urdu-English pamphlet, *The Khilafet*, in which he explored the reasons for the end of the caliphate. For him, "*Khilafet* had been an engine for the aggrandisement of Islamic despotism."[80] The Ottoman dynasty was ruthlessly tyrannical.[81] For Barkatullah, if the Khilafat was to be restored, it was imperative that the power of the Sultan be limited by law. A striking illustration of this contention was "the king of England, who presided over the government of a unique empire...but [who] owing to limitation of his powers was unable to harm anybody."[82]

Barkatullah believed that mischief proceeded not just from the sultan, but "rather the very existence of the spiritual and temporal authority in one person puts the premium upon despotism, tyranny and abuse."[83] For this reason "THE KHALIF MUST BE THE SPIRITUAL LEADER ONLY".[84]

> The spiritual head of the Islamic world must religiously eschew every, and any, kind of interference in political affairs of the Faithful the world over. He must shun politics as poison...and ensure that the religion of God is not affected by political prejudices, racial limitations, selfish motives and fetishistic superstitions, but it is broad enough to include the whole of humanity under its spiritual care.[85]

In his view, "no Moslem king today can fulfil the conditions of a Khalif of Islam," and "none of the Moslem countries is in a position to discharge its obligations."[86]

But Barkatullah found it too painful to give up on Pan-Islamism completely. In early 1925, he was on the move again, traveling on a Turkish passport, his destination Germany. Having spent some time with old Muslim friends, such as Abdul Jabbar Kheri in Berlin, he went to Paris in July 1925, where he began to bring out a paper in Arabic titled *El-Islah*, which once again dealt with the Khilafat question. In a declaration on September 28 that year, he reiterated his call for representatives of Muslims from all over the world to gather "in the near future in Mecca, Medina or some other place and elect a Caliph, with a Council, as their spiritual head who would offer leadership and guidance on religious affairs"; and he suggested Cairo as an appropriate venue for such a conference.[87] The General Islamic Congress for the Caliphate did indeed take place at a facility of the historically famous *Al-Azhar* Seminary in Cairo from May 13, 1926,[88] with delegates from many parts of the so-called Muslim world attending its proceedings, but, given the continuing divisions within the Muslim *umma*, in its purpose of setting up a caliphate it failed miserably, as the record of its proceedings in Rashid Rida's periodical, *Al-Manar*, reveals. Barkatullah himself did not attend.

After the publication of only one edition, *El-Islah* was suppressed by the French government. In November, at the instigation of the British, French police arrested Barkatullah, alleging that he was provoking Arabs against the French Republic and spreading Bolshevik ideas. This was tantamount to subversion at a delicate moment. Pan-European negotiations were about to start at Locarno and conflicts were taking place in Morocco and other French protectorates and colonies. Within a few hours, he was expelled to Germany.

Dismayed by the lack of progress with regard to the caliphate, Barkatullah's focus now shifted sharply to looking at strategies for the liberation of all the people of India. Back in Berlin, he published an article titled "Hindu—Sikh—Mussalman Unity" that was reproduced in the Urdu weekly *Suchch* (January 29–February 5, 1926) in India, containing a detailed analysis of the causes of India's subjugation and poverty under colonial rule. In it, he suggested that workers and peasants in India should follow the struggles of the workers in England, elect their own leaders and give political and economic issues priority above all else. Moving away from traditional Pan-Islamist ideas and in line with his secularist approach, he suggested that Indians should keep political matters completely separate from temples, mosques, and gurudwaras, which should be used solely for spiritual purposes. To become a powerful group they, the ordinary people, needed to form a political organization—an Indian Independence League with a democratic political and socialist economic program would, he argued, have a strong appeal for the masses.[89]

Thus, by June 1926, Barkatullah seemed to have moved decidedly away from Pan-Islamism. That he had drawn closer to the Comintern was evident in his letters of May 1926 and February 1927.[90] He was reported to have reinvigorated his association with activists in the Indian nationalist networks, such as Iqbal Shaidai (who had acted as a channel between Kabul, American Ghadarites, and Moscow) and Dr. M. A. Ansari (one of the main leaders of the Khilafat agitation in India, but now a key member of the Indian National Congress [INC]). On receiving a request from Ansari, he had met Jawaharlal Nehru, a rising star of the INC, in Switzerland. Interestingly, while Barkatullah quickly grasped Nehru's criticisms of Comintern's anti-imperialist strategy in India and was keen to arrange mutually beneficial discussions, Nehru's impression of Barkatullah on meeting him was somewhat patronizing: "He was a delightful old man, very enthusiastic and

very likeable. He was rather simple, not very intelligent, but still trying to imbibe new ideas and to understand the present-day world."[91]
Nehru again met Barkatullah at the International Congress Against
Colonial Oppression and Imperialism held in Brussels in February
1927. Supported by all manner of left-wing nationalists, socialists
and communists, its rather diffuse aim was to "deter imperialist governments from oppressing weak nations." It was broad enough to
comfortably accommodate, on the one hand, Nehru, the sole representative of the secular INC, and, on the other hand, someone like
Shakib Arsalan (1869–1946), a well-connected Pan-Islamist from
Lebanon and a prime mover in Berlin's émigré circles. Barkatullah
was participating as the official delegate of the San Francisco-based
Ghadr Party. Reflecting back, Nehru was more respectful in acknow-
ledging Barkatullah's political stature describing their tryst in Brussels
as the "first and last meeting" of the first prime ministers of the governments of India, Barkatullah of the one established in parallel to
the colonial government (the PGI in Kabul in 1915), and Nehru, of
the postindependence one in 1947.[92]

After returning from Brussels, Barkatullah was invited by the
Ghadr Party to attend its annual general meeting in San Francisco
in November 1927. At the end of August, Barkatullah and his old
companion Mahendra Pratap together sailed for the United States
from Bremen in Germany.[93] On his arrival in New York, however,
his chronic diabetes returned with a vengeance. All the same, he was
determined to attend the Ghadr Party meeting. That he was still an
inspirational figure was evident in the rousing welcome he received
from hundreds of supporters in Detroit and Chicago, crowds chanting
Bande Mataram (Hail to the motherland) as he made his way from
New York to San Francisco. By the time he reached his destination
he was on his last legs—at a large meeting of Indians in Marysville,
California, he got up to speak but weakness overtook him; he sat
down without uttering a word, tears rolling down his cheeks; he died
soon after on September 20 on his way to San Francisco and was buried in Sacramento. The headstone on his grave reads: "World famous
scholar and patriot, great leader of Indian nationalism and reformer
of modern Islam."[94] As this epitaph made clear, Barkatullah remained
a passionate Muslim revolutionary nationalist to the last.

CONCLUSION

So what was/is Barkatullah's legacy? He began his exile as a radical
Pan-Islamist and ended it as a cosmopolitan revolutionary still actively

engaged in global anticolonial networks. As a political activist, he had pursued his radical anti-imperialist and anti-British strategy in indefatigable fashion and largely in a Muslim idiom. While some have found his retrieval of support from such politically diverse regimes as the German Reich, the Bolsheviks, and the Italian Fascists to be intriguing, when considered closely the consistency of his strategy can be clearly understood within the context of his priorities, which themselves evolved over time.

In Barkatullah's militant anticolonial Pan-Islamism, the key enemies were imperial England and France. His writings in 1913 regarding the Balkan war unequivocally laid the blame for all the "evils" on England, especially denouncing its "robbing and plundering of India."[95] As the war began, Germany's strategy converged with Barkatullah's own program: along with many of his compatriots he had concluded a while before that "England's difficulty would be India's opportunity."[96] With the Germans and the Ottomans defeated, Barkatullah then turned to the Bolsheviks. The methods that they had recently deployed to demolish the tsarist regime, their annulment of all secret treaties imposed by the imperialist governments, and their proclamation of "the right of all peoples, no matter how small they be, to determine their own destiny," had impressed him greatly. Nevertheless, he was explicit that he was "neither a Communist nor a Socialist, but [his] political programme [was] the expulsion of the English from Asia....In this [he] concurred with the communists and in this respect [they were] genuine allies."[97] Likewise, his brief sojourn to Rome, undertaken with Chicherin's blessing, for the purpose of mobilizing financial resources on behalf of the Berlin-based Indian revolutionaries cannot be construed as Barkatullah's condoning of Italian Fascism's oppression.

The abolition of the Ottoman Caliphate in 1924 had left him grappling with the reality of Muslim political fragmentation along national lines as Muslims increasingly identified themselves as Turks and Arabs—the citizens of emerging nation-states. Not that Pan-Islam, contrary to the popular view, had ever historically been a unitary movement. In the past it had served different political objectives for different Muslim collectivities: the Ottomans emphasized fraternal ties to bind their diverse Muslim populations; the Sharifians reclaimed caliphal entitlement invoking its Arab authenticity; and, beyond these polities, Muslim populations sought support for their resistance to imperialist control. Nevertheless, like al-Afghani, Rashid Rida, and Shakib Arsalan, Barkatullah's first priority had been to secure the political independence of Islam—and, though dismayed by the caliphate's abolition by Ataturk's Turkish nationalists, he must have taken heart from their success at repelling the attempts by "the British Crusader [to eradicate] all independent Muslim power in the world."[98]

But, as we have seen, Pan-Islam's emancipatory beat—a struggle for justice and dignity against foreign oppression that used a religious idiom—continued to pulsate within Barkatullah for the remainder of his life. Despite having concluded that "no Muslim king to-day can fulfil the conditions of a *Khalif* of Islam,"[99] he believed that a caliphate reformed along democratic lines, with a permanent secretariat charged with organizing representative gatherings where political priorities could be defined and disputes resolved, might indeed be able to unify the Islamic world and become a formidable force in resisting and challenging its enemies. That Barkatullah's vision maintained a considerable appeal especially among Muslim cosmopolitans can be gauged from the many congresses that were called in the interwar period (Mecca 1924 and 1926; Cairo 1926, Jerusalem 1931). Particularly notable was the European Muslim Congress held in Geneva in September 1935 under the leadership of Shakib Arslan, the doyen of Pan-Islamist exiles based in Europe.[100] While these congresses failed in their central purpose of establishing a caliphate-like structure, the reconciliation of a supposedly medieval political system with the requirements of "modernity" that Barkatullah pursued is still seeking resolution today.

And in the period since World War II, Barkatullah's thinking has continued to resonate, albeit with two forms of Pan-Islamism: radical (which would eliminate borders and create a single Muslim state) and moderate (which only seeks harmony between Muslim states). As a transnational militant, he can be viewed, in some ways, as a precursor of those present-day would-be Islamist revolutionaries who find in their religion the ways and means to mount challenges to the postimperial order as well as the basis for opposition to regimes in Muslim countries. But the seeds of the moderate approach can also be found in Barkatullah's post-caliphate writings. A transnational Muslim subjectivity (the desire to relate internationally; and an imagined community, not a separate nation, nor a unified economic market, nor a distinct civilization, but a reconfigured globalised cultural formation), though unable to fully articulate itself politically, continues to resonate powerfully around the world. For some, this might be symbolized by the Organisation of Islamic Co-operation established in 1969, a project that is arguably very distant from the kind of post-caliphate purely spiritual polity envisaged by Barkatullah. His was also a very different vision from the program of some twenty-first-century trans-national radical Islamist groups, which, though also committed to armed struggle against the perceived Western/"crusader" onslaught and to reestablishing the caliphate, endow it with a global political mission, something that, in the end, he rejected.

Notes

1. N. Keddie, *An Islamic response to Imperialism: Political and Religious Writings of Sayyid Jamāl Ad-Dīn 'al-Afghānī'* (Berkeley: University of California, 1968), 39–41.
2. *The Crescent* 20 (June 3, 1896).
3. *The Crescent* 44 (November 19, 1893).
4. *The Pall Mall Gazette*, November 10, 1906.
5. "Moslemism in Liverpool," *Liverpool Review*, November 28, 1891.
6. Extract from Report by New Scotland Yard, July 30, 1924, 1, British Library (hereafter BL).
7. Ibid.
8. *The Times*, September 26, 1890.
9. *The Standard*, June 5, 1895.
10. *The Times*, December 22, 1894.
11. R. Geaves, *Islam in Victorian Britain: The Life and Times of Abdullah Quilliam* (Leicester: Kube, 2010), 73.
12. A. C. Bose, *Indian Revolutionaries Abroad: 1905–1927* (New Delhi: Northern Book Centre, 2002), 54.
13. See Report by New Scotland Yard, July 30, 1924, 5, BL.
14. M. Irfan, *Barkatullah Bhopali* (Bhopal: n.a., 1969), 92–93.
15. J. Campbell Ker, *Political Trouble in India, 1907–1917* (Calcutta: Superintendent Government Printing, 1917), 226–227.
16. Campbell Ker, *Political Trouble*, 114.
17. Campbell Ker, *Political Trouble*, 222.
18. K. H. Ansari, *The Emergence of Socialist Thought Among North Indian Muslims 1917–1947* (Lahore: Book Traders, 1990), 20–21.
19. L/P&J/12/758, 83, BL.
20. Campbell Ker, *Political Trouble*, 133.
21. Campbell Ker, *Political Trouble*, 133.
22. Campbell Ker, *Political Trouble*, 134.
23. Campbell Ker, *Political Trouble*, 134–135.
24. Bose, *Indian Revolutionaries Abroad*, 114.
25. Supplementary History Sheet of Maulvi Barkatullah (henceforth, SH of MB), L/PJ/12/213, File 1103/24, 8, BL. The real name of the Ghadr Party was "The Hindi Association of the Pacific Coast"; it was founded in 1913 by Har Dayal, regarded by the British as one of the most dangerous but outstanding revolutionaries. With the publication of its periodical the *Ghadr*, it popularly became

known as the Ghadr Party. See T. R. Sareen, *Indian Revolutionary Movement Abroad (1905–1921)* (New Delhi: Sterling Publishers, 1979), 72–73; when Bhagwan Singh and Barkatullah arrived in San Francisco in May 1914, they were, apparently, appointed president and vice-president of the Association—see H. Puri, "Revolutionary Organisation: A Study of the Ghadar Movement," *Social Scientist* 9.2–3 (September–October 1980), 61.

26. Bose, *Indian Revolutionaries Abroad*, 89.
27. Bose, *Indian Revolutionaries Abroad*, 88.
28. Campbell Ker, *Political Trouble*, 261.
29. Campbell Ker, *Political Trouble*, 126–127.
30. M. Freiherr von Oppenheim, *Denkschrift betreffend der Revolutionierung der islamischen Gebiete unserer Feinde*, Berlin, 1914, Archive Sal. Oppenheim jr. & Co. 25/10.
31. Campbell Ker, *Political Trouble*, 297.
32. These were: Barkatullah, Taraknath Das, Birendranath Dasgupta, Bhupendra Nath Dutta, Mandayam P. Trimul Acharya, Basant Singh, Chandrakant Chakravarty, Rishi Kesh Latta, Shiv Dev Singh Ahluvalia, S. C. Mukherjee, A. C. Sharma, Laxman Prasad Varma, Abdul Hafis, Sarat Dutta, Kedarnath Seauldin, Jodh Singh, Heramba Lal Gupta, Safia Caderwail, K. S. Rao. See No. 21074–1(77), No. 21074–2(74,152), No. 21074–3(218), No. 21075–1(12), No. 21075–2(144), No. 21076–2(113), No. 21076–3(222), No. 21117–2 (188), Politisches Archiv des Auswärtiges Amt (henceforth PAAA).
33. No. 21076, 178–179, January 10, 1915, PAAA.
34. H. Morgenthau, *Ambassador Morgenthau's Story*, Chapter XIV, "Wangenheim and the Bethlehem Steel Company—A 'Holy War' That Was Made In Germany," accessed November 15, 2011, http://net.lib.byu.edu/~rdh7/wwi/comment/morgenthau/Morgen14.htm.
35. No. 21244, 155, PAAA.
36. No. 21252, 24, 131, 255, PAAA; No. 21253, 455–456, PAAA.
37. No. 21095–1, 8, 76, PAAA.
38. Baron von Oppenheim's memorandum "Organisation der Behendlung der muhammedanischen und indischen Kriegsgefangenen," February 27, 1915, No. 21245, 78, PAAA.
39. No. 21255, 3, March 18, 1916, PAAA.
40. Report on propaganda among Indian PoWs, April 11, 1915, No. 21246, 116–117, PAAA.
41. D. Omissi, *Indian Voices of the Great War: Soldiers' Letters, 1914–18* (London: Macmillan Press, 1999), 199.
42. No.21250, 192–193, PAAA.
43. H. N. Gardezi, ed., *Chains to Lose: Life and Struggles of a Revolutionary: Memoirs of Dada Amir Haider Khan*, vol. I (Karachi: University of Karachi, 1986), 88.
44. Campbell Ker, *Political Trouble*, 261.

45. T. L. Hughes, "The German Mission to Afghanistan 1915–1916," in *Germany and the Middle East* ed. W. Schwanits (Princeton: Markus Weiner Publishers, 2004), 38.
46. Hughes, "The German Mission," 39.
47. Campbell Ker, *Political Trouble*, 132.
48. Bose, *Indian Revolutionaries Abroad*, 176.
49. Campbell Ker, *Political Trouble*, 304.
50. U. Sims-William, "The Afghan Newspaper, Siraj al-Akhbar," *Bulletin (British Society for Middle Eastern Studies)* 7.2 (1980): 120.
51. Ansari, *Emergence of Socialist Thought*, 22.
52. Sareen, *Indian Revolutionary*, 180.
53. *Documents of the History of the Communist Party*, vol. 1, 1917–1922 (New Delhi: Peoples Publishing House, 1971), 118–120. For the two policy declarations "To the Muslim Toilers of Russia and the East," and "Declaration of the Rights of Toiling and Exploited Peoples," see Secretary of State for India to Viceroy, No 968a, December 13, 1917, Chelmsford Papers, MSS Eur E 264, BL.
54. M. H. Khan and A. R. Kamal, eds., *The Contribution of Raja Mahendra Pratap and Prof. Barkatullah Bhopali in Freedom Struggle and Its Importance in Contemporary Society* (Kolkata: Towards Freedom, 2008), 10–11.
55. Ansari, *Emergence of Socialist Thought*, 47.
56. *Documents of the History of the Communist Party*, 118–120.
57. L/PS/11/173, BL.
58. For the full text of the pamphlet "Bolshevism and the Islamic Body Politics," see L/P&S/10/836, 52–63, BL.
59. HS of MB, 9.
60. *Muslim Outlook*, November 6, 1919 and October 30, 1919.
61. G. Krishna, "The Khilafat Movement In India: The First Phase (September 1919–August 1920)," *Journal of the Royal Asiatic Society of Great Britain and Northern Ireland* 1.2 (April 1968), 39.
62. Krishna, "The Khilafat Movement," 44.
63. Sareen, *Indian Revolutionary*, 220.
64. Bose, *Indian Revolutionaries Abroad*, 322.
65. Sareen, *Indian Revolutionary*, 220.
66. C. Kaye, *Communism in India, 1919–1924, with Unpublished Documents from National Archives of India, 1919–1924*, compiled and edited by S. Roy, with an introduction and explanatory notes by M. Saha (orig. 1926, reprint Calcutta: Editions Indian, 1971), 145.
67. Kaye, *Communism in India*, 156.
68. Kaye, *Communism in India*, 170.
69. Kaye, *Communism in India*.
70. HS of MB, 12.
71. Kaye, *Communism in India*, 56.
72. Kaye, *Communism in India*, 223.
73. HS of MB, 10.

74. Kaye, *Communism in India*, 56.
75. HS of MB, 10.
76. Kaye, *Communism in India*, 91.
77. This circular appeared on December 11, 1923 and, on January 5, 1924 the *"Independent"* (Allahabad) reproduced it in full. It purported to be issued by the "Executive Board of India Independence Party."
78. Kaye, *Communism in India*, 56; also HS of MB, 9–10.
79. N. Qureshi, *Pan-Islam in British Indian Politics: A Study of the Khilafat Movement, 1918–1924* (Leiden, Netherlands: Brill, 1999), 376.
80. Professor Mohammad Barakatullah (Maulavie) of Bhopal, India, *The Khilafet* (London: Luzac, 1924), 57.
81. Barakatullah, *The Khilafet*, 52.
82. Barakatullah, *The Khilafet*, 7.
83. Barakatullah, *The Khilafet*, 8.
84. Barakatullah, *The Khilafet*, 59.
85. Barakatullah, *The Khilafet*, 61.
86. Barakatullah, *The Khilafet*, 54, 55.
87. Irfan, *Barkatullah Bhopali*, 260–261.
88. M. Kramer, *Islam Assembled: the Advent of the Muslim Congress* (New York: Columbia University Press, 1986).
89. Irfan, *Barkatullah Bhopali*, 265.
90. RGASP 495–68–186 and RGASP495–68–207, Russian State Archives of Socio-Political History, Moscow.
91. Jalal Nehru, *An Autobiography: With Musings on Recent Events in India* (London: John Lane, 1936), 151.
92. Cited in Irfan, *Barkatullah Bhopali*, 277.
93. R. 2302352, No. 78315, June 26, 1947, PAAA.
94. A. Khan, "Mawlana Barakatullah: An Indian Muslim Revolutionary in America," *The Muslim Observer* (Sacramento, USA), July 1, 2009, accessed November 15, 2011, http://www.ilmgate.org/mawlana-barakatullah-an-indian-muslim-revolutionary-in-america/.
95. Campbell Ker, *Political Trouble*, 134.
96. Campbell Ker, *Political Trouble*, 261.
97. *Documents of the History of the Communist Party*, 118.
98. "Safara l-turkb i'l yunan," *al-Manar* 23 (November 19, 1922), 714–717.
99. *The Khilafet*, 54–55.
100. Kramer, *Islam Assembled*, 142–153.

References

Ansari, K. H. *The Emergence of Socialist Thought Among North Indian Muslims 1917–1947.* Lahore: Book Traders, 1990.
Barakatullah, Professor Mohammad (Maulavie), of Bhopal, India. *The Khilafet.* London: Luzac, 1924.

Bose, A. C. *Indian Revolutionaries Abroad: 1905–1927.* New Delhi: Northern Book Centre, 2002.

Campbell Ker, J. *Political Trouble in India, 1907–1917.* Calcutta: Superintendent Government Printing, 1917.

Documents of the History of the Communist Party, vol. 1, 1917–1922. New Delhi: Peoples Publishing House, 1971.

Gardezi, H. N., ed. *Chains to Lose: Life and Struggles of a Revolutionary: Memoirs of Dada Amir Haider Khan,* vol. I. Karachi: University of Karachi Press, 1986.

Geaves, R. *Islam in Victorian Britain: The Life and Times of Abdullah Quilliam.* Leicester: Kube, 2010.

Hughes T. L. "The German Mission to Afghanistan 1915–1916." In *Germany and the Middle East,* edited by W. Schwanits, 25–63. Princeton, NJ: Markus Weiner, 2004.

Irfan, M. *Barkatullah Bhopali.* Bhopal: n.a., 1969.

Kaye, C. *Communism in India, 1919–1924, with Unpublished Documents from National Archives of India, 1919–1924,* compiled and edited by S. Roy, with an introduction and explanatory notes by M. Saha. First published 1926. Reprint, Calcutta: Editions Indian, 1971.

Keddie, N. *An Islamic Response to Imperialism: Political and Religious Writings of Sayyid Jamāl Ad-Dīn 'al-Afghānī.'* Berkeley: University of California Press, 1968.

Khan, A. "Mawlana Barakatullah: An Indian Muslim Revolutionary in America." *The Muslim Observer* (Sacramento, USA), July 1, 2009. Accessed November 15, 2011. http://www.ilmgate.org/mawlana-barakatullah-an -indian-muslim-revolutionary-in-america/.

Khan M. H. and A. R. Kamal, eds. *The Contribution of Raja Mahendra Pratap and Prof. Barkatullah Bhopali in Freedom Struggle and Its Importance in Contemporary Society.* Kolkata: Towards Freedom, 2008.

Kramer, M. *Islam Assembled: The Advent of the Muslim Congress.* New York: Columbia University Press, 1986.

Krishna, G. "The Khilafat Movement In India: The First Phase (September 1919–August 1920)." *Journal of the Royal Asiatic Society of Great Britain and Northern Ireland* 1–2 (April 1968): 37–53.

Nehru, J. *An Autobiography: With Musings on Recent Events in India.* London: John Lane, 1936.

Omissi, D. *Indian Voices of the Great War: Soldiers' Letters, 1914–18.* London: Macmillan Press, 1999.

Puri, H. "Revolutionary Organisation: A Study of the Ghadar Movement." *Social Scientist* 9.2–3 (September–October 1980): 53–66.

Qureshi, N. *Pan-Islam in British Indian Politics: A Study of the Khilafat Movement, 1918–1924.* Leiden, Netherlands: Brill, 1999.

Sareen, T. R. *Indian Revolutionary Movement Abroad (1905–1921).* New Delhi: Sterling, 1979.

Sims-William, U. "The Afghan Newspaper, Siraj al-Akhbar." *Bulletin (British Society for Middle Eastern Studies)* 7.2 (1980): 118–122.

CHAPTER 8

Victims, Wives, and Concubines: The Spanish Civil War and Relations between Moroccan Troops and Spanish Women*

Ali Al Tuma

It has generally been argued that during and after the Spanish Civil War the issue of Moroccan troops interacting with Spanish women was both a difficult and highly charged matter for the Spanish Nationalists. One scene in a Spanish film *Libertarias* sums up the standard perception of this interaction. Toward the end of the film, a contingent of Moroccan soldiers takes a group of *milicianas* by surprise and slaughters them with knives. At the same time, a nun, who had accompanied the militia-women, is forcefully undressed by two Moroccans while others are seen expressing sadistic enjoyment at the sight. Fortunately for the nun, a Spanish officer intervenes in time to save her from rape and possible death.[1] This film represents the typical view of relations between Moroccan soldiers and Spanish women during the Civil War—a relationship of sexual aggressors and sexual victims. Given this common viewpoint, it would be difficult to imagine that there were in fact voluntary carnal encounters, love stories, and marriages between the two groups. However, these existed—even to an extent that suggests that they were more than incidental.

The intent of this essay is to furnish an overview of the interracial and intercultural relations between Moroccan soldiers who fought in Spain during the Civil War and the Spanish women of that time, and how the Spanish Nationalist authorities viewed and regulated these relations. The focus will be on the voluntary relations between these two groups. These relationships were an important indicator of how officials, and especially military authorities, in a European country, regarded the interaction with what were effectively temporary Muslim immigrants in a European civilian society. In this regard, the reader will notice that the prevalent attitude in contemporary Spain—even among those who sympathized with Muslim immigrants—that romantic relationships between Muslim men and Spanish women are doomed to failure,[2] was also reflected in the outlook of the Spanish military authorities who brought Moroccan soldiers to Spain during the Civil War, despite their generally sympathetic attitude toward these soldiers and their culture.

I. The Victims

When segments of the Spanish military (Nationalists) rose up against the Popular Front Government (Loyalists) on July 17, 1936, it very quickly became apparent that their victory would not be a swift one. It also became clear that the Nationalists would need the army of Africa, composed in its majority of Moroccan *Regulares* and *mehallas* from the Spain's Moroccan Protectorate,[3] as well as the *Tercio* (the Spanish version of the Foreign Legion), to secure their base in Andalusia against the Loyalist counterattacks. The Army of Africa's intervention proved decisive and its military efficacy, as attested by the unit decorations it received, far exceeded its numbers.[4] As growing numbers of Moroccan soldiers were either airlifted or shipped to southern Spain, they came increasingly in contact with Spanish civilians in the areas they occupied.[5] Soon stories of Moroccan atrocities and the wholesale rape of Spanish women started to spread among the Loyalist populace and their proponents. These were generally reinforced by the traditional Spanish image of the "Moor" as a lustful irrational being. There are a small number of testimonies of people who claimed to have actual firsthand information of these charges. These will be the starting point in the discussion of this first and most controversial aspect of the interaction of Moroccan males and Spanish females during the Civil War.

At some point in October 1936, at the crossroads outside Navalcarnero (to the west of Madrid), the American journalist John Whitaker wrote, in a classic and frequently cited account, how he met a Moroccan officer, Mohamed El Mizzian, who would eventually rise to the rank of general in Franco's army. El Mizzian, according to Whitaker, had brought two young girls (presumably Republican militia-women) for interrogation and then taken them to a school-house where 40 "Moorish" soldiers were resting. When Whitaker asked what would happen to them, El Mizzian responded, "Oh, they'll not live more than four hours."[6] Of course the reason that this anecdote is frequently quoted is that it probably is the only one that reported a rape in progress. Moreover, it cogently highlighted the reputation of Moroccan soldiers as the Civil War's prime rapists. For propaganda purposes this reputation was also strongly promoted by General Queipo de Llano, the man who almost single-handedly took control of Seville in July 1936. During one of his infamous and terrifying evening radio speeches of that year, Queipo luridly noted: "Our brave Legionnaires and Regulares have shown to the reds what it means to be a man. Also to the red women, who now have finally come to know real men."[7] While Queipo frequently mixed truth and lies in his speeches, his propaganda chief Antonio Bahamonde, who later defected to the Loyalists, is, along with Whitaker, one of the authorities cited concerning accusations of Moroccan troops raping Spanish women. For instance, he mentioned in his memoirs that in a number of Andalusian villages "the Moors raped the women they found on their way and killed them later."[8] Though there is some truth in his claims, he might have exaggerated the scale of the rapes.[9] The question then is how extensive and frequent were those cases of Moroccan soldiers raping Spanish women during the Civil War?

First, there is evidence that during the first weeks of the Civil War there were sexual assaults committed against suspected Loyalist women by Nationalist males (and one would assume that Loyalist males committed similar acts against Nationalist women). These would seem to have been the work mostly of Spaniards. Carlota O'Neill, the Mexican wife of a Loyalist pilot executed early in the war, for instance, tells of females with Loyalist sympathies being raped in Melilla during 1936. The perpetrators were always Spanish Falangists.[10] Consequently, perpetrators of such acts, if they occurred on a wide scale, were not solely Moroccans. Nor is there any evidence to suggest that Moroccans constituted the majority of the offenders. Second, unlike those quantitative studies of rapes committed by Allied troops, both Western and Soviet, in post–World War II Germany and Eastern Europe,[11] there are no comparable studies concerning similar behavior of Nationalist troops, including Moroccan troops, during the Spanish Civil War. While there can be little doubt that such acts did take place, it is not known whether the numbers were in thousands, hundreds, or dozens. Historians have never managed to translate these probabilities into bottom-line figures. Francisco Sánchez Ruano is unique in attempting to quantify rape cases that Moroccan troops committed, or might have committed, though in the end he does not produce solid numbers. Based on his research of mainly municipal archives, he concludes that large-scale cases of rape committed by Moroccan troops were confined to the initial stage of the war in a few villages of Andalusia, Extremadura, and in the zone of Toledo (in Castilla la Mancha) as well as during the last phase of the war in Catalonia.[12]

Third, except in cases where it was the deliberate policy of the regional commander (Queipo de Llano, for instance) to use sexual violence or the threat of it as a weapon, it seems that Moroccan troops generally, as the testimonies of individual Moroccan veterans assert, did not overstep discipline. When individual soldiers did, punishment would many times follow quickly and harshly.

Charges of rape committed by Moroccan soldiers cannot be dismissed, but the assessment of this phenomenon at times lacks a clear basis in documents and testimonies. For example, Gustau Nerín claims, in his otherwise valuable work, that "many of the Moroccans who were convicted during the war, were accused of sexual abuses, but the sentences were very light (months, including days of imprisonment)." However, the archival sources, which he uses to support this claim, contradict his conclusion.[13] Among hundreds of offences ranging from drunkenness to murder, seven cases are related to rape (*violación*). In three of these, the offenders received life sentences, while the military courts handed out two other Moroccans 30 years of imprisonment each. There is also one case of sexual assault (*abusos deshonestos*) for which a sentence of 14 years, 4 months, and 1 day was given. The lightest sentence, mentioned in this source, for an offender convicted of rape was 6 years, 1 month, and 16 days. These judgments hardly validate Nerín's claim of "light" sentences.[14]

Western historians have usually neglected the Moroccan side of the rape issue that has been elicited in the recent past through interviews of aging veterans. Despite the necessary caution that one should take while considering these interviews, they cannot be ignored given the pejorative historical legacy and reputation that has been associated with the actions of Moroccan troops during the Spanish Civil War. This legacy and reputation continues to this day to be linked in Spanish public discourse to the "Moor."

In these interviews, the majority of Moroccan veterans indicated that they had not witnessed, participated in, or had any knowledge of cases of Moroccan troops raping Spanish women. All agreed that their superiors forbade them, on the pain of death, from attacking civilians or hurting women.[15] At the same time, some admitted that looting was permissible upon first entering an enemy village or town. One of the veterans noted that "there never was aggression against civilians. It was the finest army. It was forbidden to touch women or any house. The major, San Martin, told the Tabor [a battalion sized unit]: 'no touching of women, no touching of anything.'"[16]

Still there were a few Moroccan veterans who did confirm that some soldiers were involved in cases of rape. One veteran even confirmed more than one instance. He noted that when the army entered a city the soldiers were free to loot as they liked, but that civilians were, according to him, off-limits. Failing to respect that order entailed a *consejo de guerra* (i.e. court martial). He witnessed the trials of two cases of rape that Moroccan soldiers had committed—one had occurred in Seville, where the perpetrator received the death sentence; The other took place in Catalonia, when three soldiers raped two girls of one family. Two soldiers were subsequently executed after interrogation while the third fled to the "*rojos*" (the reds).[17] This last incident is suspiciously similar to one recounted by another veteran, in whose version three Moroccans raped girls from one family and killed the parents. Two of the perpetrators were caught and executed, while the third managed to flee and eventually find his way back to Morocco.[18] Both accounts could be of the same incident. But in the second version, General Muñoz Grandes played a part as he spoke to one Moroccan *caïd* (native officer), asking him: "We were at war in Morocco. Did we do such things?" The *caïd* answered in the negative, whereupon the general asked "Then why did they kill [these] people?"[19] The native officers of the unit then put their signatures on the execution order. Another veteran relayed how on one occasion a girl was raped. After dismissing the first two groups of soldiers that were brought to her, she identified the supposed perpetrator in the third group, and thereupon he was executed by his own unit "so that others would not be able to do it. Therefore when we entered an inhabited place we could not do anything." The chief of his unit had told its members that Spain was not like Morocco. In Morocco, "the women do as you want from them," but in Spain if a woman "wants to, then it does not matter to anyone. But if she does not want to, then there is nothing [that can happen] by force."[20] In fact the Moroccan veterans who expressed their views on this issue always approved of the shooting of a rapist, whether they witnessed an actual rape or not. But punishment was not always taken for granted, as rape charges were sometimes disputed by fellow soldiers. One death sentence for two Moroccans accused of rape and killing, for instance, prompted a Tabor of the Mehalla—who thought the soldiers were innocent—to refuse to follow orders and to start marching toward Salamanca with the intention of protesting to Franco that they were "dying in times of war and in times of peace."[21]

In conclusion, the testimonies of the Moroccan veterans concerning the issue of rape leave one with the impression that Moroccan troops were strongly discouraged by their Spanish officers from committing rape. Further, if they did in fact commit the act and were caught, they generally suffered harsh penalties ranging from extended incarceration to execution.

II. The Wives

For all the horror of individual and gang rape, relations between Moroccan soldiers and Spanish women during and after the Spanish Civil War were in fact much more nuanced and complex. Despite their propaganda-inspired reputation as lustful aggressors, a number of Moroccan soldiers had romantic relationships with Spanish women. In fact, there were a sufficient number of these relationships to alarm the Nationalist military and to motivate it to take measures to impede them.

The following anecdote, by a veteran of Regulares Ceuta, El Hussein ben Abdesselam, is illustrative of the general attitude of Spanish society and the military toward Moroccan-Spanish romantic relations ending in marriage. El Hussein's Tabor arrived one day at the Extremaduran village of Puebla de la Calzada, and the soldiers were quartered on the opposite side of a workshop where several girls worked sewing clothes. The owner, a wealthy Spanish woman, used to invite a number of soldiers to sit with them. During these gatherings, the Spanish owner fell in love with a corporal from Larache named Abdesselam, who apparently was well-versed in Spanish, and in the end they decided to marry. Upon hearing of the marital intentions of this Spanish woman, indignation arose among the people of the village, and a number of them went to complain to the commanding officer of the Tabor who promised to prevent the intended marriage. He summoned the Moroccan corporal and assigned him fixed office duty, and prevented him from leaving his quarters, until the unit left the village. When the Spanish lady realized what had happened, she took her car and drove south, crossed into Morocco and headed toward Tetouan where she met the Khalifa, Mulay El Hassan ben El Mehdi, to seek his intercession. Commenting that he had no problem with a Spanish woman marrying a Moroccan subject, the Khalifa reassured her that he would intercede with Franco in the matter. Whatever the Khalifa might have written or said, it seems that it had the intended effect. Sometime later the Tabor commander summoned the people who had complained to him about the Spanish-Moroccan marriage, and told them that he had received instructions from Franco not to hinder the marriage of the corporal and the Spanish lady. Within a matter of months the marriage documents were ready and the corporal stayed in Spain with his Spanish wife.[22]

The happy ending to the story of the Moroccan corporal and his wealthy Spanish wife was not representative of the majority of the cases of romantic relationships between Moroccan soldiers and Spanish women. The difficulties that these couples faced were extensive. As one veteran pointed out: "It was not easy to marry a Spanish woman. Not like today. They [the military superiors] would forbid it."[23] Indeed, this was the policy that the Spanish military, and the Protectorate authorities through their controllers of native affairs (*interventores*), sought to implement. Franco's positive attitude in the aforementioned anecdote was the exception to the rule.

It is important to note that in the majority of documented cases of mixed marriages, intended marriages, or other romantic relationships, the soldiers in question could be divided into two groups. The first consisted of wounded men who obviously had enough free time to stroll outside the hospitals and make contact with girls of the cities where the military hospitals were located. "The nurses loved the Moroccans," asserts one veteran, "the correspondence between the soldier and the nurse continued even after he returned to the front."[24] The other group, a smaller one, consisted of those who were assigned duties that left them behind the front lines, like the Moroccan military police, the *mejasnia*, or those performing guard duties for high Spanish figures, such as General Franco. It was these circumstances that facilitated the relationships that started to worry the Spanish military authorities.

In May 1937, the Delegation for Native Affairs of the High Commissariat reported the case of a young Spanish girl form Saragossa, where a Muslim hospital existed, who tried to accompany an injured Moroccan back to Morocco so that they would contract a civil marriage. The report expressed relief that the lack of necessary documentation kept the girl from crossing the border at Castillejos into the Protectorate.[25] However, it expressed concern that such instances might take place in the future and that such unions not only produced insurmountable problems but also impeded the protecting mission, though it does not state how. The report asked for adequate measures to impede such journeys, preferably cutting them short in the places of origin, usually cities where Muslim hospitals existed.[26]

Another case of intended Moroccan-Spanish marriage that illustrates one of the justifications the Nationalist authorities used to oppose this type of relationships was that of the military policeman, or *mejasni*, also a member of Franco's Moroccan Guard, Ben Brahim Susi. In March 1938, the Delegation of Native Affairs was informed that Susi had divorced his Moroccan wife and intended to marry a Spanish woman from Salamanca. The *interventor* in north Spain (the Spanish military controller of native affairs), who was charged with investigating the matter, noted that the Spanish woman had a limp and judging from "her physical look," concluded that the Moroccan *mejasni* intended to benefit materially from marrying this much older woman. The *interventor* visited the Spanish lady and ascertaining that she was not pregnant, tried to convince her of her mistaken choice. His argument was interesting. The Spanish officer told her that "the Moors in a European environment are only useful for military service." He also argued that Moors are "such friends of fantasy" that he must have created grand stories about his personal attributes and great possessions.[27]

The "problem" of interreligious marriages emerged with such frequency that it eventually became a matter for ministerial consideration. In July 1938 the Nationalist minister of national defense issued an order prohibiting "illegal marriages" between "Muslim soldiers" and Spanish women. The order came as a result of a lengthy complaint concerning these marriages, which the Legal Department of the Ministry of Defense had previously formulated. The specific incident that prompted this complaint and the subsequent order was a marriage in Melilla between a Moroccan corporal of the Regulares and a Spanish woman who had come from the peninsula. What was even more egregious and reflected a "lack in morality" was that her father even gave "authorization" to the marriage. The Legal Department outlined in its report the possible consequences of such marriages. One negative effect mentioned, citing the opinions of military authorities in the Protectorate's eastern region, was that these unions would enrage native women. As the report noted, the differences in tradition would "degenerate into quarrels that would cause continuous bitterness between women of both religions."[28] In addition, the report expressed a concern for the well-being of "our [female] compatriots" who would gain neither spiritual nor material advantage from these marriages. The ministry's Legal Department urged civilian authorities in the peninsula to do their utmost to legally hinder interreligious relationships, and noted that the Church's cooperation should not be a problem, as it can, within its functions, work to encumber such marriages. The report also lamented the fact that the civil code on marriage contained no prohibition regarding differences of faith. On the other hand, it noted that the defense minister could use the current law to insist on prior authorization for any soldier wishing to contract marriage, and thus could legally require civilian authorities in Spain and Spanish Morocco to refuse to register such marriages without this authorization. Finally, the report recommended that all sectors and commanders of Moroccan units be informed of this policy, but that it be done as discreetly as possible, given the "delicate" nature of the matter. Further, the units should be ordered to keep authorizations to a minimum.

The defense minister's instructions did ultimately achieve the desired result. It prohibited the Muslim religious personnel attached to military units from actually sealing marital contracts, which was easy to do since many of them held the rank of officer. In March 1938, the director of the Muslim hospital in Saragossa informed the *interventor* of Moroccan affairs in northern Spain that he learned about an intended marriage between a Spanish woman and one of the Moroccan patients who had asked the hospital's imam and the catib (notary) to arrange the marital union. The director managed, in time, to instruct his two subordinates to stop the arrangements. Additionally, the *interventor* ordered the hospital's religious staff to refrain from effectuating any further marriages without the authorization of his office and without first providing the *interventor* with information on the "Moor" and the "Christian" woman and the circumstances of their relationship.[29]

In the light of the efforts of the Spanish military authorities to forestall, as much as possible, marriages between Spanish women and Moroccan soldiers, due to religious and cultural differences, one might imagine that conversion to Christianity would have raised fewer objections to such unions. In 1938, there was just such an instance. The military Muslim hospital of Medina del Campo reported that a member of the *mejasnia* intended to marry a Spanish woman and would convert to Christianity to do so. This, however, presented the Spanish military with a more explosive issue since the intended conversion might give the appearance that the hospital administrators were condoning proselytizing activities that were strictly forbidden in Muslim hospitals. The hospital's director was eager to communicate that no such forbidden conversions were taking place.[30] This sensitive issue was very important to Franco and his followers who presented themselves as "men of God," whether Christians or Muslims, fighting the "Godless Reds." As Carmen Franco, the daughter of the generalissimo, stated, her father "had much respect for Islam." For instance, he never advocated that the members of his Moorish Guard, who had married Spanish women, convert to Christianity. He thought that the Moroccans should not change their religion because they were "very impervious and it was a complication to mix both religions."[31] While it probably can be concluded that Franco was not a supporter of these types of marriages, at least in the case of the Moorish Guard he did not actively oppose them.

In the 1940s when a sizable numbers of Moroccan soldiers were still stationed in Spain and conducted operations against anti-Franco guerillas, the issue of Moroccan-Spanish marriages continued to concern the Franco government. As in the past, the same uncomfortable questions of religious and cultural differences dominated these alliances. As one veteran remembered during this period:

> The captain would be informed about the marriage. They will call the woman and ask her if she agrees to marry with him. She says yes, he says yes. Then they [the military superiors] would say: "he is a Moro and you are Spanish, how will you marry? If you agree to marry him according to his religion, then fine. If no, then you stay with your religion and he the same, but without marriage." But when the children are born, that is a problem. When the child is born, they come and say: "what name will you give it?" Many times, they went to the priest, and the priest talks with the soldier: "the children must have the same religion, they cannot be parted, you have the Moorish religion, the Muslim one, and she has the Spanish religion. It must be given a careful thought." One of them must fall in the trap, the man or the woman. If the man loves her and wants to marry her then he must become a Spanish subject. They go to the priest and he baptizes him. And if not, they remain like this [in un-marital relationship].[32]

As such, the end of the Civil War in April 1939 did not end the troubling issue of Moroccan-Spanish marriages. Though large numbers of Moroccan troops returned to Morocco, others remained for garrison duty and to mop up remnants of Loyalist resistance. This meant the continued presence of some Moroccan troops in the Spanish peninsula's population centers led to continued romantic attachments leading to marriages, despite the restrictions imposed by the Spanish state, which grew stronger in 1941 when it forbade municipal judges from authorizing civil marriages, except for those who were not Catholic and those who could prove that they were not baptized.

A July 1939 report highlighted yet another aspect of this issue: the question of the nationality of the Spanish female who contracted marriage with a Moroccan. The report noted an increase in the frequency with which Spanish women were entering into civil marriages with Moroccans in front of either Spanish municipal judges or justices of peace in Spanish Morocco.[33] A problem arising from these unions was the question of the woman's nationality. According to Article 22 of the Spanish Civil Code at the time, a Spanish woman who married a foreigner lost her Spanish nationality and automatically assumed the nationality of her husband. At the same time, Moroccan law did not automatically grant Moroccan nationality to a foreigner marrying a Moroccan subject.[34] The report also indicated that the local Moroccan authorities were too inflexible in providing these Spanish women, who decided to move with their husbands to Morocco, with the necessary Moroccan documentation. On the other hand, some Spanish women found it difficult to obtain the necessary Spanish documentation to travel with their Moroccan husbands in the first place, since they were now considered noncitizens by the Spanish authorities. As noted in both, the documents of the Protectorate authorities and of the Spanish Ministry of Foreign Affairs, there were also concerns for the political and legal well-being of these Spanish women. They were losing the protection of Spanish laws, and while these were not the most liberal during this era, the Spanish most certainly considered them more "progressive" than those that existed in Morocco. This was yet another reason for the Spanish Nationalist authorities to feel uncomfortable with Moroccan soldiers having lasting relationships with Spanish women. In legal terms, this concern was solved in March 1941 by prohibiting Catholics from contracting civil matrimonies.

During the Civil War, the Nationalist policy with regard to romantic relationships was still taking its nascent steps. The policy was not yet well-defined. It was not until the mid-1940s that the Spanish Protectorate authorities, especially the Delegation of Native Affairs, developed a "doctrine" with regard to impeding relations between Moroccan men (who now included, in addition to soldiers and ex-soldiers, also many students) and Spanish women.[35] The delegation deemed such relationships damaging for the prestige of the protecting power, and resolved to cooperate with the Spanish "National Board for the Protection of Women" to avoid their continuation. The delegation found that Spanish women who consorted with Moroccan men did so out of "pretentiousness, ignorance, vice or greediness," and considered the cultivated and suave "Moor" the most dangerous type. But by this time the delegation had a well-established practice in place, starting with intercepting letters between Spanish women and Moroccan men, gathering information to establish the nature of the relationship (is it merely friendly or is it romantic?) and taking steps to prevent the Spanish woman in question from moving to Morocco and the Moroccan man from coming to Spain,[36] as well as informing Spanish family members so that they would take action.[37] The mere interception of letters that never reached their destination was probably enough in some cases to end the relationships as it gave the impression to lovers that their partners neglected or had abandoned them.

The Spanish military and the Protectorate's Spanish authorities generally tried to prevent Moroccan soldiers from marrying Spanish women. In their "protective mission," the Spanish proclaimed their desire to prevent their Moroccan subjects from lapsing out of their religion, to preserve the harmony of family and village life in the Protectorate and to placate the sensitivities of the native women.[38] But the Nationalist policy toward interreligious marriages also stemmed from the decided viewpoint that romantic and marital relationships between people of two different cultures and faiths were incompatible and thus ultimately doomed to failure. The Spanish military officers and officials who considered themselves to have the closest cultural and personal ties to Morocco and its people, given their years of military service in the Protectorate, and who had no issue with the Moroccan military presence in Spain, were the ones who probably had the greatest concerns about their Moroccan brothers-in-arms establishing personal liaisons with Spanish women.

Despite the policy of obstructing interreligious marriages between Moroccans soldiers and Spanish women, the Spanish Army never actually resorted to penalize, during the Civil War in any case, those soldiers who had relationships with Spanish women, nor did they resort to physically preventing Spanish women (by imprisonment, for example) from consorting with Moroccan soldiers. And the law did not, until the end of the Civil War, prohibit such marriages. In practice, interreligious marriages or romantic relationships continued to take place during and immediately after the war, giving the obviously mistaken impression to some Moroccan veterans that the Spanish Army not only tolerated but also looked positively upon mixed marriages.[39] Yet, the majority of Moroccan veterans conceded that such unions were either difficult or totally forbidden.

There are no estimates as to how many Moroccan soldiers serving in Spain married Spanish women or had a relationship with the intention of marriage. But fragmentary and anecdotal evidence gives an insight into the contexts of these marriages. All of the Moroccan veterans who personally knew other Moroccan soldiers who had married Spanish women and brought them back home, confirmed that these women had left Morocco in the wake of Moroccan independence either with their husbands or alone (often after the demise of the husband) and moved to the Spanish enclaves of Ceuta and Melilla or returned to their original *pueblos*. Those Moroccans who married Spanish women and lived in Ceuta and Melilla or in the Spanish peninsula, remained in place, acquiring the Spanish nationality.[40] In hindsight, this would seem to have vindicated official Spanish skepticism that Spanish women could make a life in a country so alien to their culture and religion.[41]

Now that we have seen how the Spanish Nationalists viewed mixed marriages, the final issue is how they approached and dealt with another kind of relations between Moroccan soldiers and Spanish women.

III. The Concubines

The Spanish Civil War witnessed a significant growth in the number of women turning to prostitution. Many of these were the wives and daughters of Republicans who had either died, were imprisoned, or had fled Nationalist repression. In turn, the Nationalist camp experienced a relaxation of sexual morality that saw an increase in regulated or tolerated prostitution.[42] Even the Spanish religious hierarchy, that supported the Nationalists, does not seem to have protested—in the name of Catholic morals—against the tolerance of prostitution.[43]

The tendency of the Spanish military authorities to limit relationships between Moroccan soldiers and Spanish women also echoed in its policy toward prostitution. The term "policy," however, must be used in this case with extreme caution. For, in contrast to the instructions with regard to Moroccan-Spanish marriages, no documentary material has so far come to light that explicitly prohibited Moroccan soldiers from using the services of Spanish prostitutes. Still, there are some indications that seem to confirm the aforementioned tendency. Moreover, as a rule, Moroccan troops were generally serviced by Moroccan prostitutes.

In the early days of the war, the presence of Moroccan troops in southern Spain contributed to an increase in prostitution. In Seville, for instance, prostitutes frequented the gardens where the Regulares camped.[44] To control this, the Spanish Nationalist military, in the tradition of older armies, expended some effort to facilitate pros-titution for their Moroccan troops by establishing special broth-els for them.[45] These brothels were generally staffed with women from Morocco; military authorities took care to facilitate the move-ment of Moroccan prostitutes to the Spanish peninsula. There was, for example, a request sent by the commander of the Army of the North to Franco in April 1938, asking for permission to establish a "Concubines Centre" in the neighborhood of the city of Fraga to service the needs of 11 Moroccan units belonging to the Moroccan Army Corps. Franco agreed to the proposal.[46]

There were earlier efforts to accommodate this need. In December 1936, General Orgaz, the Spanish high commissioner in Morocco at the time, planned to organize an effort to move dozens of "Chejas" and musicians whom he intended to use to build a Moorish quarter in Spain that would serve to entertain the troops.[47] In a December 1937 report, a Republican spy also noted the transport of "Arab" women to Spain. He stated that after trouble arose among the Moroccan soldiers who had been isolated in "special camps," the military administration felt compelled to bring these women and settle them in farmhouses near these camps. The reason for this "isolation" of the soldiers, this Republican report claimed, was that the Regulares continued raping even after conquered territory was organized.[48]

In Morocco itself, the sending of Moroccan prostitutes to Spain had provoked, early in the war, the outrage of the wives of the Moroccan soldiers fighting in Spain. According to Rosalinda Powell Fox, the British mistress of Colonel Juan Beigbeder (high commissioner of Morocco from 1937 to 1939), a group of Moroccan wives stormed the Larache train station where a train of female "camp followers" was ready to follow the troops. The wives attacked the prostitutes in a battle where "hair was pulled out by the roots," "earrings wrenched from a delicate ear," and "dresses were torn and bosoms exposed," managing to prevent the departure of the prostitutes that day. Only under the cover of the early hours of the next morning did the train with "its fallen human cargo" leave the city.[49]

There is no hard evidence to indicate the total number of Moroccan women who traveled to Spain to provide sexual services to the mem-bers of the Moroccan units or how long they remained. Only shreds of information are available. For example, in September 1938, 21 women were en route to a brothel in the village of Valmanya (in Lérida, and not far from the already mentioned Fraga), where a little less than 50 women were already stationed. However, in a report from the commander of the Aragon Army Corps, these women were no longer needed since there were no more Moroccan units in the sector.[50] This again demonstrated that Moroccan women had the task of servicing exclusively Moroccan troops.

Why did the Spanish military take the trouble of importing prostitutes from Morocco for its Moroccan soldiers? Certainly there should have been, in a time of war and devastation, no shortage of available prostitutes in Spain itself.[51] One answer may be that Moroccan prostitutes doubled as dancers and singers and thus created an overall entertainment environment that was more familiar to and in accordance with Moroccan culture. It is not clear from the source materials whether the Moroccan soldiers preferred Moroccan "concubines" over local Spanish women. However, the obvious objective was to discourage Moroccan soldiers from having sex with Spanish women. In some cases, the Moroccan troops were forbidden from going into cities during their free time but not explicitly forbidden from soliciting Spanish prostitutes. One veteran specifically noted this prohibition but then indicated that he and his comrades would "go secretly to the places of vice" during the night only to return to their positions in the morning.[52]

The Nationalist military policy concerning the use of prostitutes was to separate, as best possible, Spanish and Moroccan troops. This separation was based on a very practical rationale. Some Spanish prostitutes simply did not want the Moroccans. One such veteran prostitute recalled that "nobody wanted the Moors, because they came accustomed to the carte blanche that they gave them and they wanted to do whatever they desired. In one village in Asturias they left the majority of the women there pregnant."[53] But the separation in the prostitution sphere also reduced the instances of friction that might have arisen in the brothels between Moroccan and Spanish soldiers,[54] especially had some Spanish soldiers objected to a Moroccan having sexual contact with a Spanish woman even if it was consensual. It would also reduce tensions with other European soldiers such as the substantial number of Italians in Nationalist Spain. In Seville, for instance, during the early phases of war, the "Moors" were forbidden from visiting night clubs so as to avoid contact with the Italians who called them "Abyssinians" and had frequent and violent clashes with them.[55] Since efforts by the Spanish military authorities existed to prevent marital relations between Moroccans soldiers and Spanish women, it is safe to assume that the Spanish military sought to apply this policy to prostitution as well. The difference being that the Moroccan troops were offered an alternative in the form of imported Moroccan prostitutes.[56]

CONCLUSION

The Spanish Nationalist military felt uncomfortable with the issue of Moroccan soldiers interacting with Spanish women. The Nationalists faced a fundamental dilemma. They had brought Muslim Moroccans to Christian Spain and expended considerable effort to justify their presence as true allies in the crusade against the godless "reds." At the same time, the Nationalists portrayed themselves as fighting for traditional Catholic Spain: the same Spain that had put to an end the Moorish political presence at the end of the fifteenth century and its demographic presence in the early seventeenth century. These were also the same individuals who did everything they could to impede interactions and marriages between Moroccan soldiers and Spanish women.

The interracial and interreligious relations between Moroccan soldiers and Spanish women are a good example of the ambivalence with which the Spanish Nationalists looked upon their Protectorate in Morocco. Contrary to what colonial France was doing in its colonies, the Spanish tried to strengthen the Arab and Muslim identity of Spanish Morocco, while at the same time clinging to it desperately as a part of a grand Spanish empire. Their policy toward the Moroccan-Spanish male-female relationships echoed this approach. As much as the Nationalists deemed the Moroccan soldiers an essential part of the Spanish Nationalist Army and their "crusade," their policy was to ensure that these "Moors" retained their Muslim identity and space and were kept, as much as possible, separate from the Spanish population, particularly its female inhabitants. Interracial marriages were deemed destructive to this aim.

In her work on the cultural Spanish responses to modern Moroccan immigration in Spain, Daniela Flesler discusses today's public opinion about romantic relationships between Muslim men in general and Moroccan men in particular, and Spanish women. She notes that contemporary Spanish literary works as well as feature movies that have dealt frankly with this issue, and have generally criticized racist attitudes toward such relationships, have nevertheless tended in the end to judge these intercultural and interreligious romantic bonds as almost always doomed to failure. In this regard, and if one can cautiously speak of continuities in attitudes, it probably should be noted that Spanish society, civilian and military alike, whether Francoist or democratic, sympathetic or not to the "Moor," whether in the 1930s, 1940s or in the twenty-first century, has displayed a relative consistency in its attitude toward romance between the Muslim Moroccan male and the Spanish female.

NOTES

*Acknowledgments: I am immensely grateful to Shannon E. Fleming who spent time and effort in reviewing this paper and providing suggestions that considerably contributed to its improvement. I also thank my supervisors Henk te Velde and Eric Storm for their continuous feedback and challenging questions. I am indebted to the association of Moroccan ancient combatants, its secretary El Amine Rqibate and its branches in Alcazarquivir, Tetouan, and Nador for bringing me in touch with war veterans. Also many thanks to the people in the *Cuartel de Regulares* in Ceuta who helped me track and interview Moroccan veterans in that territory. I am especially thankful to Mustafa El Merroun for granting me exclusive access to the transcripts of interviews that he conducted in the 1990s.

1. Directed by Vicente Aranda, Spain, 1996.
2. Daniela Flesler, *The Return of the Moor: Spanish Responses to Contemporary Moroccan Immigration* (West Lafayette: Purdue University Press, 2008).
3. The *Regulares* were units composed of Spanish officers and mostly Moroccan soldiers, but were part of the Spanish army. The *Mehal-las* on the other hand were considered Moroccan units that fell under the authority of the government of the Khalifa, the official representative of the sultan in the Spanish protectorate and the highest native authority in the zone.
4. Ali Al Tuma, "The Participation of Moorish Troops in the Spanish Civil War (1936–1939): Military Value, Motivations and Religious Aspects," *War & Society* 30.2 (2011), 91–107.
5. The total number of Moroccan troops that fought in Spain reached 80,000 according to Madariaga. See: María Rosa Madariaga, *Los moros que trajo Franco: La intervención de tropas coloniales en la guerra civil española* (Barcelona: Ediciones Martínez Roca, 2002), 172.
6. John T. Whitaker, *We Cannot Escape History* (New York: Macmillan, 1945), 114. "I suppose Franco felt that women had to be given to the Moors," concludes Whitaker, since the Moors "were unpaid." The military historian Jesús María Ruiz Vidondo denies, in his article, Whitaker's version of the events, arguing that the Regulares group Nr.5 (Alhucemas), of which El Mizzian was a Tabor commander, did not advance through Navalcarnero but through Boadilla. He does not provide evidence for his argument. See Jesús María Ruiz Vidondo, "Ben Mizzian, el general moro de Franco," *Arbil* 119 (2009), accessed September 4, 2013, http://revista-arbil.es/119ruiz .htm. However, the records of Mizzian's military career, kept in the military archives of Segovia, credit him and his Tabor for playing a part, on October 29, 1936, in the occupation of Navalcarnero. Whitaker was therefore correct about, at least, the month and the location in which Mizzian was present. Archivo General Militar de Segovia, Caja 746, Exp.6/pag. 59.

7. Ian Gibson, *Queipo de Llano: Sevilla, verano de 1936 (Con las charlas radiofónicas completas)* (Barcelona: Ediciones Grijalbo, 1986), 84. See Gibson's comment on the different versions of this quote.

8. Antonio Bahamonde y Sánchez de Castro, *Un año con Queipo: memorias de un nacionalista* (Barcelona: Ediciones españolas, 1938), 96.

9. An example of such exaggeration is the estimation of Bahamonde of 150,000 execution in the area of command of General Queipo. Bahamonde claimed that Moroccan troops were brought by planes to Jerez, and were tied to the wings so as to transport the greatest possible number. He claimed to have witnessed two "Moors" in Seville who showed the marks of ropes that were used to tie them on the wings. See Bahamonde, *Un año con Queipo*, 26. How could they have survived such an experience, and how this legend continues to be believed, one wonders.

10. Carlota O'Neill, *Trapped in Spain* (Toronto: Solidarity Books, 1978), 42–43.

11. For example, J. Robert Lilly estimated that American soldiers committed 17,800 rapes in England, France, and Germany. Antony Beevor estimates the number of rape victims of Soviet troops in Germany to be around two million. Soviet troops even raped "liberated" women prisoners from Polish, Ukrainian, or Russian nationalities. See Robert J. Lilly, *Taken by Force: Rape and American GIs in Europe during WWII* (New York: Palgrave Macmillan, 2007) and Antony Beevor, *Berlin: The Downfall 1945* (London: Penguin, 2002).

12. Francisco Sánchez Ruano, *Islam y Guerra Civil Española: Moros con Franco y con la República* (Madrid: La esfera de los libros, 2004). He studied and documented 34 cases of rape and murder in Catalonia committed by Moorish troops and believes that those practices were widespread in Catalonia, see his conclusions in Ruano, *Islam y Guerra Civil*, 381. He leaves the question undecided as to whether the geographical concentration of the crimes in mainly Catalonia and Andalusia has something to do with a lack of research on other regions or with different behavior by Moorish troops in different places. He takes precautions in his conclusions though. Sometimes troops of different origin operated together in the same region, making pointing a finger to particular units difficult, besides the fact that after the effective ending of military operations the Moorish units were moved out, being followed by a period of post-combat repression in which the actors were Spanish. (Ruano, *Islam y Guerra Civil*, 371, 374, 375, 378).

13. Gustau Nerín, *La guerra que vino de África* (Barcelona: Critica, 2005), 287. The source that he gives in his *La Guerra* is Archivo General de la Administración (hence AGA), M-1686.

14. Whether or not the convicts served their full sentences is another matter, which the source does not clarify.

15. Among testimonies that claimed the strict prohibition on rape, usually to be punished by death, are those of Mohamed Mhaouesh, Mohamed

ben Omar el Hashmi, Abdullah El Omari, El Massari, El Boubekra, as well as other testimonies in the personal archive of El Merroun, and those of most of the veterans interviewed for this study.

16. Interview with Ahmed Mohamed Ahmed, Alqazarquivir, February 21, 2011.

17. Testimony of El Bekkouri Mohamed El Ayashi who served in the headquarters of his unit working on legal and native affairs. El Merroun archive.

18. Testimony of El Bubakra. El Merroun archive.

19. Testimony of El Bubakra. El Merroun archive. However, the reference with regard to the Rif war, though it might be the experience of Muñoz Grandes himself, does not apply to the Rif war in general. During that war, Spanish and Spanish-led forces used sexual aggression against women in rebel territories. According to some accounts, Franco and Varela (the only officer to receive the most distinguished San Fernando laureate twice) were brought women as war prizes by their troops but that both men magnanimously refused the gift. Nerín, *La Guerra*, 285–286.

20. Interview with Masoud Ballah a veteran of the *Tiradores de Ifni* battalion, Brussels, November 5, 2011.

21. Testimony of Abdelkader El Dukhri El Shaoui. El Merroun archive. This witness did not experience the incident himself, but heard it from soldiers of the Mehalla involved, while he was receiving treatment in the hospital.

22. Interview with El Hussein ben Abdesselam, Ceuta, January 24, 2011. Years after the events he met in Ceuta the mixed couple which had produced two children.

23. Interview with Abdelkader Ahmed, Alcazarquivir, February 21, 2011.

24. Testimony of Ahmed ben Abdullah Al Omari. El Merroun archive.

25. Castillejos is modern-day Fnideq, the Moroccan locality closest to the border of Ceuta.

26. AGA, Af, 81/1122 Leg. 3763/3. "Orden sobre prohibición de casamientos ilegales de soldados musulmanes con españolas."

27. AGA, Af, 81/1113, Leg. 3746/3, report nr. 1650, on April 1, 1938. The report concluded that it was futile to convince the Spanish woman to desist from her intention.

28. AGA, Af, 81/1122, Leg. 3763/5. "Informe de la sección de Justicia del Ministerio de Defensa Nacional, sobre matrimonios de soldados musulmanes con españolas."

29. See AGA, Af, 81/1113, Leg. 3746/3, cables nr. 471 and 1673.

30. See AGA, Af, 81/1113, Leg. 3746/3, cable nr 2556.

31. Jesus Palacios and Stanley G. Payne, *Franco, mi padre: Testimonio de Carmen Franco, la hija del Caudillo* (Madrid: La esfera de los libros, 2008), 8.

32. Interview with the Regulares veteran Dandi Mohamed, Tetouan, February 15, 2011. Notice that becoming a Spanish subject, in the eye of this veteran, amounts to or equals converting to Christianity.

33. See AGA, Af, 81/11023, Exp.108.

34. A foreign woman who married a Spanish man automatically obtained, according to the Spanish Civil Code, the Spanish nationality.

35. Fernando Rodriguez Mediano, "Delegación de Asuntos Indígenas, S2N2. Gestión Racial en el Protectorado Español en Marruecos," *Awraq: estudios sobre el mundo árabe e islamico contemporáneo* 20 (1999), 181.

36. Rodriguez Mediano, "Delegación de Asuntos Indígenas," 188.

37. Ibid., 173, 174.

38. In the case of Moroccan soldiers who divorced their wives in Morocco to marry Spanish women, the Regulares groups paid the divorced women their due *sadak* (dowry, in this case the portion to be paid after separation) and deducted the amount from the soldier's pay. See for example AGA, Af, 81/1113, Leg. 3746/3 "El cabo de Regulares de Larache Mohammed Ben Yilud número 3004 intenta casarse con una española."

39. Interviews with Abdessalam El Amrani and Mohammed Ayyashi El Zerki, Ceuta, June 30, 2011.

40. Interviews with: Mohamed Abdullah Susi and El Hussein ben Abdessalam in Ceuta, respectively January 19 and 24, 2011; Dandi Mohamed in Tetouan, February 15, 2011; Abdelkader Ahmed and Ahmed Mohamed Ahmed in Alcazarquivir, February 21, 2011; Al Kendoussi ben Boumidien ben Mohamed in Nador, July 4, 2011. See also for the Moorish guard soldiers who married Spanish women and remained in Spain, Archivo General Militar de Guadalajara, *La Guardia Mora del Generalísimo, expedientes personales de Moros.* AGMG. UCOS. Regimiento de la Guardia del Jefe del Estado, Índice N. 32.

41. It should be noted here that the Moroccan veterans interviewed for this study almost never, in retrospect at least, complained of racist attitudes by either their Spanish direct superiors or the Spanish Nationalist military in general, even when some of these veterans were aware of the generally unfavorable Spanish attitude toward mixed marriages. They generally agreed that the treatment by their superiors was good, that they were treated on an equal footing with the Spanish soldiers, and they generally regarded their Spanish officers and remembered them with affection. Perhaps they thought that such marriages were not fruitful either, though I must admit that their own general attitude to the viability of such marriages is something that their testimonies did not touch upon.

42. Jean-Louis Guereña, *La prostitución en la España contemporánea* (Madrid: Marcial Pons, 2003), 412. This culminated, in 1941, in the official repealing of the 1935 prohibition on prostitution. In 1956, prostitution was made once again illegal. Guereña, *La prostitución*, 415, 436.

43. Guereña, *La prostitución*, 410.
44. Bahamonde, *Un año con Queipo*, 28.
45. For references to various women from Morocco working or running brothels in Spain, see for example AGA, Af, 81/1150. Some of these women obtained permission to cross to Spain using safe-conducts provided by army divisions. Requests by some of these women included permission to carry large quantities of Kif (which is used in various sorts of drugs).
46. Archivo General Militar de Ávila, A.1, L.50, Cp. 45.
47. AGA, Af, 81.1150, Exp.5429. "Cheja," the female form for the Arabic word "sheikh" refers in this context to women professionalizing in singing and dancing and who, says Madariaga in her study, doubled as prostitutes. See Madariaga, *Los moros que trajo Franco*, 286.
48. Report by the Servicio de Información Exterior, December 1937, in International Institute for Social History, Archivo FAI, CP, 33A/5.
49. Rosalinda Powell Fox, *The Grass and the Asphalt* (Puerto Sotogrande, Spain: J. S. Harter and Associates, 1997), 81–82.
50. Letter to Lieutenant Colonel Antonio García, September 12, 1938, AGA, Af, 81/1125, Leg.3370, Cp 2 "Varios."
51. For example, upon the entry of Nationalist troops in Barcelona, recalls one veteran, women in the city called on the Moroccan soldiers to sleep with them "for there was hunger." Testimony of Ihmido El Ma'dani. El Merroun archive.
52. Testimony of Mohammed ben Omar ben El Hashmi. El Merroun archive.
53. J. R. Saiz Viadero, *Conversaciones con la Mary Loly: 40 años de prostitución en España* (Barcelona: Ediciones 29, 1976), 18. By "they gave them" I presume she meant that Nationalist authorities gave the Moroccans the "carte blanche."
54. For examples of quarrels at prostitution houses between Moroccan and Spanish soldiers see AGA, Af, 81/1125, Leg. 3770, "escándalos— reyertas." In one such incident, a Moroccan military policeman was beaten up by a Requeté and a Legionnaire. The madam of the house claimed that he had mistreated one of the prostitutes, while he accused the two Spanish men of attacking him without any reason. While being interrogated he threatened to take revenge on the madam for testifying against him.
55. Bahamonde, *Un año con Queipo*, 43. The Italians, who acted like they were in a "conquered country" used to have "many incidents with the Moors, some grave," and even deadly ones. Bahamonde, *Un año con Queipo*, 147.
56. A number of veterans refer to comrades who used the services of Spanish prostitutes or had otherwise extramarital sexual relationships with Spanish women, though denying that they themselves ever indulged in such contacts.

REFERENCES

Archivo General de la Admanistración.
Archivo General Militar de Ávila.
Archivo General Militar de Guadalajara.
Archivo General Militar de Segovia.
Archivo FAI (International Institute for Social History).
Bahamonde y Sánchez de Castro, Antonio. *Un año con Queipo: memorias de un nacionalista.* Barcelona: Ediciones españolas, 1938.
Beevor, Antony. *Berlin: The Downfall 1945.* London: Penguin, 2002.
Flesler, Daniela. *The Return of the Moor: Spanish Responses to Contemporary Moroccan Immigration.* West Lafayette: Purdue University Press, 2008.
Gibson, Ian. *Queipo de Llano: Sevilla, verano de 1936 (Con las charlas radiofónicas completas).* Barcelona: Ediciones Grijalbo, 1986.
Guereña, Jean-Louis. *La prostitución en la España contemporánea.* Madrid: Marcial Pons, 2003.
Lilly, J. Robert. *Taken by Force: Rape and American GIs in Europe during WWII.* New York: Palgrave Macmillan, 2007.
Madariaga, María Rosa. *Los moros que trajo Franco. La intervención de tropas coloniales en la guerra civil española.* Barcelona: Ediciones Martínez Roca, 2002.
Nerín, Gustau. *La guerra que vino de África.* Barcelona: Critica, 2005.
O'Neill, Carlota. *Trapped in Spain.* Toronto: Solidarity Books, 1978.
Palacios, Jesus and G. Stanley Payne. *Franco, mi padre: Testimonio de Carmen Franco, la hija del Caudillo.* Madrid: La esfera de los libros, 2008.
Powell Fox, Rosalinda. *The Grass and the Asphalt.* Puerto Sotogrande, Spain: J. S. Harter and Associates, 1997.
Rodriguez Mediano, Fernando. "Delegación de Asuntos Indígenas, S2N2. Gestión Racial en el Protectorado Español en Marruecos." *Awrāq: estudios sobre el mundo árabe e íslamico contemporáneo* 20 (1999): 173–205.
Ruiz Vidondo, Jesús María. "Ben Mizzian, el general moro de Franco," *Arbil* 119 (2009). Accessed September 4, 2013. http://revista-arbil.es /119ruiz.htm.
Saiz Viadero, J. R. *Conversaciones con la Mary Loly: 40 años de prostitución en España.* Barcelona: Ediciones 29, 1976.
Sánchez Ruano, Francisco. *Islam y Guerra Civil Española: Moros con Franco y con la República.* Madrid: La esfera de los libros, 2004.
Thomas, Hugh. *The Spanish Civil War.* London: Penguin, 1965.
Tuma, Ali Al. "The Participation of Moorish Troops in the Spanish Civil War (1936–1939): Military Value, Motivations and Religious Aspects." *War & Society* 30.2 (2011): 91–107.
Whitaker, John T. *We Cannot Escape History,* New York: Macmillan, 1945.

CONTRIBUTORS

Humayun Ansari OBE is professor of Islam and Cultural Diversity and Director of the Centre for Minority Studies at Royal Holloway, University of London. His research interests include the history of Muslims in the West, radical Islamic thought, ethnic diversity, identity, and migration. His published works include, *The Emergence of Socialist Thought Among North Indian Muslims, 1917–1947;* "*The Infidel Within," Muslims in Britain Since 1800*; and *The Making of the East London Mosque, 1910–1951.*

Mohammed Alsulami is lecturer at the Department of Languages and Literature of Islamic Nations, Umm al-Qura University (Saudi Arabia). He obtained his MA at the Department of Middle Eastern Studies, Leiden University. He defended his PhD thesis, *Notions of the Other in Modern Iranian Thoughts*, at Leiden Institute for Area Studies (LIAS), 2014. His research interests focus on Iranian nationalism and national identity, modern history of Iran, and the Arab-Iranian relations.

Nathalie Clayer is professor at the EHESS (Paris), a senior research fellow at the CNRS (Paris), and head of the CETOBAC department (Centre d'études turques, ottomanes, balkaniques et centrasiatiques, CNRS-EHESS-Collège de France). Her main research interests are religion, nationalism, and state-building process in the Ottoman Empire and in Balkans, especially among the Albanians. Among her recent publications are *Aux origines du nationalisme albanais. La naissance d'une nation majoritairement musulmane en Europe* (2007); *Islam in Inter-War Europe* (2008) coedited with Eric Germain; and *Les musulmans de l'Europe du Sud-Est* with Xavier Bougarel (2013).

Richard van Leeuwen is currently lecturer in Islamic Studies at the Department of Religious Studies of the University of Amsterdam. His research focuses on the history of the Middle East, Arabic literature, and Islam in the modern world. His academic positions include a PhD position (University of Amsterdam, 1986–1991), a postdoc grant by the Royal Dutch Academy of Arts and Sciences (1992–1996), and a senior research grant by the Deutsche Forschungsgemeinschaft (1997–2001). He also works as a translator of Arabic literature. Among his publications are *The Thousand and One Nights; Space, Travel and Transformation* (2007) and *Waqfs and Urban Structures: The Case of Ottoman Damascus* (1999)

David Motadel is research fellow at Gonville and Caius College, University of Cambridge. He studied history at the University of Freiburg and completed his MPhil and PhD in history at the University of Cambridge, where he was a Gates scholar. He has held research positions at Harvard, Yale, and Oxford.

Götz Nordbruch is researcher at the The Georg Eckert Institute for International Textbook Research in Brunswick. He completed his PhD in Islamic Studies at Humboldt Universit—Berlin (2007) with a thesis examining *Encounters with National Socialism in Syria and Lebanon, 1933–1945*. From 2008 to 2009 he was a postdoctoral researcher at the "Institut de recherches et d'études sur le monde arabe et musulman" in Aix-en-Provence. From 2009 to 2012 he was assistant professor at the Centre for Contemporary Middle East Studies of the University of Southern Denmark in Odense. His research focuses on European–Middle Eastern intellectual encounters in the early twentieth century.

Umar Ryad is associate professor of Islamic Studies, University of Utrecht. In 2008–2014, he has been working as assistant professor of Islamic Studies at Leiden University. He studied at al-Azhar University in Cairo (BA Islamic Studies in English, 1998) and obtained his MA degree in Islamic Studies (cum laude) from Leiden University (2001), where he also received his PhD degree with the thesis *Islamic Reformism and Christianity: A Critical Study of the Works of Muhammad Rashid Rida and His Associates (1898–1935)* (2009). His current research focuses on the dynamics of the networks of Islamic reformist and pan-Islamist movements, Muslim polemics on Christianity, the history of Christian missions in the modern Muslim World, and transnational Islam in interwar Europe. He has recently received an ERC Starting Grant (2014–2019) for the study of Muslim Networks in Interwar Europe and European Trans-cultural History.

Ali Al Tuma is a PhD candidate at Leiden University Institute for History. For his thesis he is researching the participation of the Moroccan troops in the Spanish Civil War, particularly the relation between race, culture, and war. He has published a number of articles on this topic in English, Arabic, and Dutch. Among his publications are "The Participation of Moorish Troops in the Spanish Civil War (1936–1939): Military Value, Motivations, and Religious Aspects," *War & Society* 30.2 (2011): 91–107 and "Tangier, Spanish Morocco and Spain's Civil War in Dutch Diplomatic Documents," *The Journal of North African Studies* 17.3 (2012): 433–453.

INDEX

Printed in the United States of America